Preteen

BIG BOOK of Bible Puzzles

DAVID C COOK

transforming lives together

BIG BOOK OF BIBLE PUZZLES FOR PRETEENS
Published by David C Cook
4050 Lee Vance Drive
Colorado Springs, CO 80918 U.S.A.

Integrity Music Limited, a Division of David C Cook
Brighton, East Sussex BN1 2RE, England

ISBN 978-0-8307-7242-1

The content included in this book was originally published in *Through the Bible Puzzles for Kids 8–12* by Standard Publishing in 2001 © Standard Publishing, ISBN 978-0-7847-1171-2.

Cover Design: James Hershberger

Printed in the United States of America

5 6 7 8 9 10 11 12 13 14

081524

Contents

How to Use This Book

Welcome to *Big Book of Bible Puzzles for Preteens*, a learning adventure for the preteens in your classroom or home! Preteens will be excited to review Bible stories and verses through completing mazes, codes and ciphers, hidden pictures, and a variety of other enticing puzzles. The puzzles contained in this book teach Bible stories and verses in an age-appropriate way for preteens and highlight over 150 Bible stories.

How to Use This Book in Your Classroom

Use this book as a fun way to review Bible stories and reinforce what your preteen learns through Bible study. Follow these easy steps for successful use of the puzzles:

- Find the puzzle that matches your lesson's Bible story or verse. Select one or more puzzles to use.
- Make multiple copies of the puzzle you have selected.
- Check the puzzle's directions for any extra materials you will need.
- Give a puzzle to each child.
- Assist children as needed to complete the puzzle.
- Talk with children while they work on the puzzle. The printed copy on each puzzle will help you communicate the important link between a Bible story and the everyday lives of the children in your class.

How to Use This Book in Your Home

This book gives you a wonderful opportunity to help your preteen learn what the Bible says about loving God and following Him every day. Follow these steps for a fun and valuable time of learning together:

- For most puzzles, nothing more than a pencil is necessary. Crayons, colored pencils, scissors, or tape are needed for a few puzzles.
- Invite your child to work on several puzzles a week.
- Encourage your child to complete only one or two pages at a time.
- Encourage your preteen to read the puzzle's Bible verse.
- Briefly talk with your preteen about the life-application ideas presented in the puzzles and about the responses appropriate to your preteen's own life. Tell how you obey the verse too.
- Look back together at the puzzles your preteen has finished. Review the Bible stories and verses.

Leading a Child to Christ

One of the greatest privileges of serving in children's ministry is to help guide children to become members of God's family. Pray and ask God to prepare the kids you know to understand and receive the good news about Jesus. Ask God to give you the sensitivity and wisdom to communicate effectively and to be aware as opportunities occur.

When talking with children about salvation, use words and phrases they understand; never assume kids understand a concept just because they can repeat certain words. Avoid symbolic terms that will confuse literal-minded thinkers. As you watch and pray, you will see kids developing relationships with God.

Here are some questions you can ask and things you can discuss with a child who is interested in accepting Jesus as their Lord and Savior. Encourage the child to look up and read the Bible verses along with you.
Read John 3:16. **Why did God send Jesus to earth?** (God loved us so much that He wants us to have eternal life with Him.)

First John 3:1 says that God wants us to be His children. But sin, doing wrong, separates us from God. Read Romans 6:23. **What do you think should happen to us when we sin?** (die) **But what is God's gift to us?** (eternal life in Jesus)

Jesus willingly died on the cross to take the punishment for our sins. Read 1 Corinthians 15:3. **But Jesus didn't stay in the tomb. After three days, He came back to life! Jesus died so that we can live forever in heaven with Him.**

Are you sorry for the wrong things that you've done? If you are, what should you do? Read 1 John 1:9. **Our sins are wiped away when we're truly sorry for what we've done and when we turn to God.**

Read Ephesians 2:8. **How are we saved?** (by God's grace, through faith) **Christian faith is a life-long adventure here on earth. With Jesus as Lord of our lives, we build a life of submitting to God, following Jesus, and keeping in step with the Spirit.**

At this point, continue to talk with the child about accepting Jesus as Lord and Savior. Include what your church teaches about how this happens. If you have any questions about salvation, talk with your pastor or children's ministry leader.

God wants every person to accept the free gift of eternal life that He's offering. What do you need to do about this?

Let There Be ...

Read Genesis 1:1–25. Starting with Day 1, find the correct path through the maze to the things God created on that day. Do this until you have matched all the days with the correct pictures.

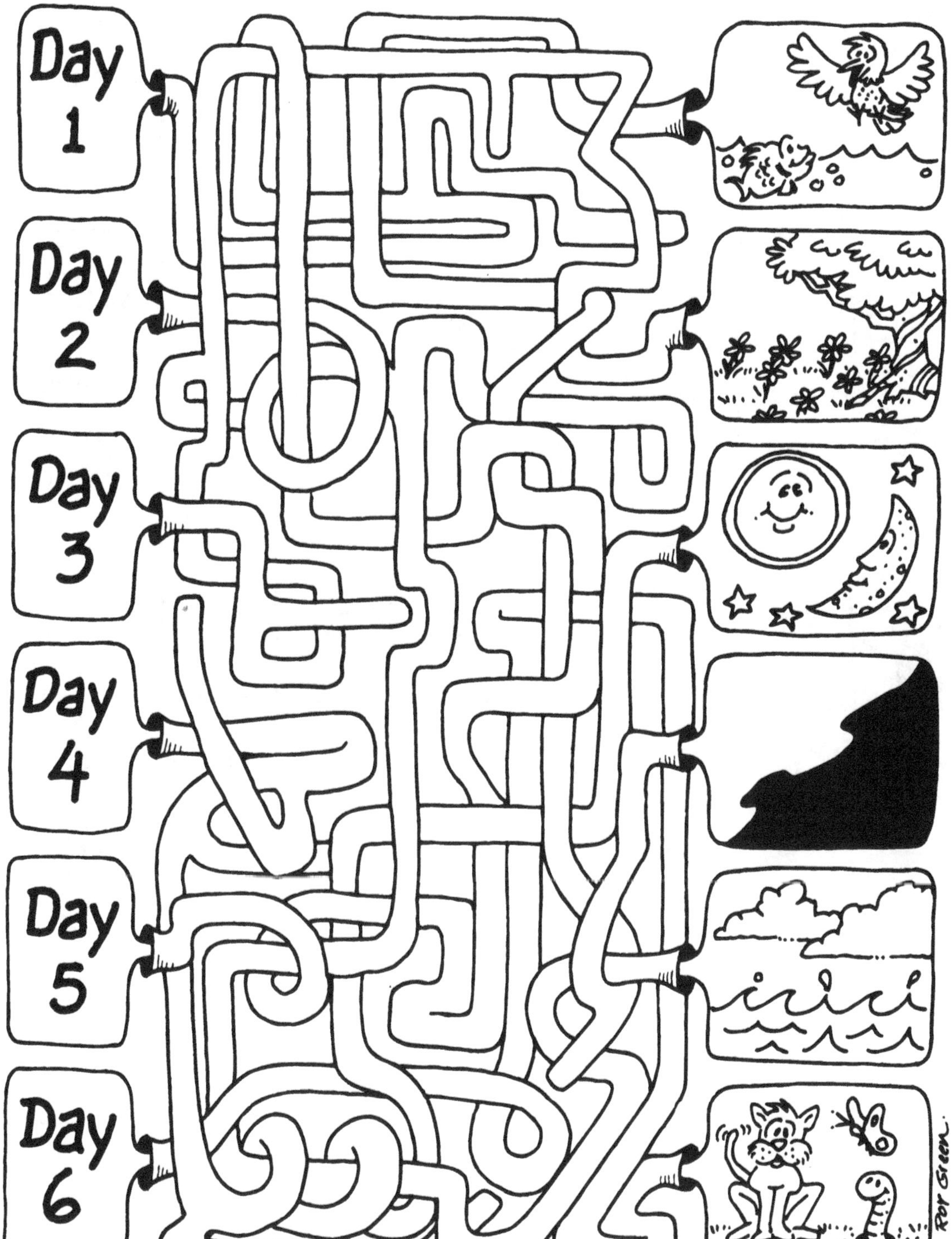

The Beginning

Do you know how the world began? Use the graph to find out. Each column has a number and each row has a letter. Use the number and the letter combination to solve this puzzle. (Example 5C = G) Read the story in Genesis 1:1—2:3.

	1	2	3	4	5	6	7	8
A	A	L	T	H	D	W	I	C
B	T	E	O	G	Y	H	W	I
C	L	T	S	A	G	A	T	H
D	O	R	G	I	E	L	A	N
E	I	S	H	E	M	R	D	P

___ ___ ___   ___ ___ ___ ___ ___ ___ ___   ___ ___ ___

5C 3B 7E   8A 2D 4E 1A 7C 2B 5A   4C 6D 1C

___ ___ ___ ___ ___ ___   ___ ___ ___ ___   ___ ___ ___

3A 6B 1E 8D 4B 3C   6A 4D 1B 3E   4A 8B 2E

___ ___ ___ ___ ___ ___ ___ ___   ___ ___ ___ ___ ___.

6C 2A 5E 7A 3D 8C 2C 5B   8E 1D 7B 5D 6E

Something Special

Beginning with column 1, go down each column until you come to a dot. Copy the letter found to the left of the dot onto the corresponding blank below. Some columns will have more than one letter. For extra help, put a piece of paper on the right side of the puzzle. Move it to the right to reveal one column at a time. When complete, you will find out about God's special creation. Read Genesis 1:27.

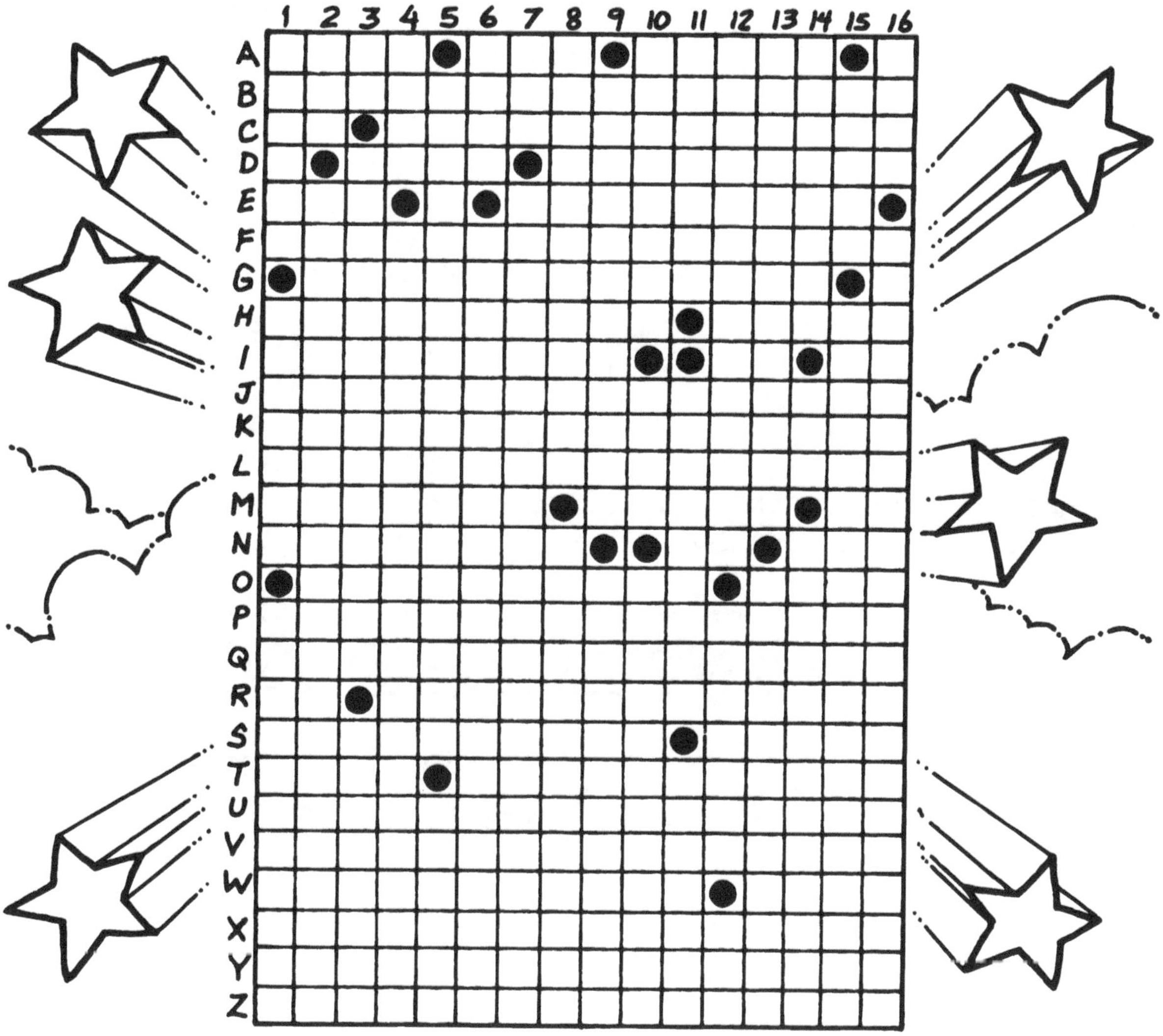

___ ___ ___   ___ ___ ___ ___ ___ ___ ___
1 1 2   3 3 4 5 5 6 7

___ ___ ___   ___ ___   ___ ___ ___
8 9 9   10 10   11 11 11

___ ___ ___   ___ ___ ___ ___ ___ .
12 12 13   14 14 15 15 16

Strange Tree

A sad event occurred at a tree in God's garden. Use the code from the strange tree below to solve the puzzle. Read the story in Genesis 2:15–17 and 3:1–23.

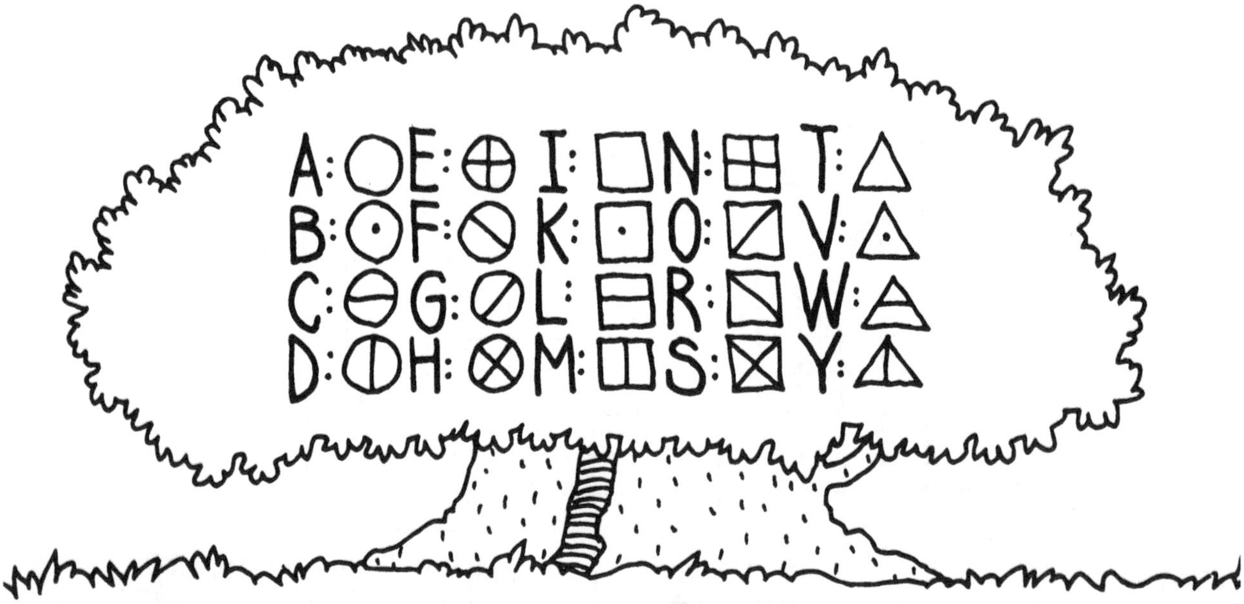

Where Are You?

Starting with the first puzzle box, copy the letter directly below the number 1 to the blank space under the number 1 in the second puzzle box. Move all the letters in each column to the empty boxes before you move on to the next number. Cross out each letter after you move it. When complete, read the question in the second puzzle box. Then answer the question on the blank lines below. Read Genesis 3:6–19.

1	2	3	4	5	6	7	8	9	10	11	12	13	14
K	I	D	H	Y	F	D	I	T	R	Y	D	T	M
A	N	W	E	E	V	E	O	M		G	O	A	O
		D				R		D		A		D	?

1	2	3	4	5	6	7	8	9	10	11	12	13	14
■	■	W		Y	■				■	A			
	N		■			E	■	T			■	T	
H				■	F			M	■		O		?

____

____

Offerings

To solve this puzzle, collect all the letters in each shape below. Unscramble the letters found in the same shape to discover why God looked with favor on Abel's offering and not with favor on Cain's offering. Then read the story in Genesis 4:1–15.

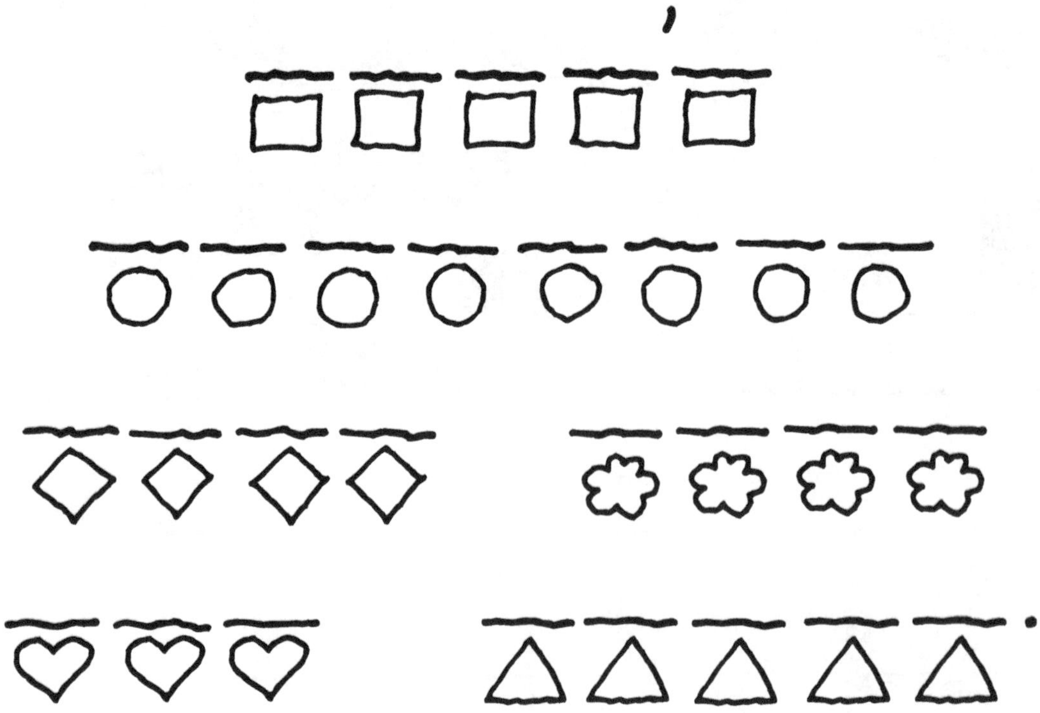

Rainbows

God put the rainbow in the sky as a sign of the covenant He made with all people. Use the code to discover the covenant God made with us. Read about the promise in Genesis 9:8–15.

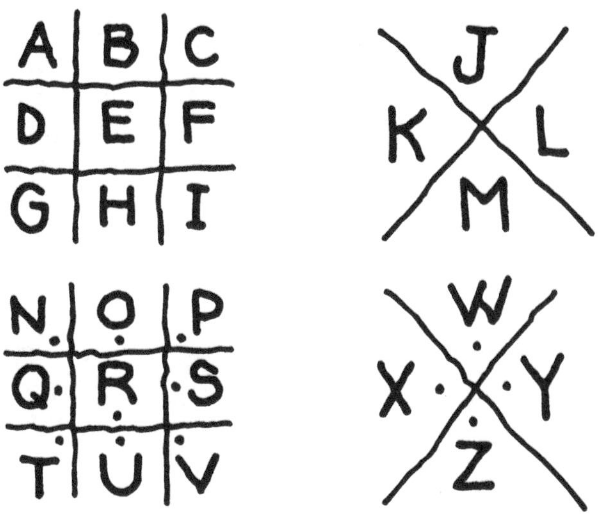

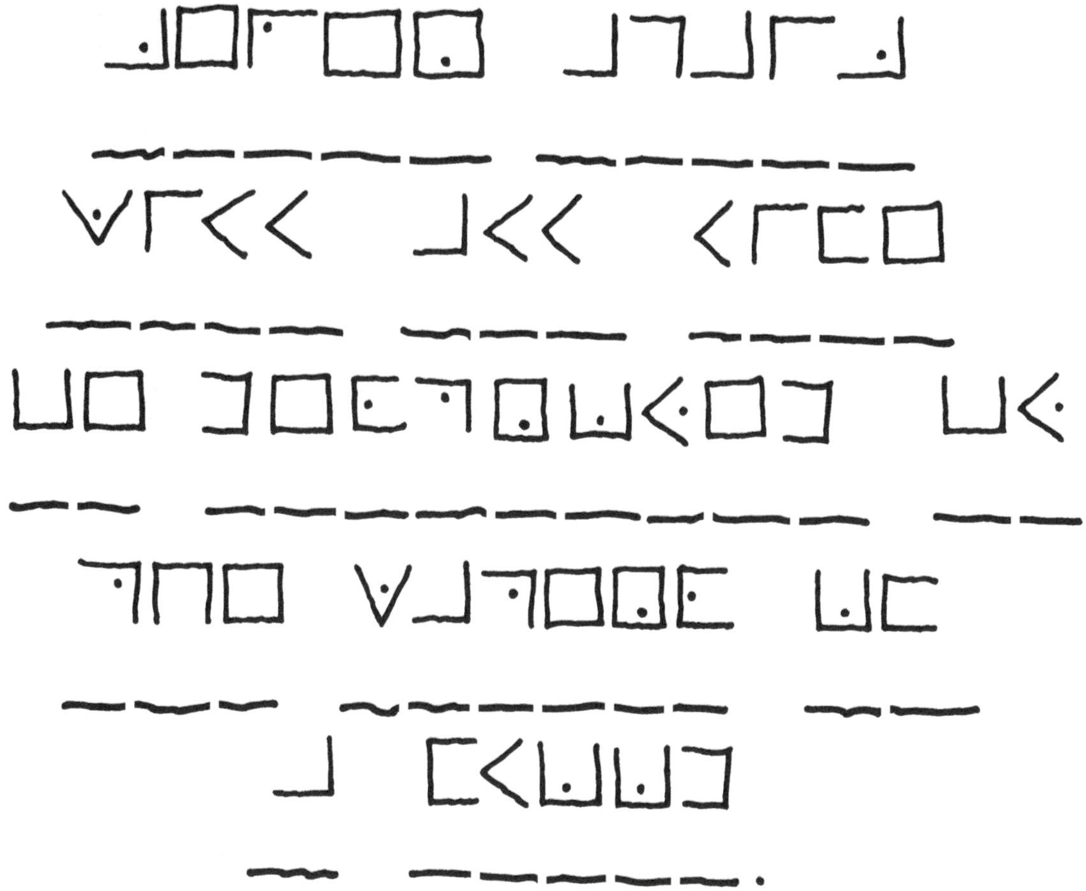

The Promise

God told Abram to go to a new land. Complete the math problems and decode the promise God gave Abram. Check your work in Genesis 12:2. Read about Abram's journey in Genesis 12:1–7.

A = 1 • B = 2 • C = 3 • D = 4 • E = 5 • F = 6 • G = 7 • H = 8 • I = 9 • J = 10
K = 11 • L = 12 • M = 13 • N = 14 • O = 15 • P = 16 • Q = 17 • R = 18 • S = 19
T = 20 •U = 21 • V = 22 • W = 23 • X = 24 • Y = 25 • Z = 26

5 + 4 | 12 + 11 | 6 + 3 | 4 x 3 | 8 + 4

6 + 7 | 8 – 7 | 6 + 5 | 3 + 2 | 5 x 5 | 5 x 3 | 14 + 7

7 + 2 | 7 + 7 | 5 x 4 | 8 + 7 | 5 – 4

4 + 3 | 6 x 3 | 4 + 1 | 1 + 0 | 10 + 10

7 x 2 | 9 – 8 | 10 x 2 | 8 + 1 | 6 + 9 | 9 + 5

3 – 2 | 6 + 8 | 2 + 2 | 3 x 3

16 + 7 | 12 – 3 | 6 x 2 | 7 + 5

1 + 1 | 9 + 3 | 9 – 4 | 12 + 7 | 4 + 15

15 + 10 | 11 + 4 | 7 x 3

Separation

Abram and his nephew Lot agreed to separate because there was not enough grass on the land to feed both of their flocks. Follow the directions carefully for a wonderful example of unselfish love shown by Abram. Read the story in Genesis 13:1–9.

(1) Change the letter O to T • (2) Change the letter E to G • (3) Change the letter H to I
(4) Change the letter T to O • (5) Change the letter G to E • (6) Change the letter I to H
(7) Keep the other letters the same.

H F   Y T U   E T   O T   O I G   L G F O,

___ ___   ___ ___ ___   ___ ___   ___ ___   ___ ___ ___   ___ ___ ___ ___,

H' L L   E T   O T   O I G   R H E I O;   H F

___'___ ___   ___ ___   ___ ___   ___ ___ ___   ___ ___ ___ ___ ___;   ___ ___

Y T U   E T   O T   O I G   R H E I O,   H' L L

___ ___ ___   ___ ___   ___ ___   ___ ___ ___   ___ ___ ___ ___ ___,   ___'___ ___

E T   O T   O I G   L G F O.

___ ___   ___ ___   ___ ___ ___   ___ ___ ___ ___.

Who's Who?

Read Genesis 18:1–14. Use the clues below to fill in the answer boxes on the right. If some of the letters appear in the next answer, the arrows will show you where to place them.

1. Man near the great trees of Mamre (v. 1).
2. The visitors (v. 2).
3. The visitors asked about whom (v. 9)?
4. The one who prepared the meal (v. 7).
5. The visitor who spoke (v. 13).
6. "Will I really have a ____ now that I am old?" (v. 13).

Unscramble the circled letters to solve the puzzle below. The three visitors came to give Abraham and Sarah a

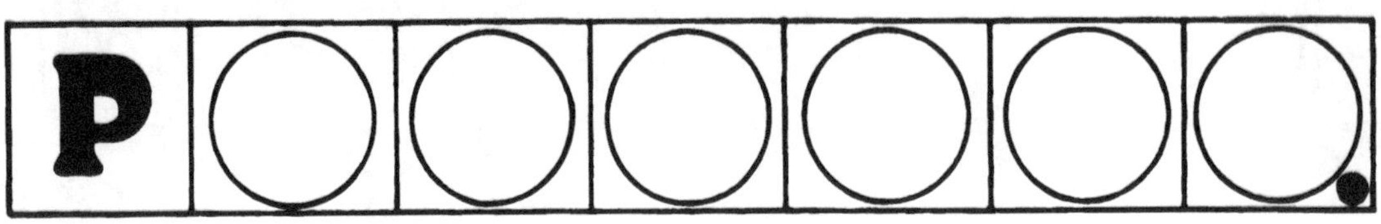

A Lot to Learn

Read Genesis 19. Fill in the missing words in each sentence below. Place an X through the letters that spell the missing words in each line of the box. Then write the remaining letters from left to right, line by line, in the blanks at the bottom. These letters will spell out an important lesson from Genesis 19.

1.	S	S	O	I	D	N	O	M
2.	B	R	L	I	N	O	T	G
3.	D	E	S	S	T	R	O	Y
4.	P	W	I	U	F	N	E	I
5.	S	U	S	L	F	U	H	R
6.	M	P	I	L	E	L	A	R
7.	R	I	N	S	T	I	N	G

1. The two angels arrived at ______________________ (v. 1).
2. The angels spoke to ______________________ (v. 12).
3. They told him the Lord was about to ______________________ the city (v. 14).
4. They told him to flee with his ______________________ and daughters to the mountains (vv. 16–17).
5. Then the Lord rained down burning ______________________ on Sodom and Gomorrah (v. 24).
6. But Lot's wife looked back and became a ______________________ of salt (v. 26).
7. The next morning Abraham looked toward Sodom and Gomorrah and saw dense smoke ______________________ from the land (v. 28).

_ _ _   _ _ _ _ _ _ _   _ _ _ _ _ _ _ _ _ _

Stop!

Abraham was going to follow God's command and offer his son Isaac as a burnt offering. Write the letter that comes after the letter given to see what an angel of the Lord said to Abraham. Read the story in Genesis 22:1–13.

"C N M N S K Z X Z G Z M C N M

_ _ _ _ _ _ _ _ _ _ _ _ _ _ _

S G D A N X," G D R Z H C. "C N M N S

_ _ _ _ _ _ _ _ _ _ _ _ _ _ _ _ _

C N Z M X S G H M F S N G H L. M N V H

_ _ _ _ _ _ _ _ _ _ _ _ _ _ _ _ _ _ _

J M N V S G Z S X N T E D Z Q F N C,

_ _ _ _ _ _ _ _ _ _ _ _ _ _ _ _ _ _

A D B Z T R D X N T G Z U D M N S

_ _ _ _ _ _ _ _ _ _ _ _ _ _ _ _ _

V H S G G D K C E Q N L L D X N T Q R N M,

_ _ _ _ _ _ _ _ _ _ _ _ _ _ _ _ _ _ _ _ _

X N T Q N M K X R N M."

_ _ _ _ _ _ _ _ _ _ _

Family Ties

Abraham's servant was sent to find a wife for Isaac. He found Rebekah. Bethuel, Rebekah's father, told the servant to take Rebekah so she could be the wife of his master's son. Finish each word with its correct ending to discover why Bethuel agreed to send his daughter to a strange land. The last part of each word is in the image. Read the story in Genesis 24:32–52.

HE___ ___ I___ REBE___ ___ ___; TA___ ___

H___ ___ A___ ___ G___, AN___ L___ ___

HE___ BE___ ___ ___ ___ T___ ___ WI___ ___

O___ YO___ ___ MAS___ ___ ___'___ S___ ___,

A___ TH___ LO___ ___ H___ ___

DIR___ ___ ___ ___ ___ ___.

Brothers

Jacob and Esau were the twin sons of Isaac. One of the twins did a very foolish thing. Discover what happened by coloring in each box where the answer does not equal 24. Then read about Jacob and Esau in Genesis 25:27–34 and 27:1–44.

84-27= A	14+10= E	24X0= O	8X3= S	41-28= R	28-4= A	4X6= U	9+9= T
12+12= S	17+7= O	20+14= A	2X12= L	47-24= E	23+14= R	6+18= D	37-8= E
3X12= B	42-22= E	51-27= H	35-11= I	64-20= H	19+5= S	9+17= T	24X1= B
4+20= I	8X6= A	55-31= R	14+10= T	81-55= O	72÷3= H	7X4= A	11+16= E
18-6= S	9+15= R	49-24= G	9X4= O	48-24= I	14+13= D	3+21= G	68-3= R
37-13= H	2+22= T	6X7= I	38-4= H	48÷2= T	7+8= T	16+8= O	68-44= J
22+22= O	30-6= A	16+7= M	24X1= C	30-5= L	25-1= O	23+1= B	3X6= Z

Heavenly Ladder

Jacob dreamed he saw angels ascending and descending a stairway to heaven. Decode the puzzle to discover why Jacob called the place "Bethel" after he awoke. Then read Genesis 28:10–22.

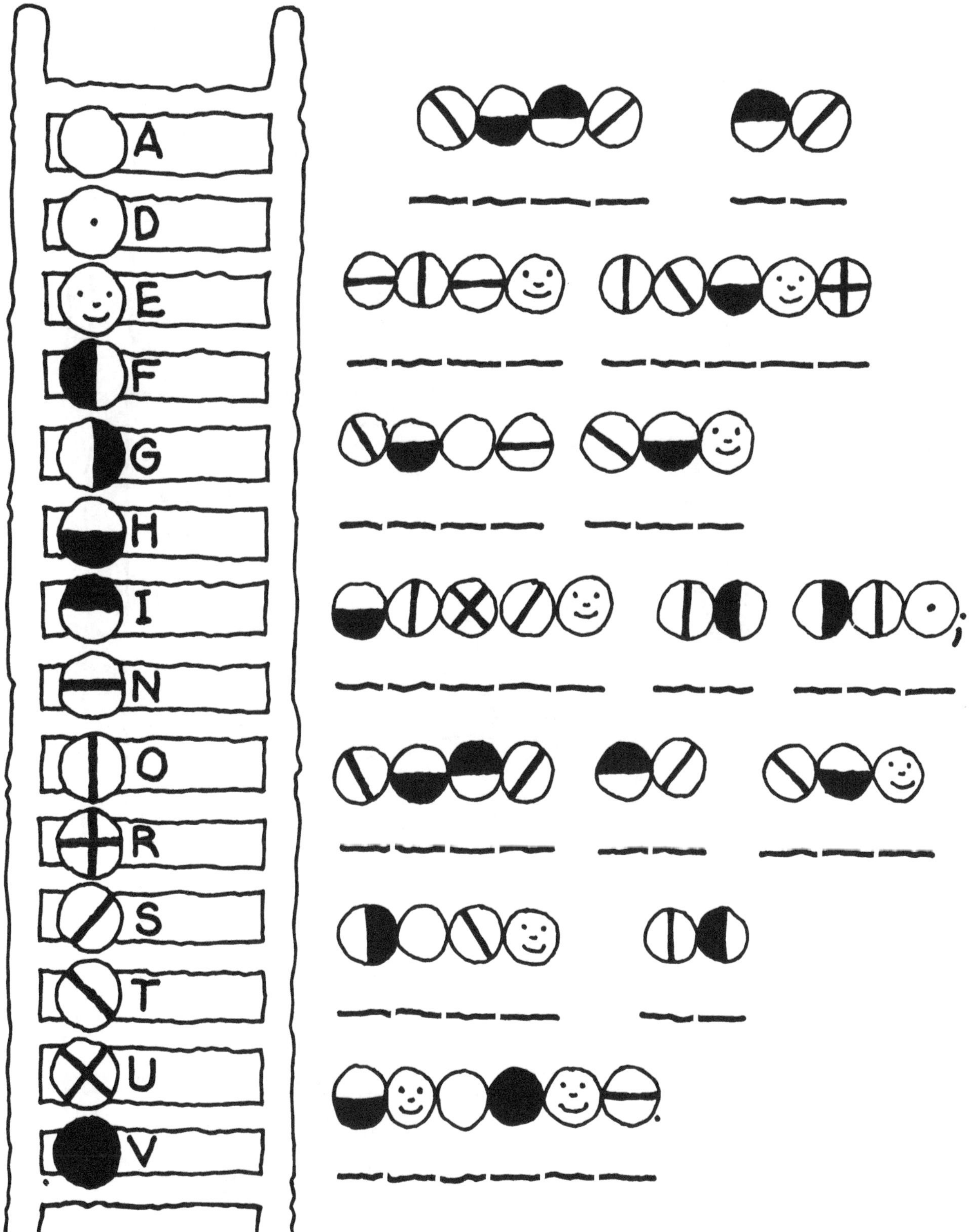

Children of Israel

The 12 sons of Israel became the 12 tribes of Israel. Their names are listed below. Each box connects to a box containing the same letter. After you find the names of the 12 sons of Israel, check your work in Genesis 35:23–26.

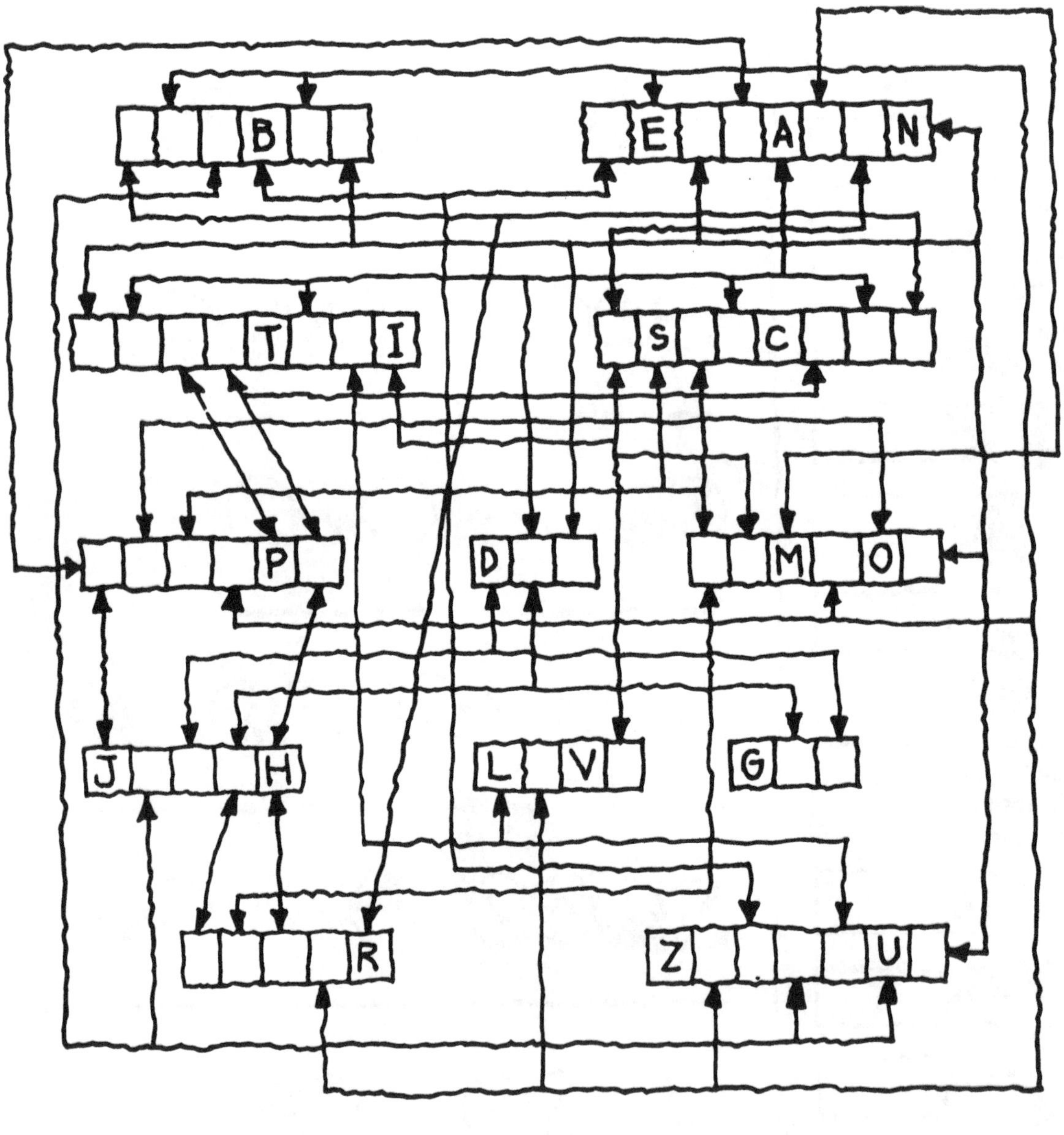

Oh Brother!

Read about Joseph in Genesis 37:3–36. Use the clues below to unscramble the words. Write the circled letters in order in the spaces at the bottom of the page.

(v. 3) ________________ loved Joseph more than any of his sons.

SEARIL ___ ___ ___ (◯) ___ ___

(v. 5) Joseph had a ________________.

MRDAE ___ ___ ___ ___ (◯)

(v. 12) Joseph's brothers had gone to graze their ________________.

COLFSK ___ ___ ___ ___ ___ ___

(vv. 21–22) This brother tried to rescue Joseph.

BUERNE ___ (◯) ___ ___ ___ ___

(v. 23) Joseph was wearing a richly ornamented ________________.

BEOR (◯) ___ ___ ___

(v. 24) Joseph's brothers threw him into a ________________.

NERTISC ___ ___ ___ ___ ___ (◯) ___

(v. 28) His brothers sold him to ________________ merchants.

NATIIMEDI ___ ___ (◯) ___ ___ ___ ___ ___ ___

(v. 36) The Midianites sold Joseph in ________________.

TGEPY (◯) ___ ___ ___ ___

Unscramble the circled letters to fill in the blanks below.

(v. 19) Joseph's brothers called him a ___ ___ ___ ___ ___ ___ ___.

Who's in Charge?

Read Genesis 41:15–57 about Joseph in Egypt. Then use the code to solve the puzzle. Find the letter in the message on the outside circle. Match it with the letter below it on the inside circle.

Z R K B K Y R   C K S N   D Y   T Y C O Z R,   "C S X M O   Q Y N

R K C   W K N O   K V V   D R S C   U X Y G X   D Y   I Y E...

S   R O B O L I   Z E D   I Y E   S X   M R K B Q O

Y P   D R O   G R Y V O   V K X N   Y P   O Q I Z D."

Hunger Strike

Read Genesis 41:38–43, 46–49, 53–57. Then write the food names from each square in the matching line of the acrostic puzzle. When complete, the shaded area will tell about the crisis that came to Egypt.

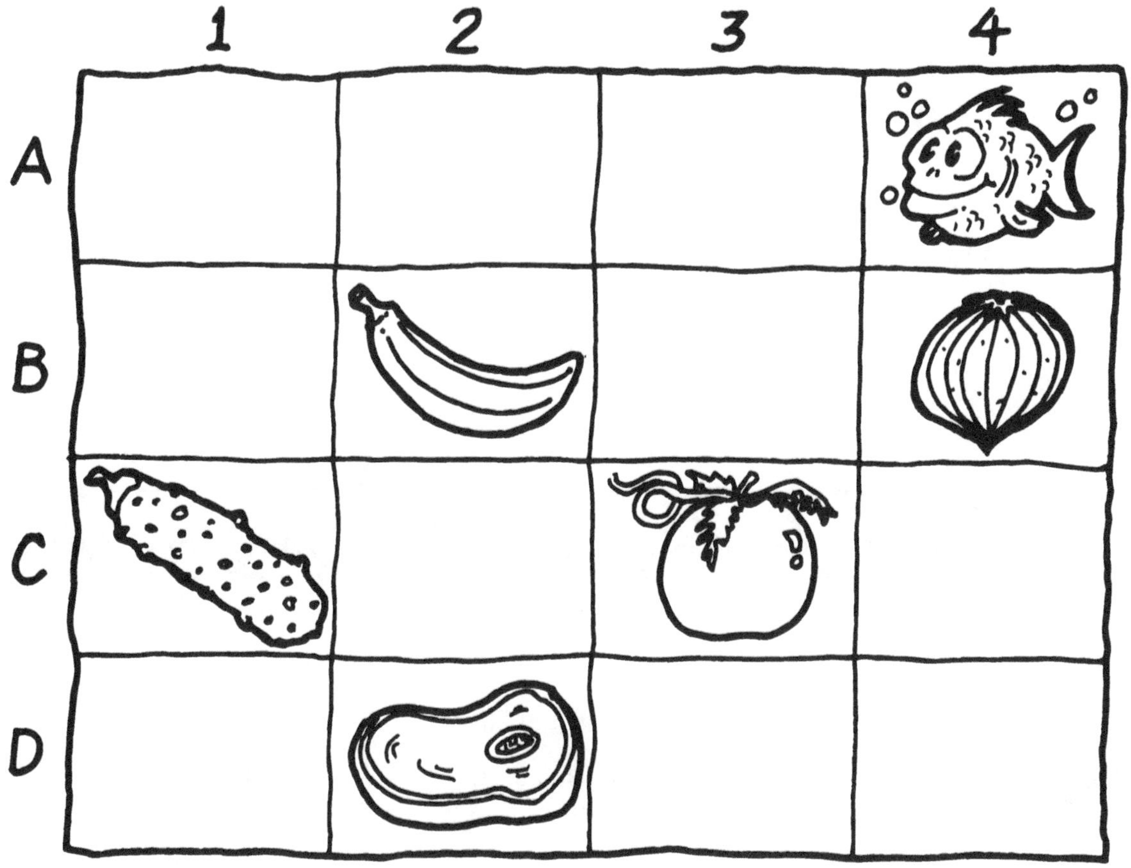

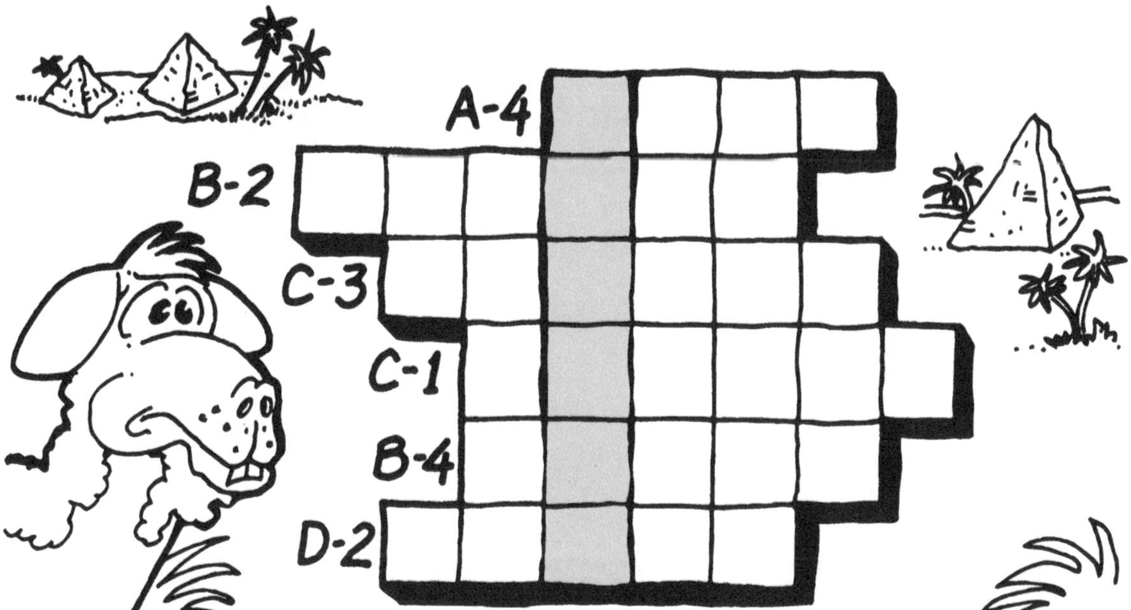

Family Reunion

Read about Joseph's reunion with his family in Genesis 42, 45, and 47. Mark an O over the statements that are true and an X over the false ones. If you're correct, you will have three Xs or Os in a row.

Ten of Joseph's brothers went to Egypt to try to buy grain.	Joseph's brothers didn't know who he was when they met him in Egypt.	Joseph was angry that his brothers had sold him into slavery.
Joseph told his brothers they should be mad at themselves for what they did.	Joseph said it was good he had been sold into Egypt because he had saved lives.	Joseph didn't want his brothers to tell his father he was alive.
Joseph's brothers were shepherds.	Pharaoh would not let Joseph's family settle in Goshen.	The Israelites increased greatly in number.

Egyptian Inscription

Read Exodus 1:1–5. These verses tell the names of the 12 sons of Israel. These men and their families moved to the land of Egypt to escape famine. The names of these 12 men are hidden in the Egyptian inscriptions below. Can you find them? Hint: hold this page up to a mirror.

Baby in a Basket

Read Exodus 2:1–10 about an important child. To solve the puzzle, first work the math problems. Then, beginning with the square that contains the answer of number 1, write the words in numerical order on the lines below.

4+4 him	23-10 he	11+8 him	43-22 saying	100-99 when	14-2 and	36-32 grew
5+6 daughter	12+12 him	25-20 older	13+15 water	100-80 Moses	100-94 she	9+7 son
20-3 She	92-90 the	20+5 out	28-14 became	18+9 the	11+11 I	7+2 to
30-20 Pharaoh's	12+6 named	8-1 took	21+2 drew	18+8 of	5-2 child	8+7 her

Scrambled Plagues

One of the ten plagues God sent to the Egyptians was frogs. Unscramble the words on the frogs to discover eight other plagues God sent. If you need help, read Exodus 7–10.

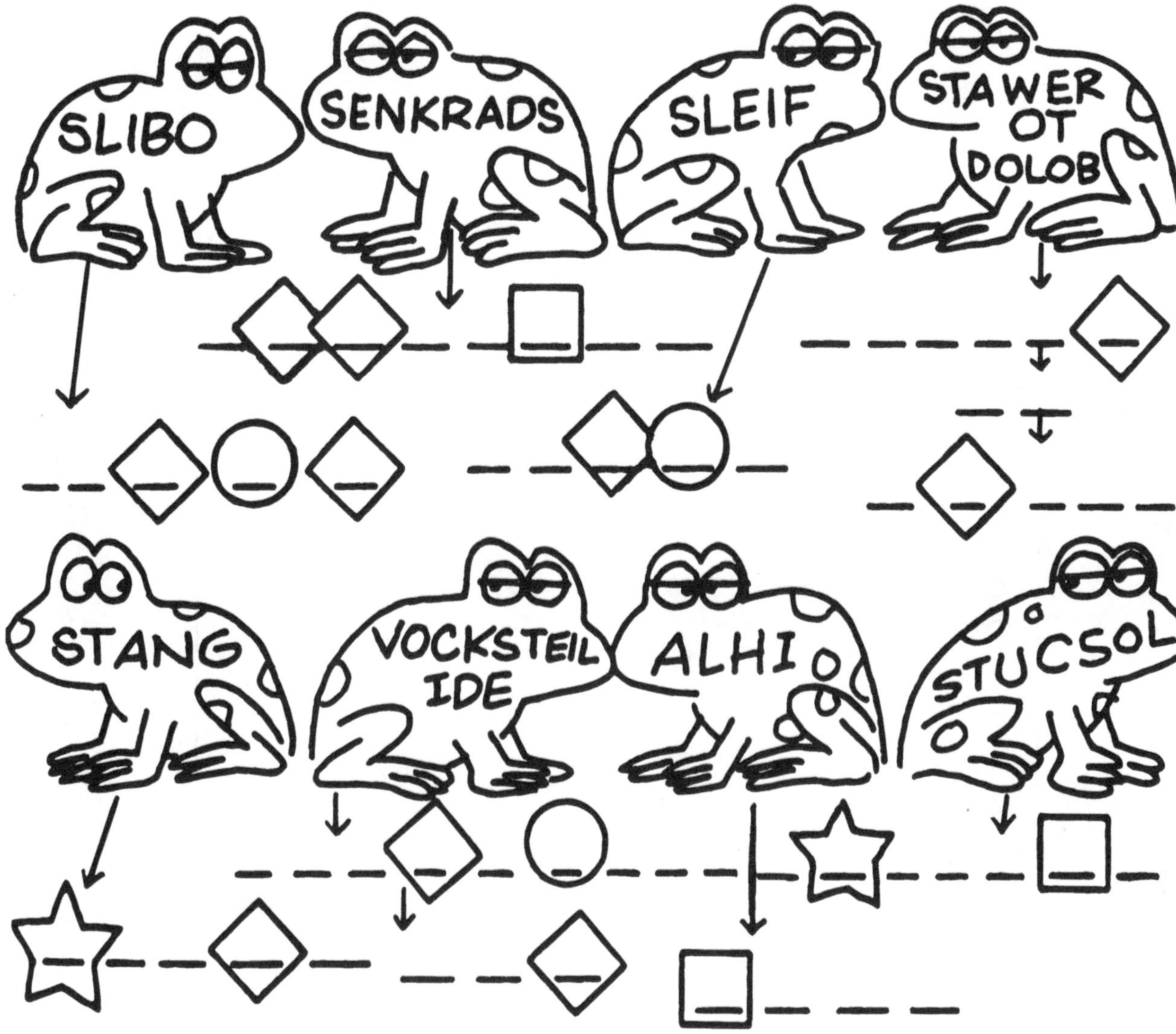

Organize the letters by shape. Then unscramble the letters to find God's message to Pharaoh.

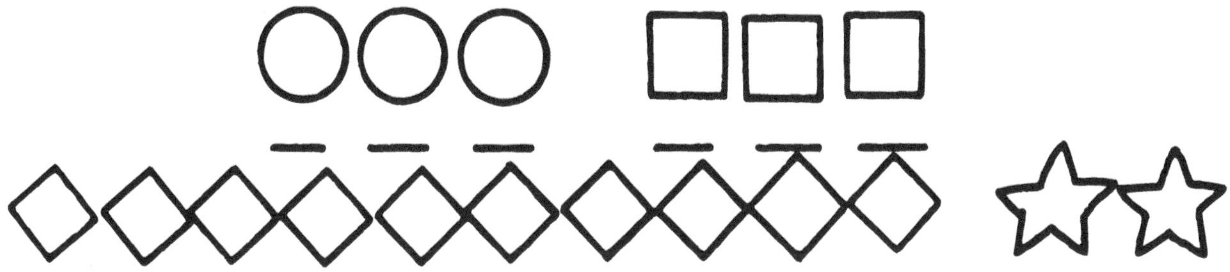

Eat and Run

Read about God's plan to free Israel in Exodus 12:3, 7–8, and 11–14. Connect the dots in order from 1 to 73 to find the Bible name for this event.

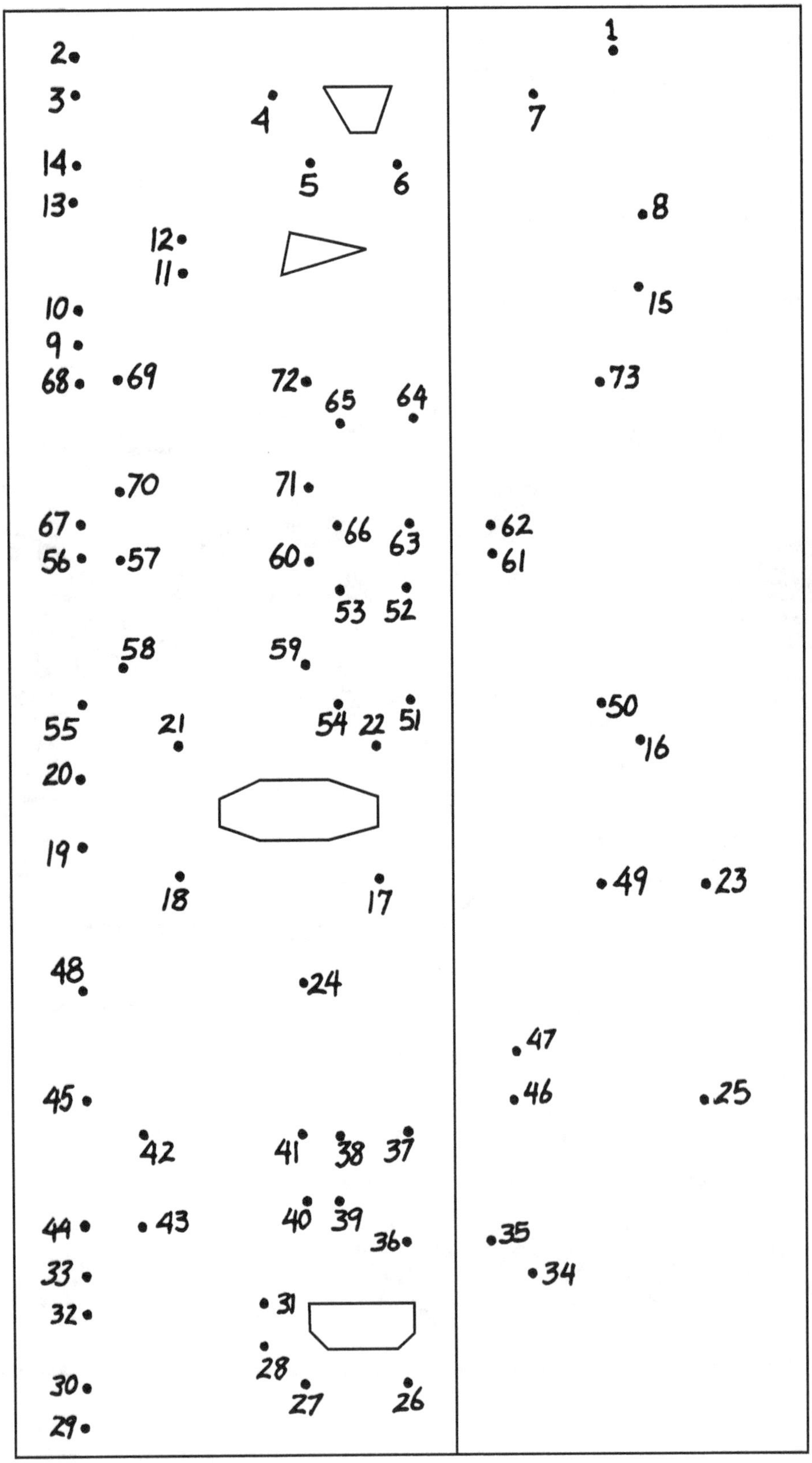

Our Passover Lamb

Read Exodus 12:21–31 to answer each question. If the answer is true, circle the letter under T. If it is false, circle the letter under F. Write the circled letters on the correct blanks below. Then read 1 Corinthians 5:7.

	T	F
1. Moses told the Israelites to put blood on the top and side of their doorframes.	H	R
2. The blood was from goats.	J	U
3. The firstborn in every family without blood on its doorframe would die.	S	M
4. The firstborn animals would die.	J	L
5. Moses told them all to stay in their homes until morning.	I	A
6. The Lord struck down the firstborn Egyptians at 2:00 in the morning.	W	C
7. Pharaoh's oldest child was killed.	E	I
8. The oldest child of every prisoner in the dungeons was killed.	T	R
9. The Lord "passed over" the homes that had blood on the doorframes.	S	D
10. The Jews remember the event by celebrating Passover.	S	U
11. While it was still night, Pharaoh told Moses to take the Israelites out of Egypt.	R	E

____ ____ ____ ____ ____   ____ ____ ____ ____ ____ ____
4 7 3 2 9   6 1 11 5 10 8

Walls of Water

Find out what happened in Exodus 14:15–31 by going through the maze. Pick up the letters as you go and write them on the lines below.

Food for Thought

Match the puzzle pieces to the shapes below. Write each word in the empty puzzle piece to complete the verse from Exodus 16.

At ______ you will ______ ______ and in the ______ you will be ______ with ______. ______ you will ______ that I am the ______ your ______. Exodus 16:12

The Ten Commandments

Use the code to find the missing word in each of the Ten Commandments. Read about the Commandments in Exodus 20:1–17.

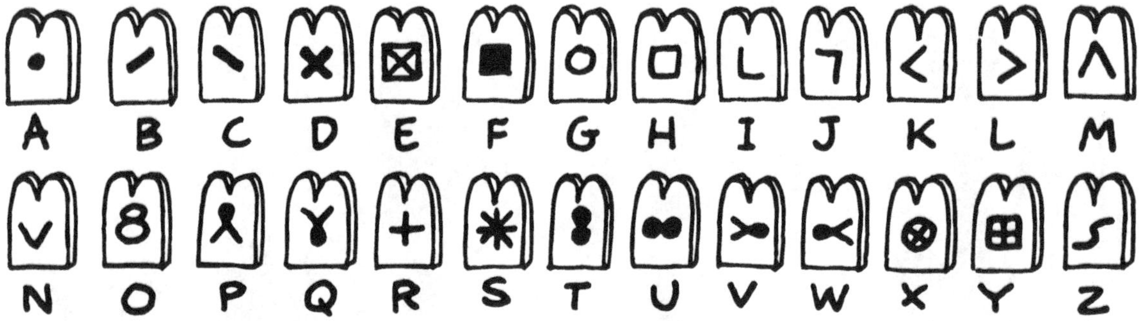

1. You shall have no other ____ before me.
   ○ 8 × ✱

2. You shall not make or worship ____.
   L × 8 > ✱

3. You shall not misuse God's ____.
   ∨ • ∧ ⊠

4. Remember the ____ day by keeping it holy.
   ✱ • / / • ⁑ □

5. ____ your father and mother.
   □ 8 ∨ 8 +

6. You shall not ____.
   ∧ •• + × ⊠ +

7. You shall not commit ____.
   • × •• > ⁑ ⊠ + ⊞

8. You shall not ____.
   ✱ ⁑ ⊠ • >

9. You shall not give ____ testimony.
   ■ • > ✱ ⊠

10. You shall not ____.
    \ 8 >- ⊠ ⁑

Beware of Imitations

Is it possible to have a substitute for God? Color in each box where the answer does not equal 24 to see what God says in Exodus 20:3.

9 x 4 = T	14 + 10 = Y	14 + 13 = H	8 x 3 = O	68 – 30 = E	6 x 7 = E	28 – 4 = U
35 – 11= S	18 – 16 = O	19 + 5 = H	48 ÷ 2 = A	49 – 24 = N	16 + 8 = L	68 – 44 = L
11 + 16 = A	24 x 1 = H	7 x 4 = U	4 + 20 = A	55 – 31 = V	81 – 55 = N	14 + 10 = E
3 x 12 = O	42 – 22 = R	72 ÷ 3 = N	64 – 20 = R	9 + 17 = Y	9 + 15 = O	8 x 6 = U
48 – 24 = O	24 x 1 = T	21 + 5 = E	63 – 39 = H	11 + 13 = E	37 – 8 = W	97 – 73 = R
51 – 27 = G	47 – 24 = A	3 + 21 = O	23 + 14 = F	99 – 75 = D	52 – 27 = O	83 – 59 = S
4 x 6 = B	12 + 12 = E	17 + 7 = F	9 + 9 = A	36 – 12 = O	2 x 12 = R	6 + 18 = E
24 x 0 = A	41 – 28 = R	37 – 13 = M	12 x 12 = H	84 – 27 = A	2 + 22 = E	20 + 14 = N

Respect

Find a shape on the outside of the puzzle that matches a shape in the tablet. Write the word from the outside shape on the matching shape. Read the rest of Exodus 20:7 to find out more about God's name. Check James 3:2–5, 7–10; and Ephesians 4:29 for more about our words.

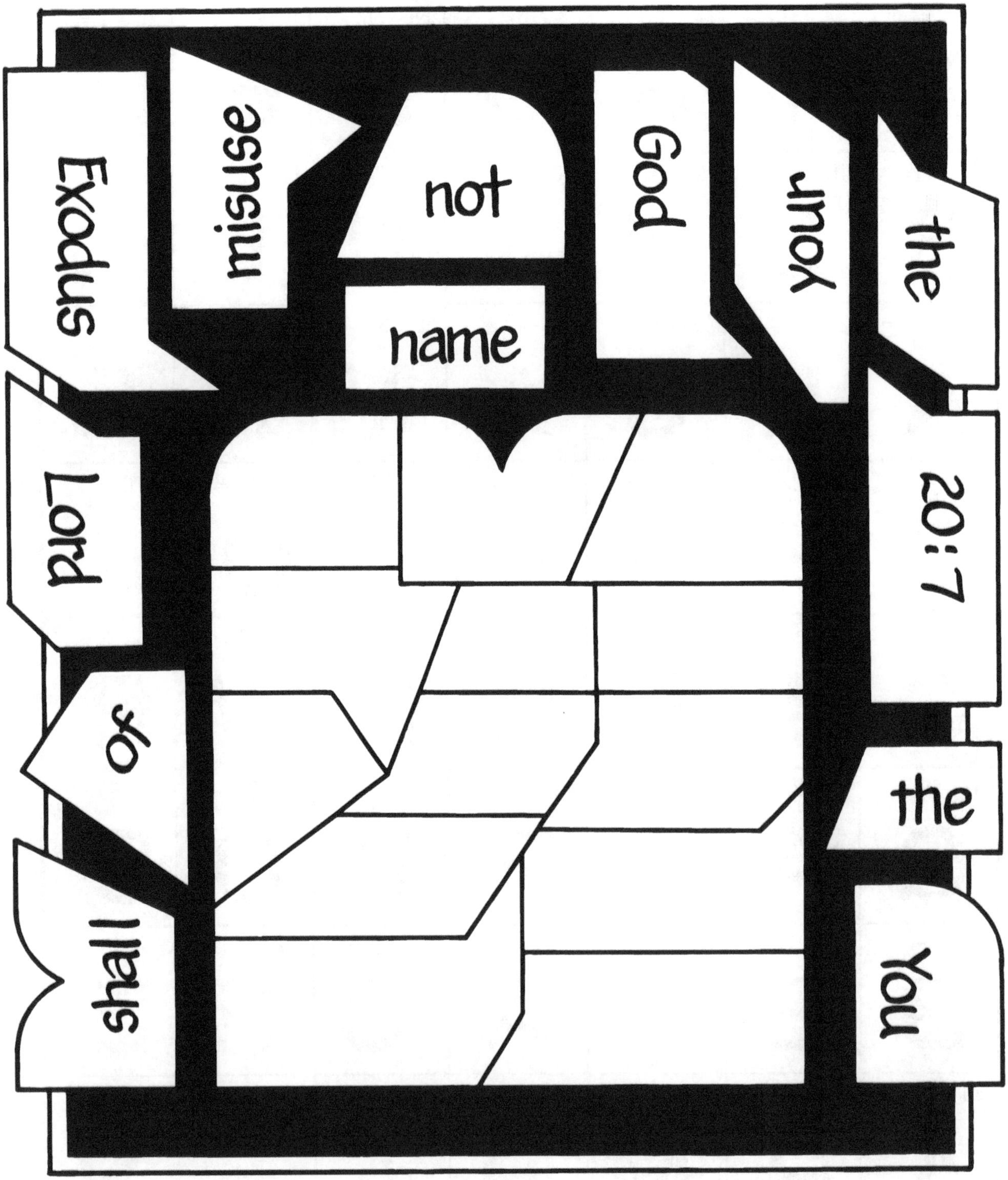

Ring the Bells

Collect all the letters with the number 1 to spell the first word below. Do the same with numbers 2 through 8. After collecting all the letters in the proper order, you will find a message about a special day. Read Exodus 20:8.

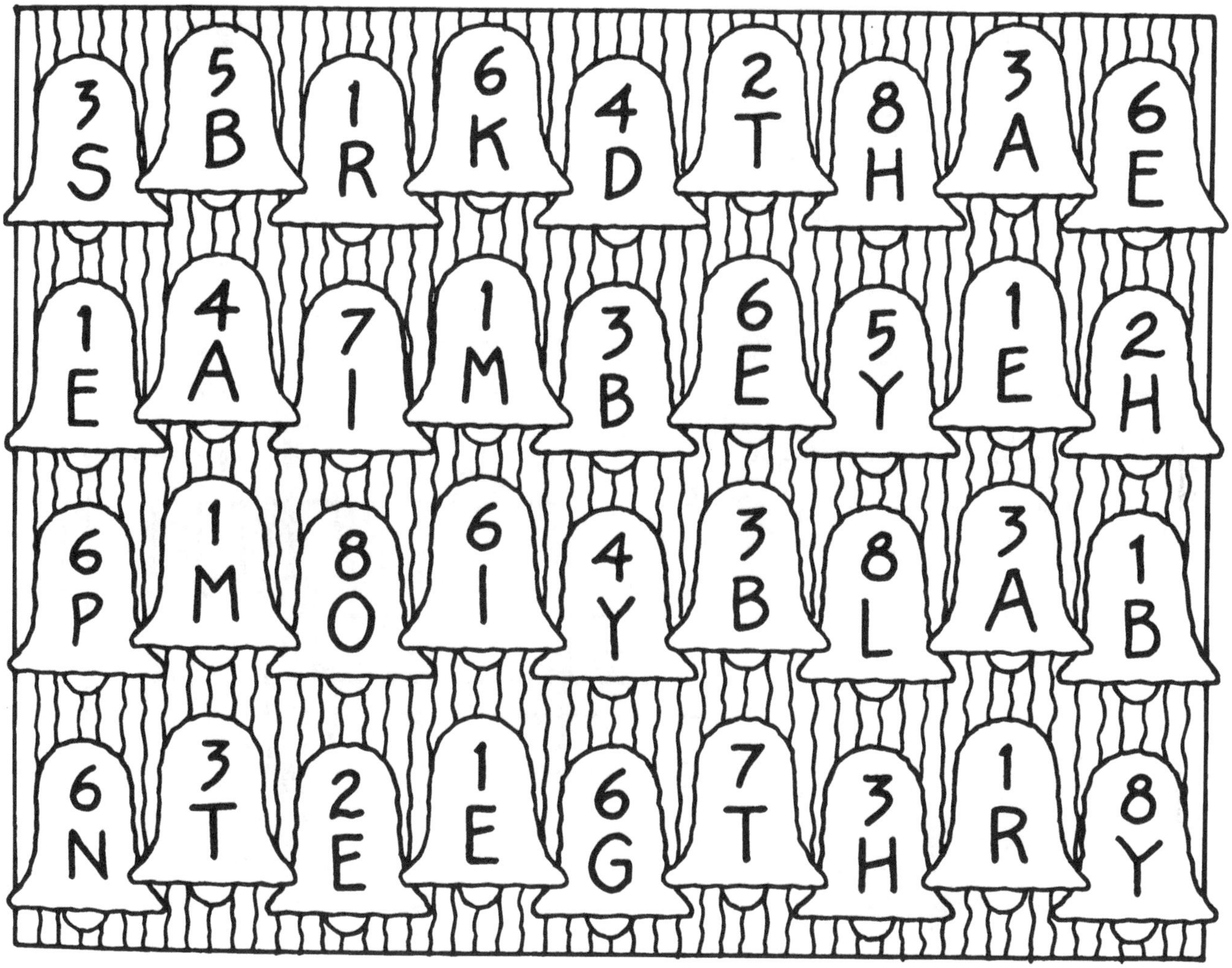

___ ___ ___ ___ ___ ___ ___ ___   ___ ___ ___
1 1 1 1 1 1 1 1   2 2 2

___ ___ ___ ___ ___ ___ ___   ___ ___ ___
3 3 3 3 3 3 3   4 4 4

___ ___   ___ ___ ___ ___ ___ ___ ___
5 5   6 6 6 6 6 6 6

___ ___   ___ ___ ___ ___.
7 7   8 8 8 8

The Promise

Complete the puzzle below to read the first commandment. Each box connects to a box containing the same letter. Use the letters given to fill in the rest of the boxes. After you finish the puzzle, check your work in Exodus 20:12.

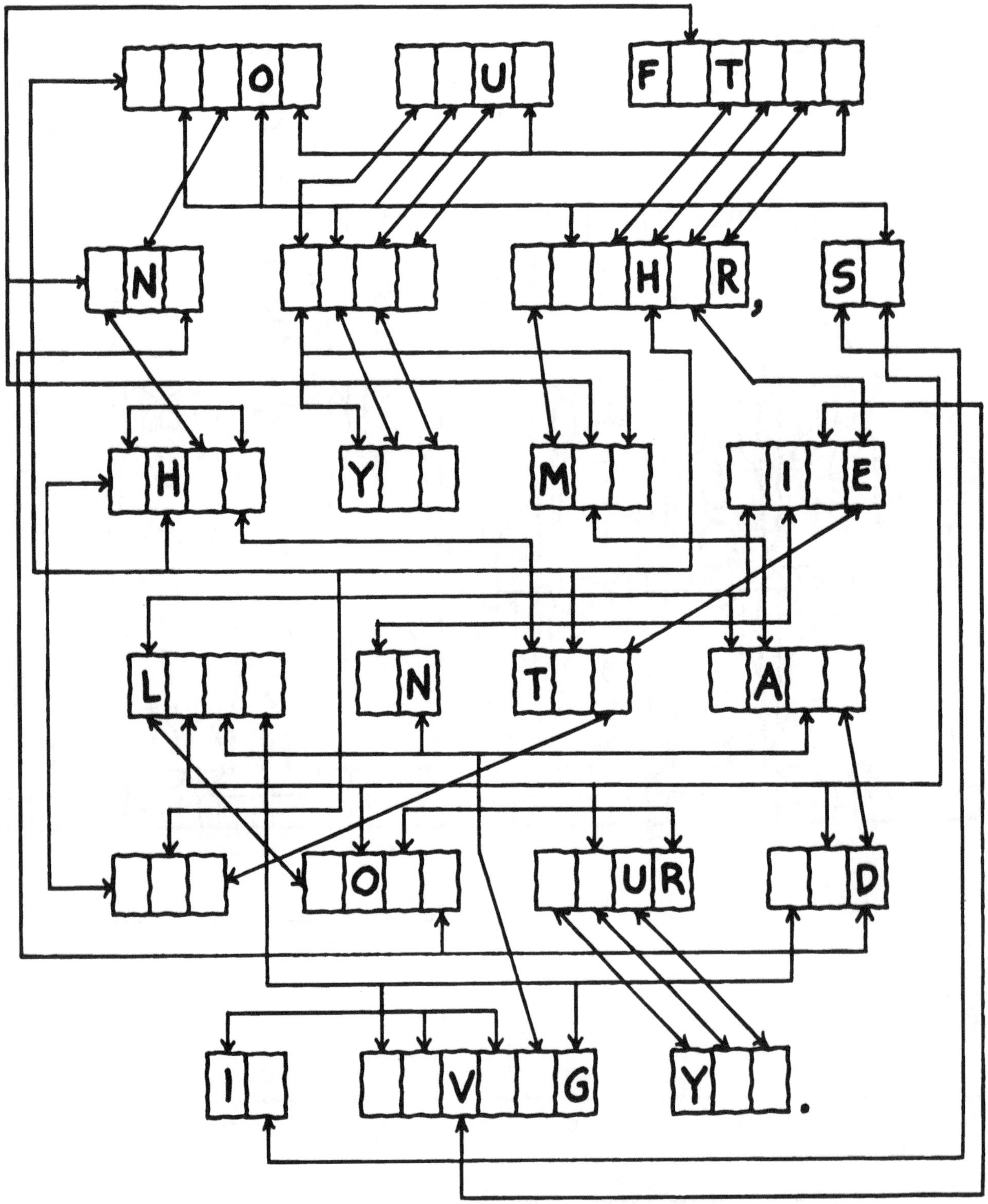

Honesty

Find Exodus 20:16 by going through the maze. Pick up the letters as you go and put them on the lines below. There is only one correct path.

Leave It Alone

Use the secret code to discover how we should behave toward our neighbors. Find each letter in the message below on the inside circle. Match it with the letter above it on the outside circle. Put those letters on the boxes below. Read Exodus 20:17.

O E K I X Q B B D E J S E L U J O E K H

D U Y W X R E H' I X E K I U.

O E K I X Q B B D E J S E L U J . . .

Q D O J X Y D W J X Q J R U B E D W I J E

O E K H D U Y W X R E H.

The Tabernacle

Read Exodus 25:1–9. Then fill in the boxes to find God's promise. Each box connects to another box containing the same letter.

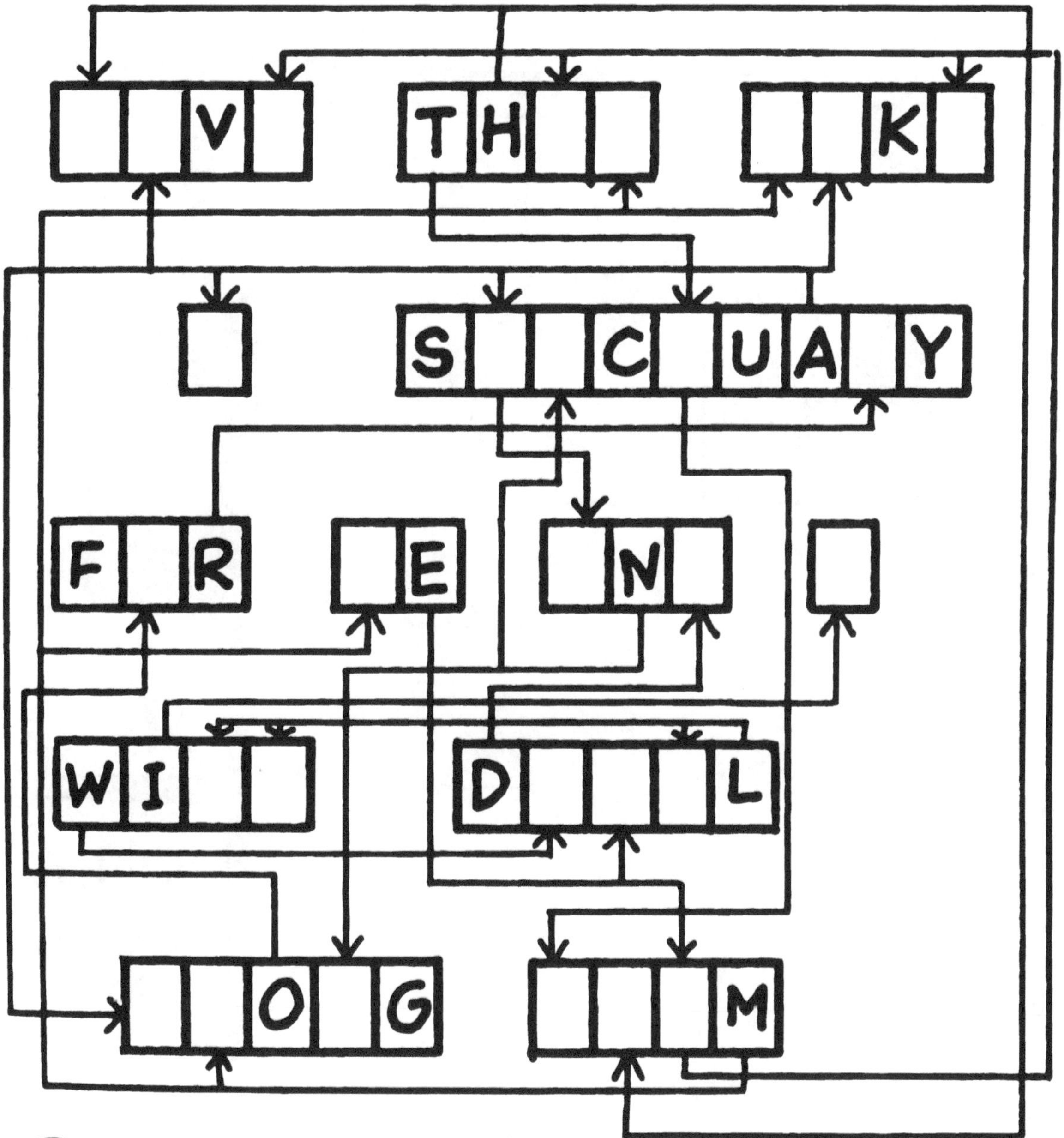

Written in Stone

Find a shape on the outside of the puzzle that matches a shape in the tablet. Write the word from that shape on the matching shape. Read Exodus 32:1–6, 15–20.

In Numbers

Below each blank are two numbers. The first number names a ROW (1–3) in the code key. The second number names a COLUMN (1–7) in the code key. For example, 13 means look in row 1 and column 3 for the letter. Read the Numbers 13–14 for help.

		C	O	L	U	M	N	S
		1	2	3	4	5	6	7
R	1	A	B	C	D	E	F	G
O	2	H	I	J	K	L	M	N
W	3	O	P	R	S	T	U	Y

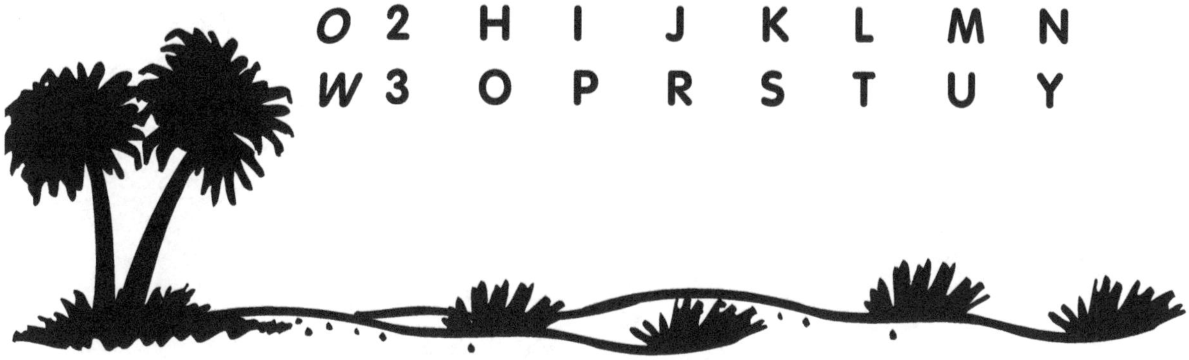

God told Moses to explore the land of ___ ___ ___ ___ ___ ___
13 11 27 11 11 27

by sending one leader from each ___ ___ ___ ___ ___.
35 33 22 12 15

These men returned after ___ ___ ___ ___ ___ days.
16 31 33 35 37

They said the land flowed with ___ ___ ___ ___ and
26 22 25 24

___ ___ ___ ___ ___. But ten men said,
21 31 27 15 37

"The people are ___ ___ ___ ___ ___ ___ ___ ___ than we are" (Num. 13:31).
34 35 33 31 27 17 15 33

___ ___ ___ ___ ___ ___ and Caleb said,
23 31 34 21 36 11

"If the Lord is ___ ___ ___ ___ ___ ___ ___ with us,
32 25 15 11 34 15 14

he will ___ ___ ___ ___ us into that land" (Num. 14:8).
25 15 11 14

Thirst Aid

Begin with the letter M on the top right of the spiral. Write that M on the first blank below. Then print every other letter on the blanks below, crossing out each letter as you use it. When you reach the center of the spiral, go back to the outside of the spiral and print the letters you have not yet used. Read Numbers 20:11.

Then ___ ___ ___ ___ ___

___ ___ ___ ___ ___ ___

his arm and ___ ___ ___ ___ ___ ___ the

___ ___ ___ ___ ___ ___ ___ ___ ___

with his ___ ___ ___ ___ ___.

___ ___ ___ ___ ___ gushed out, and

the ___ ___ ___ ___ ___ ___ ___ ___ ___ and

their ___ ___ ___ ___ ___ ___ ___ ___ ___

___ ___ ___ ___ ___.

But Why, Lord?

Read the exciting story of God giving the Ten Commandments in Deuteronomy 5:1–4, 22–29. God wants all people to keep His commandments. Use the alphabet below to find out why we should follow God's law.

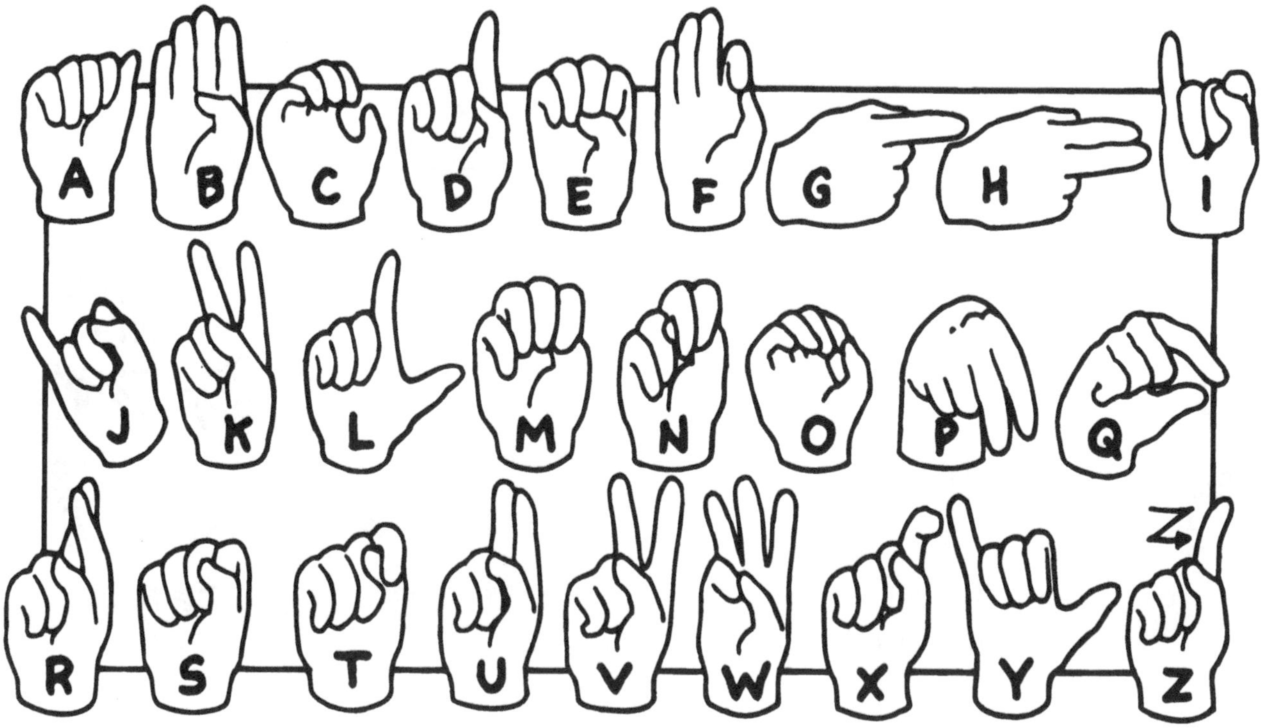

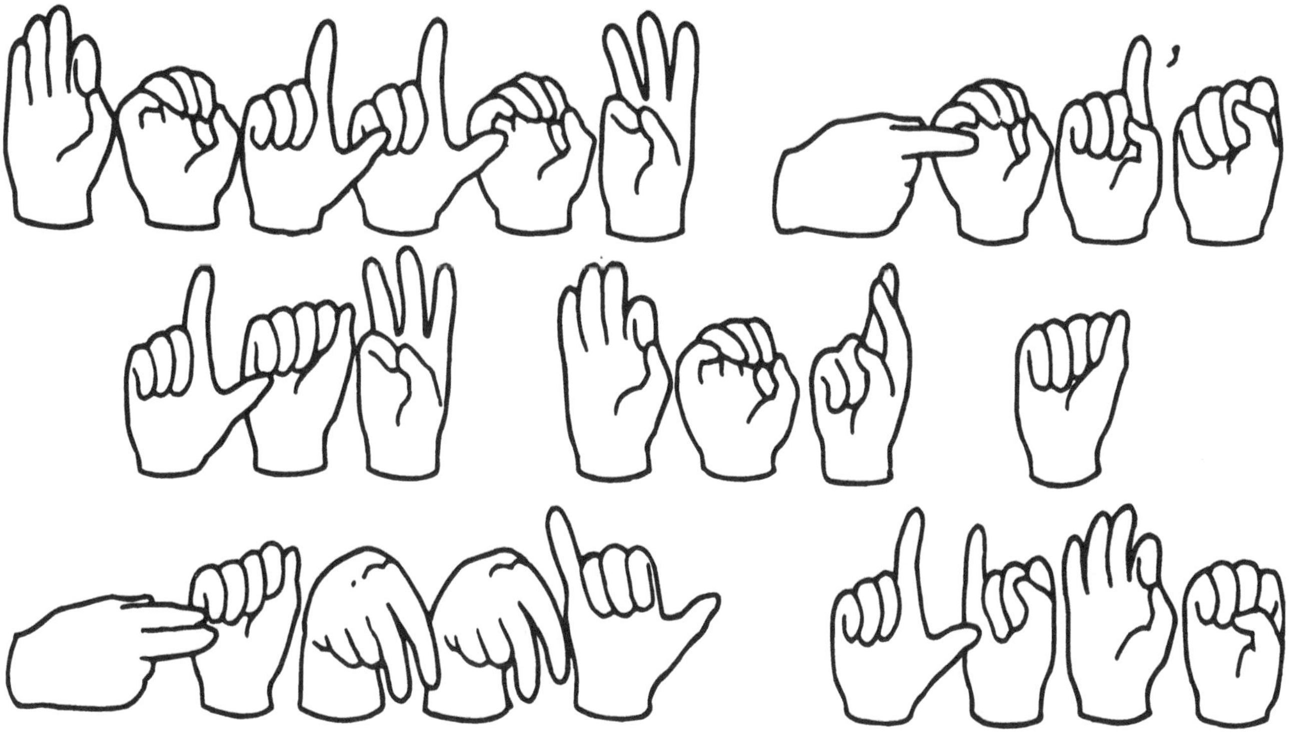

Do It Right

In the first row of letters, cross out the letters of the word REMEMBER. In the second row, cross out the letters of the word THE. Continue this for each row. Write the leftover letters in the blanks on the right. They will spell a message. Check your work in Deuteronomy 6:5.

Example: SHARE … S L H A O V E R E = LOVE

REMEMBER	R E M L E M O V B E R E	___ ___ ___ ___
THE	T T H E H E	___ ___ ___
LAWS	L L A O W R S D	___ ___ ___ ___
AND	A Y O N D U R	___ ___ ___ ___
DECREES	D E C G O R E E D S	___ ___ ___
OF	W O I F T H	___ ___ ___ ___
MOSES	M A L L O S E S	___ ___ ___
TALK	T A Y O L K U R	___ ___ ___ ___
ABOUT	H E A B O U A R T T	___ ___ ___ ___ ___
THEM	A T N H D E W M I T H	___ ___ ___ ___ ___ ___ ___
THESE	T A L L H E S E	___ ___ ___
COMMANDMENTS	C O Y M O M A N D M U R E N T S	___ ___ ___ ___
ARE	A S R O E U L	___ ___ ___ ___
TO	A N T D W O I T H	___ ___ ___ ___ ___ ___ ___
BE	B A L L E	___ ___ ___
UPON	Y O U U P O R N	___ ___ ___ ___
YOUR	Y S T R O U E N G R T H	___ ___ ___ ___ ___ ___ ___ ___
HEART	H E D E U A T R E R O N O T M Y 6:5	

___ ___ ___ ___ ___ ___ ___ ___ ___ ___ ___   ___ : ___

Welcome Home

Read Joshua 3:9–17. In the blanks blanks below, write yes if the statement is true or no if the statement is false. To find the answer to the last sentence, fold this page vertically so the arrows at A and B meet the points at A and B. Then write the answer on the line below.

A→ A•

Now the Israelites told Joshua to listen to the words of the Lord. ______

The priests were told to car-r-r y the ark as they cro s-s-s-s-s-s-s-s-s-s-s-s-sssed the Jordan River. ______

One thing to remember is the Jordan was at flood stage at this time. ______

The Israelites did not want to car-r-r-r-r-ry the ark. ______

The gr oup (the Israelites) walked ar ound the Jordan River.

B→ B•

____

Shout!

To find the answers to this puzzle, start at the circled letter on the grid below and move, one letter at a time, in the direction shown by the arrows under the blank spaces. Example: the first line begins with J so find the J in the grid below, then follow the arrow up to the O. From the O, follow the arrow up to the S. Fill in each letter in the line. Read Joshua 6 to find out more about the story.

Who did God call to lead the Israelites after Moses died?

J ___ ___ ___ ___ ___
↖ ↑ → → →

What city did the Israelites march around for six days?

J ___ ___ ___ ___ ___ ___
→ ↖ ↙ ← ↑ →

What did seven priests carry in front of the ark?

T ___ ___ ___ ___ ___ ___ ___
→ ↓ ↗ ↘ ↓ → ↓

How many times did the people march around the city on the seventh day?

S ___ ___ ___ ___
↖ ↙ ← ↗

What did the people do when the priests sounded the trumpet blast?

S ___ ___ ___ ___ ___ ___
← ↓ ← ← ↑ ↑

What did the wall of the city do when the people shouted?

C ___ ___ ___ ___ ___ ___ ___ ___
↘ → ↓ → → ↓ ← ←

(T) R M
S H U A P
H O R D N E T
(C) I (J) E V H (S)
O L T U O
L A P
D E S

Achan's Sin

Read Joshua 7:16–26 and 8:1. These verses tell us Achan disobeyed God and took some things that did not belong to him. Read the pictures below to discover a very important lesson that Achan learned the hard way.

___ ___ ___   ___ ___ ___   ___ ___ ___

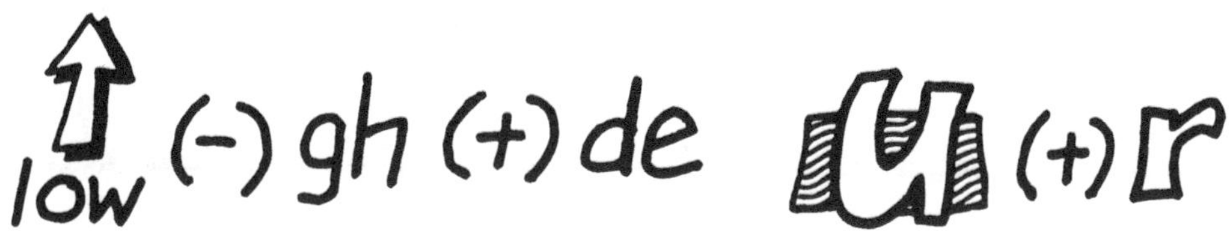

___ ___ ___ ___   ___ ___ ___ ___

___ ___ ___ ___   ___ ___ ___ ___

___ ___ ___ .

Remember the Promise

To find Joshua's message, first number the parts of the story in order. See Joshua 24:1–18 if you need help. Then fill in the puzzle message using the circled and squared letters. For example, to find the letter for [1], look for the squared letter in part 1 of the story. See verse 14 for help.

☐ You live[d] in the desert for a lo(n)g time.	☐ To I(s)aac I gav[e] Jacob and Esau.
☐ I sent Moses and Aa(r)on and brought yo[u] out of Egypt.	☐ Your (f)orefat[h]ers … lived beyond the river.
☐ I led (A)braham through[o]ut Canaan.	☐ I gave you a land on (w)hich you did not to[i]l.
☐ Jacob and his sons went do(w)n to Egyp[t].	☐ To Abraham [I] ga(v)e Isaac.

(5) [2] (8)   (4) [4] (6) (3) [4]

(7) [2] [7]   (8) [3] [5] [1]   (2) [8] [8]

(1) (2) [3] [5] [1] (1) [6] [8] (5) [4] (4) (4)

Lead the Way

Read these statements from Judges 4. If the statement is true, follow the T path. If it is false, follow the F path. Write the word at the end of each path in the blank space.

1. The Israelites once again did evil (v. 1).
2. The Lord sold them into the hands of Jabin (v. 2).
3. Jabin cruelly oppressed them for 100 years (v. 3).
4. Deborah was leading Israel at that time (v. 4).
5. Sisera was the commander of Jabin's army (v. 7).
6. Israelites came to Deborah to decide their disputes (v. 5).
7. Barak led 10,000 men against Sisera (v. 6).
8. Barak said he would never go (v. 8).
9. All the troops of Sisera fell by the sword. Only two men were left (v. 16).

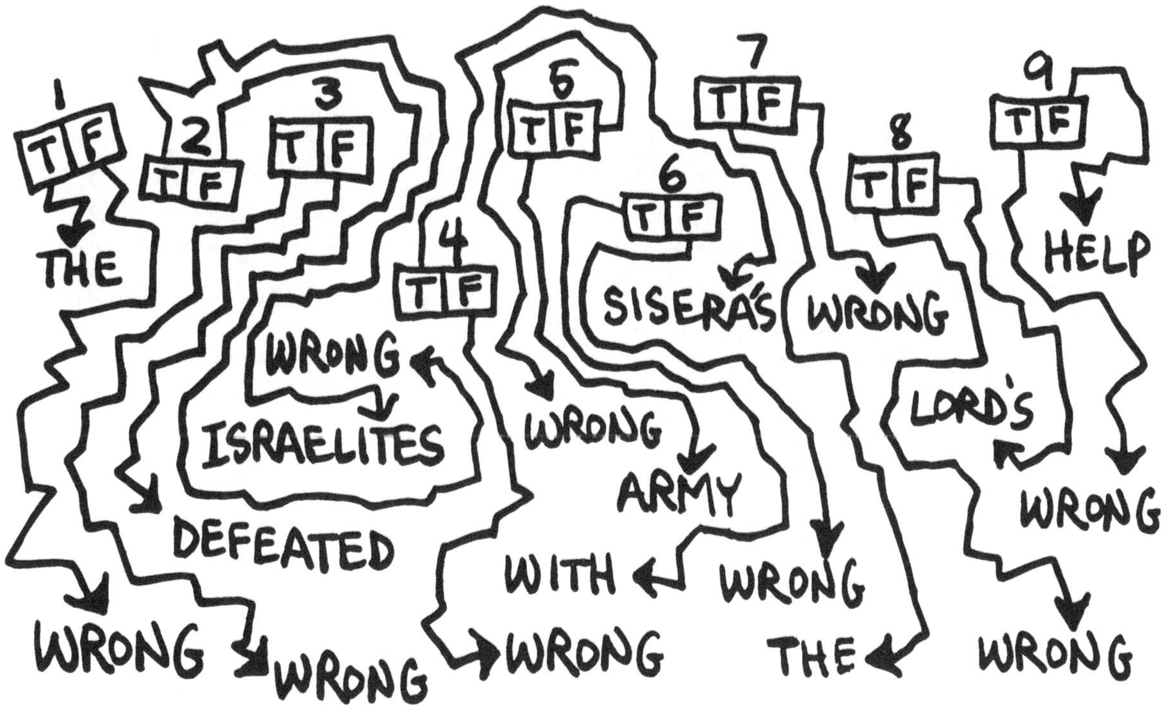

_ _ _   _ _ _ _ _ _ _ _ _ _ _

_ _ _ _ _ _ _ _ _   _ _ _ _ _ _ _'_

_ _ _ _,   _ _ _ _ _   _ _ _

_ _ _ _'_   _ _ _ _ _.

Surprise!

Israel's army was very small, but they followed God's directions. Find their battle cry from Judges 7:20 by filling in the boxes. Each box connects to a box containing the same letter.

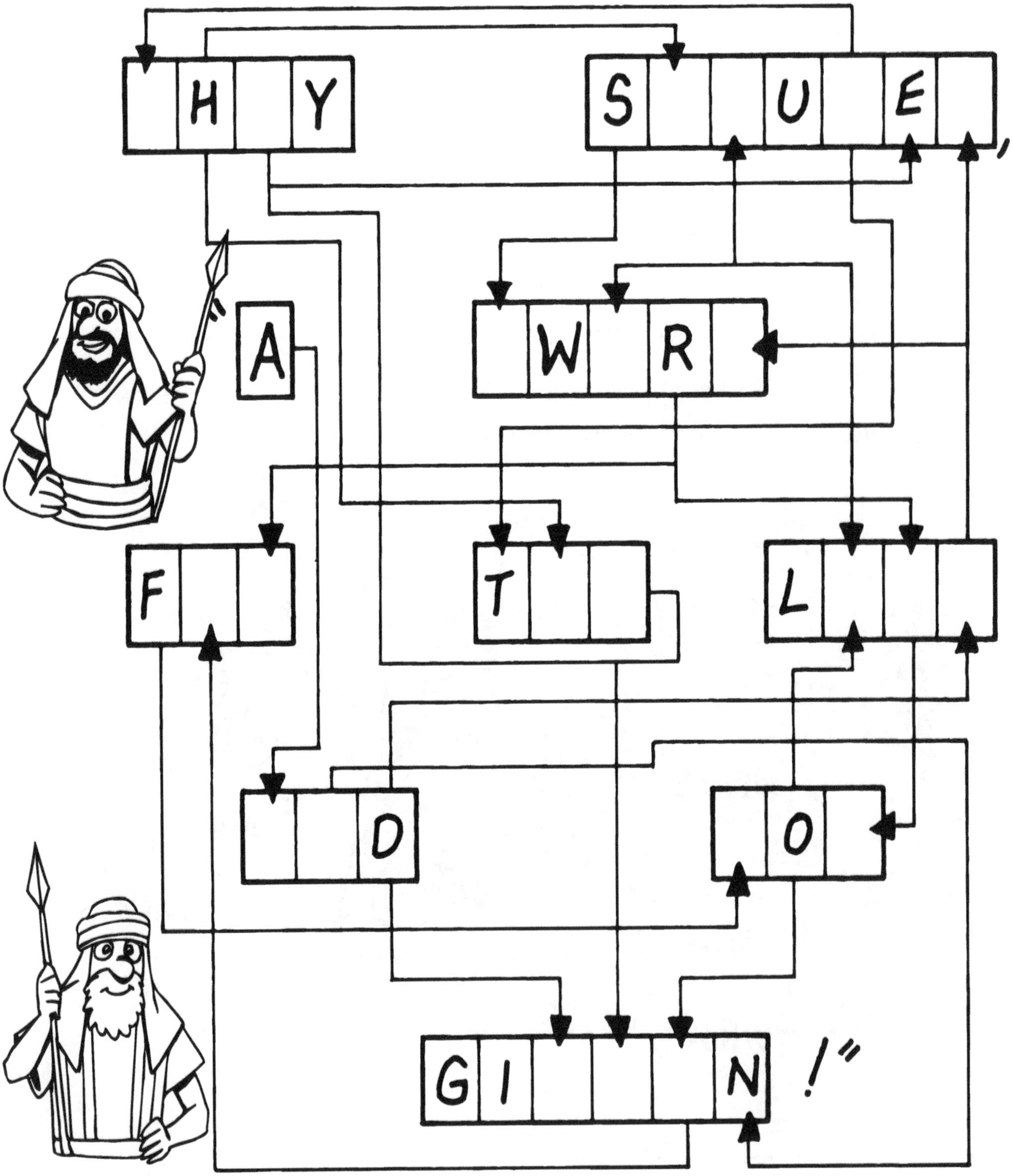

Samson's Weakness

Fifteen words in this story from Judges 13:1 and 16:4–30 have been scrambled. The first two or three letters of each scrambled word have been moved to the end of the word. Circle the scrambled words, unscramble them, and write them correctly on a sheet of paper.

Samson was born while the Israelites were vessla of the Philistines. He fell in velo with Lilahde. The Philistines asked Delilah to find the retsec of Samson's engthstr.

Samson said, "No orraz has ever been used on my head. If my head were vedsha, my strength would leave" (Judg. 13:17).

Delilah shaved off Samson's irha while he was leepas. Samson stlo his strength and the Philistines seized him and put him in sonpri.

Samson was brought out to formper for the Philistines. He yedpra to the Lord for strength.

The Lord heard Samson's prayer, and when Samson pushed the larspil of the pletem, it came down on the rulers and all the people in it.

What a Friend!

Read Ruth 1:1–10 and 14–19 to confirm if the sentences below are true. If the sentence is true, circle the letter under the YES column. If it is not true, circle the letter under the NO column. Then fill in the blanks with the circled letters in order from 1–18. Discover what kind of friend Ruth was.

		YES	NO
1.	Naomi wanted Ruth and Orpah to go back to their mothers' homes.	S	P
2.	Elimelech's family went to Bethel.	J	H
3.	His sons' names were Mahlon and Kilion.	E	R
4.	Ruth wanted to leave Naomi and go home.	S	W
5.	Orpah left Naomi and went home.	A	M
6.	Ruth and Orpah were happy to leave Naomi.	N	S
7.	Mahlon and Kilion were Ruth's brothers.	A	L
8.	Elimelech moved his family because of a famine.	O	H
9.	Ruth and Orpah were from Bethlehem.	U	Y
10.	Ruth stayed with Naomi.	A	B
11.	Ruth and Naomi went to Bethlehem.	L	R
12.	Naomi, Ruth, and Orpah went to Moab when they inherited money.	J	T
13.	Elimelech was from Bethlehem in the land of Judah.	O	A
14.	Ruth and Orpah were Naomi's daughters-in-law.	N	P
15.	Ruth wanted to follow a different God from Naomi.	U	A
16.	This story happened in the days when the kings ruled.	L	O
17.	Elimelech, Mahlon, and Kilion died.	M	B
18.	Naomi heard in Moab that the Lord had come to the aid of His people.	I	C

__ __ __   __ __ __   __ __ __ __ __   __ __   __ __ __ __ __.

Here I Am!

In 1 Samuel 3:1–20, the Lord called to Samuel. Read these verses to discover Samuel's answer. Then begin with the word SPEAK in the puzzle and find the path that matches Samuel's answer. Do not trace any line in the puzzle more than once, and change directions only at intersections marked by dots.

Sounds Like ...

In these statements from 1 Samuel 8–10, a word has been replaced with a rhyming word. Find the rhyming words and write them "across" the shapes below. Then write the correct words "down."

1. The Israelites wanted a ring (8:5).
2. God said, "Listen to them and live them a king" (8:22).
3. The Lord told Samuel he would send a can from the land of Benjamin (9:16).
4. "Anoint him jeweler over my people Israel" (9:16).
5. Samuel took a flask of soil and poured it on Saul's head (10:1).
6. "He will deliver my steeple from the hand of the Philistines" (9:16).

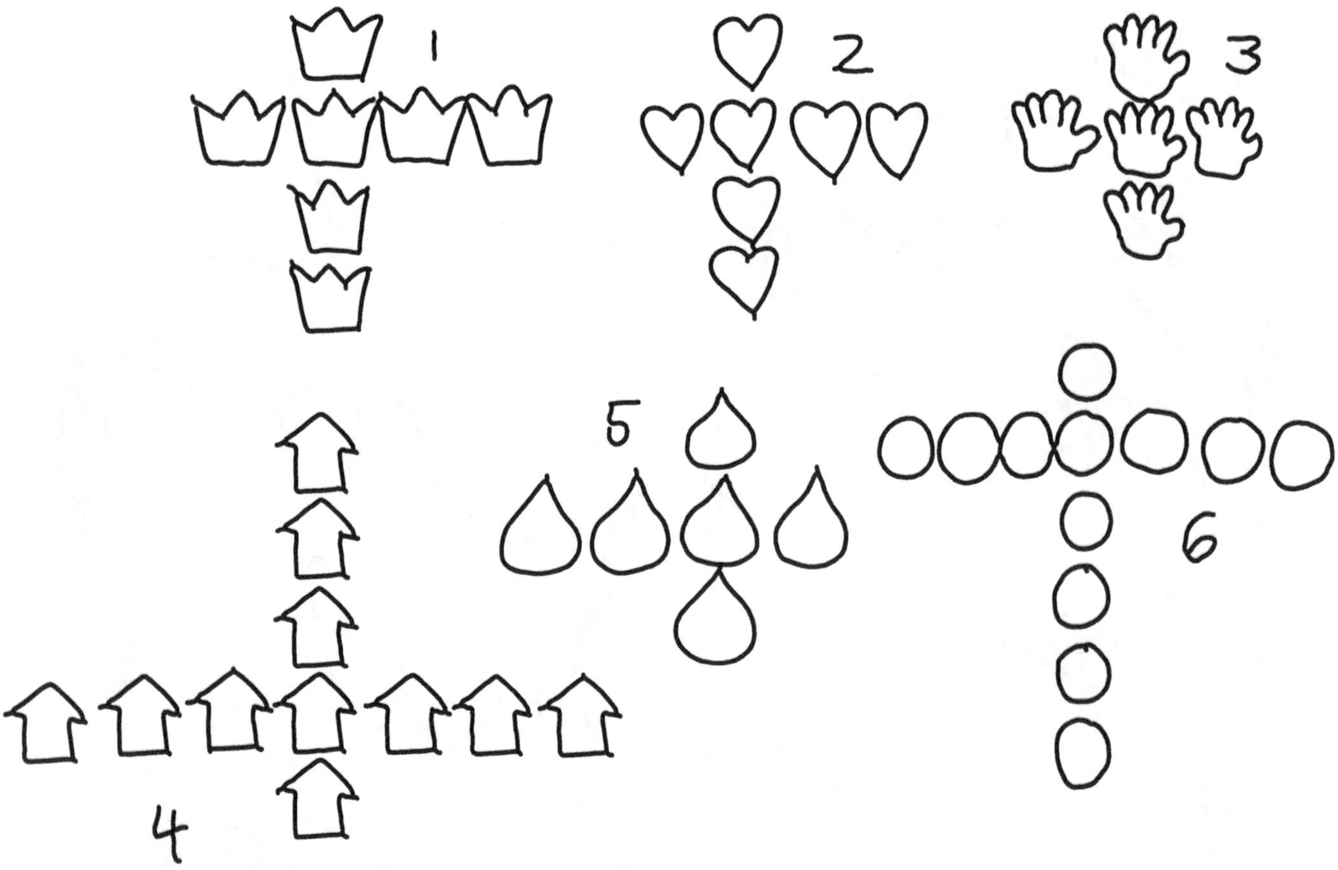

Look Inside

Look inside each of these sentences to find a hidden word. Hidden words are between other words, such as the word EGG in this sentence: (2) Peg gave out cookies. The number 2 means the hidden word starts with the second letter from the beginning of the sentence. To make the puzzle harder, cover up the number clues.The blanks after each sentence show how many letters the hidden word has. Read 1 Samuel 16:1–13 to learn more about Samuel's mission.

(11) Mary went with Ed to the park. ___ ___ ___

(6) The color does not match. ___ ___ ___ ___

(8) We ate nachos every day. ___ ___ ___ ___ ___

(9) I will send a videotape. ___ ___ ___ ___ ___

(5) Pam is one of my best friends. ___ ___ ___

(2) Go for a walk before it rains. ___ ___

(1) Jess earned straight As. ___ ___ ___ ___ ___

(3) Not one piece of mail came today. ___ ___

(3) Rob enjoyed the baseball game. ___ ___

(9) A big pumpkin grows slowly. ___ ___ ___ ___

(8) Please move Randy's bike. ___ ___ ___ ___

(1) Is Rae lending her book? ___ ___ ___ ___ ___ ___

Stones 'n Stuff

Read 1 Samuel 17:40–51 to fill in the answers to each sentence. Use the letters above the numbers to find the coded message in each stone.

1. David put the stones in a pouch of his ___ ___ ___ ___ ___ ___ ___ _5_ ' ___ ___ _2_ ___ (v. 40).

2. Goliath was a ___ ___ _13_ ___ ___ ___ _3_ ___ ___ _7_ (v. 40).

3. Goliath despised David for he was only a ___ _11_ ___ (v. 42).

4. Goliath had a _14_ ___ ___ ___ ___, ___ ___ ___ ___ ___ ___ and ___ ___ ___ _4_ ___ ___ ___ to fight David (v. 45).

5. David came to fight Goliath in the name of the ___ ___ _9_ ___ ___ ___ ___ ___ ___ ___ ___ _8_ ___ ___ (v. 45).

6. "All those gathered here will _6_ ___ ___ _12_ that it is not by sword or spear that the Lord saves" (v. 47).

7. David struck the Philistine on the ___ ___ ___ ___ _10_ ___ ___ ___ (v. 49).

8. After David ___ ___ _1_ ___ ___ ___ him, he cut off his head with the sword (v. 51).

Friends Forever

Trace the path to each star to find the scrambled words. Then fill in the sentences about the story from 1 Samuel 19–20 and 2 Samuel 9.

1. Saul told Jonathan to ____ ____ ____ ____ David.

2. Jonathan ____ ____ ____ ____ ____ ____ David that Saul wanted to kill David.

3. Jonathan ____ ____ ____ ____ ____ his friend David.

4. They swore ____ ____ ____ ____ ____ ____ ____ ____ ____ ____ with each other in the name of the Lord.

5. When David became king, he rewarded the ____ ____ ____ of Jonathan for his father's kindness.

Have Mercy on Me!

Unscramble the bold letters at the top of the grid to spell the name of a main character from 1 Samuel 24:1–17. Then write the bold letters in the correct order across the top of the empty grid. Take the word columns that appear under each bold letter and write them in order under the same letter in the empty grid. When completed, read from left to right to see what this character said to show mercy.

V	**D**	**I**	**D**	**A**
Lord	May	judge	between	the
me.	you	And	may	and
avenge	the	the	wrongs	Lord
done	you	to	me,	have
hand	but	will	not	my
	touch			you.

The Wise King

One word is missing from each of these statements from 1 Kings 3:5–15. Color the spaces containing any of the letters K, I, N, G, or S to find the missing words.

1. The Lord appeared to ____________ in a dream (v. 5).

K	S	K	G	I	N	I	Q	G	Z	A	B	S	K	I	Q	N	W	D	E	K	Q	K	I	N	V	I	A	B	S
I	C	D	F	N	M	K	R	S	Y	C	D	G	M	N	R	G	N	C	S	I	P	I	R	G	W	G	K	C	G
N	G	S	H	G	O	S	T	K	X	E	F	N	O	G	T	S	X	G	F	N	O	K	T	S	X	K	D	S	N
A	B	K	J	S	P	G	U	I	W	H	J	I	P	S	U	K	Y	B	H	G	M	I	U	K	Y	S	E	F	I
G	N	I	L	K	I	N	V	N	G	S	L	K	I	K	V	I	Z	A	J	S	L	N	G	S	Z	N	H	J	K

2. Solomon asked God for a discerning ____________ (v. 9).

K	A	I	E	I	I	I	Q	S	K	I	Z	K	I	N	L	G	S	K
G	B	N	F	N	M	O	R	G	W	N	A	I	E	G	M	V	I	W
I	K	G	H	G	G	G	T	N	I	G	B	N	K	S	O	U	N	X
S	C	S	J	S	O	P	U	K	X	S	C	G	I	H	P	T	N	Y
N	D	K	L	K	K	K	V	I	Y	K	D	S	F	N	Q	R	I	Z

3. The Lord was ____________ (v. 10).

K	I	N	R	K	T	X	Y	S	K	I	E	K	N	G	L	N	I	K	R	S	K	I	A	N	S	K	O
I	E	G	Q	K	U	Y	Z	G	C	D	F	S	H	N	M	G	P	Q	T	N	Y	Z	B	I	H	M	I
N	I	S	P	K	V	Z	A	N	I	K	D	I	G	I	O	S	K	I	U	I	S	K	C	K	J	P	N
G	F	J	O	I	W	X	B	I	A	B	E	N	J	S	P	L	O	N	V	G	X	D	E	S	L	Q	K
S	H	L	M	I	N	N	C	K	S	N	F	G	H	K	M	K	S	G	W	K	I	S	F	G	N	I	R

4. God also promised Solomon __________, _________, and a ______ ______ (vv. 13–14 ICB).

S	K	I	N	H	K	X	S	K	I	H	N	P	K	Q	G	G	S	B	N	I	K
I	A	B	G	J	I	Y	G	A	B	J	G	Q	S	R	S	V	U	C	G	Z	A
K	I	K	S	L	N	X	N	C	D	L	S	N	G	T	K	I	N	D	S	K	I
N	C	N	F	H	G	Z	I	E	F	M	K	R	I	U	I	T	A	E	X	Y	N
G	D	E	G	J	S	L	K	I	N	O	I	P	N	V	N	G	S	F	I	S	G

G	A	K	E	K	K	K	Q	S	T	X	N	A	I	G	G	L	K	K	I	N
I	B	I	F	I	M	S	R	N	I	Z	S	B	K	F	G	M	I	A	B	G
S	G	N	H	N	O	G	X	S	U	S	N	C	K	H	G	O	N	K	I	S
K	C	I	J	G	P	N	Y	K	V	Y	K	D	I	J	N	P	G	C	N	D
I	D	K	L	S	K	I	Z	S	W	X	S	E	N	S	S	Q	S	E	F	G

K	A	B	C	N	G	N	A	S	F	M	I	R	K	I	N	G	H	K	A	B	C	I	O	N	S	K	A	I	K	I
I	D	E	F	G	R	G	B	K	S	O	N	T	S	Z	A	B	C	I	X	Y	Z	K	P	G	U	V	B	N	F	H
K	H	J	L	N	T	N	C	I	H	K	G	U	K	Y	G	N	F	N	T	U	V	S	Q	S	N	G	C	G	G	S
I	M	O	P	G	U	G	D	N	J	P	S	V	I	X	D	I	E	G	W	X	Y	G	R	K	W	X	D	S	J	L
K	I	K	Q	N	G	N	E	G	L	Q	K	W	N	G	S	K	J	S	K	I	D	N	T	I	Y	Z	E	K	I	N

Good Advice

The elders and the young men gave King Rehoboam advice. Find the letters on each man to make a word. Then fill in the blanks to find the advice each group gave. Read 1 Kings 12 to find out who Rehoboam listened to.

Elders:

___ ___ ___ ___ them a ___ ___ ___ ___ ___ ___ ___ ___ ___

___ ___ ___ ___ ___ ___ (v. 7).

Young men:

Tell them you will make their ___ ___ ___ ___

___ ___ ___ ___ ___ ___ ___ ___ ___ ___ ___ (vv. 10–11).

Help from on High

In 1 Kings 17:1–6, God helped Elijah when he hid from the king. Cross out all the Cs, Gs, Ks, Os, and Qs in the stream. Then rearrange the remaining letters to find three things God provided for Elijah.

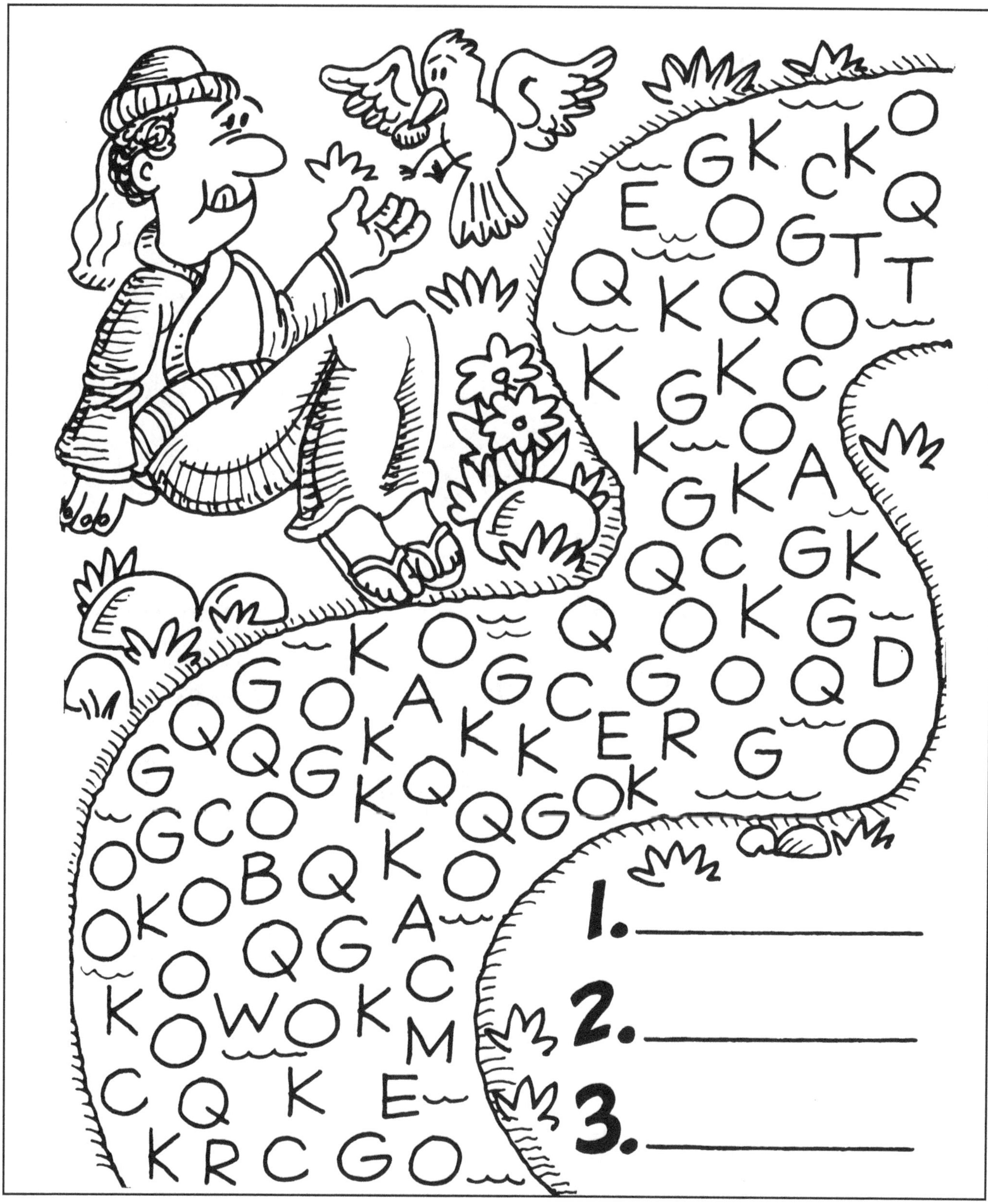

Rescue Recipe

God sent Elijah to a widow. She fed Elijah during a terrible famine. To find the recipe for the widow's food, unscramble the letters in the matching jars. Read 1 Kings 17:7–16 to find out how Elijah helped the widow.

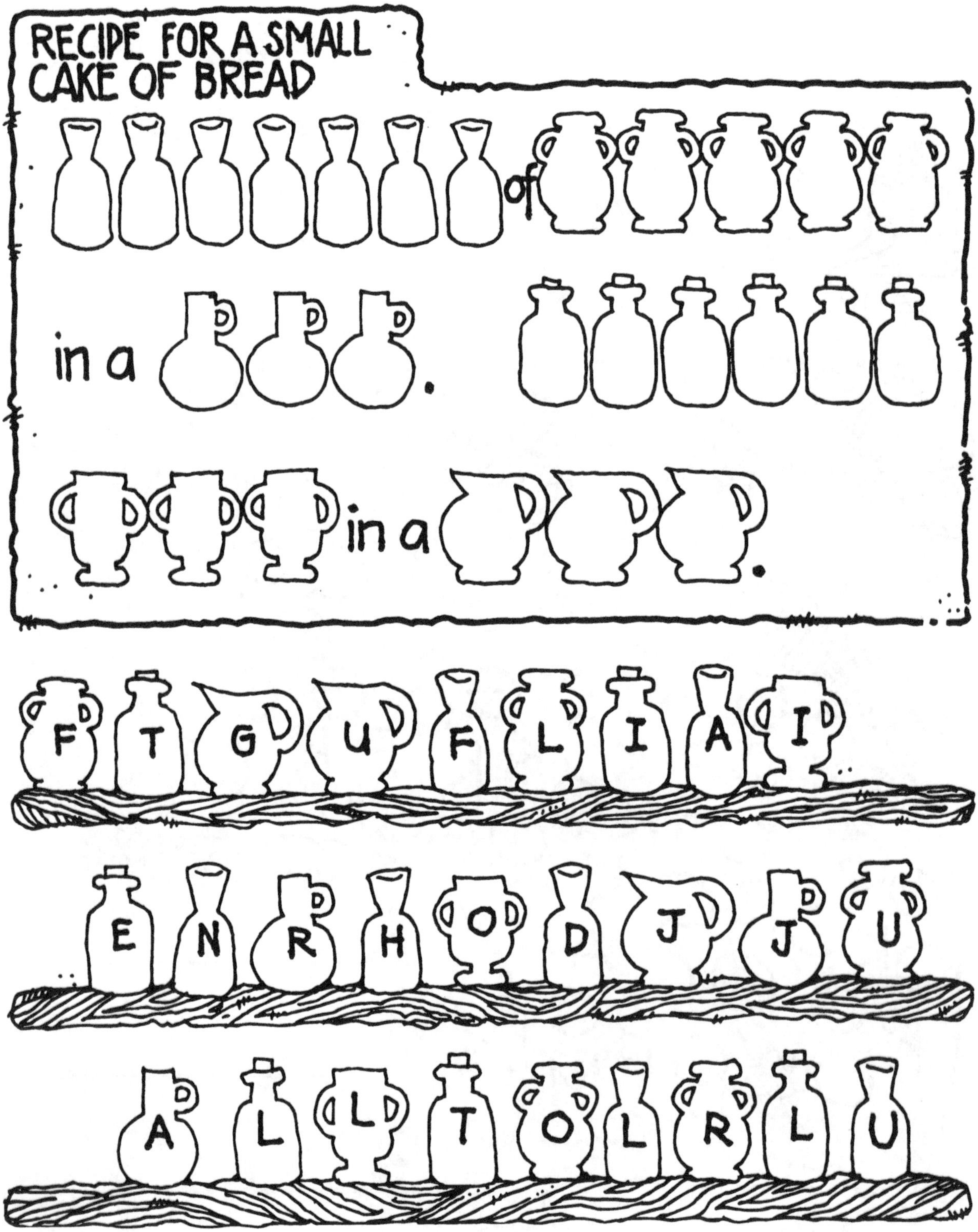

And the Winner Is ...

Read 1 Kings 18:20–39 to learn about Elijah's contest with the followers of Baal. To discover what happened to Elijah's sacrifice, find the box marked A1 at the top of the page. Copy what you see in the box into the empty A1 square in the grid. Fill in the other squares. You can also cut the squares at the top of the page apart and glue them in their proper places.

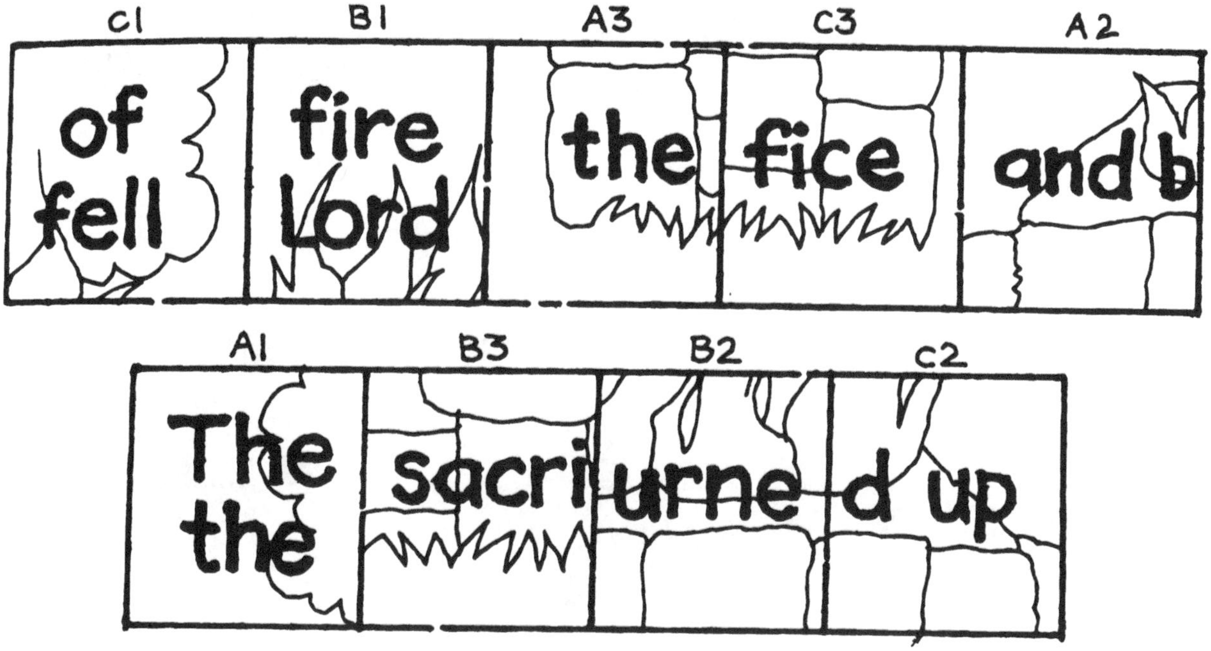

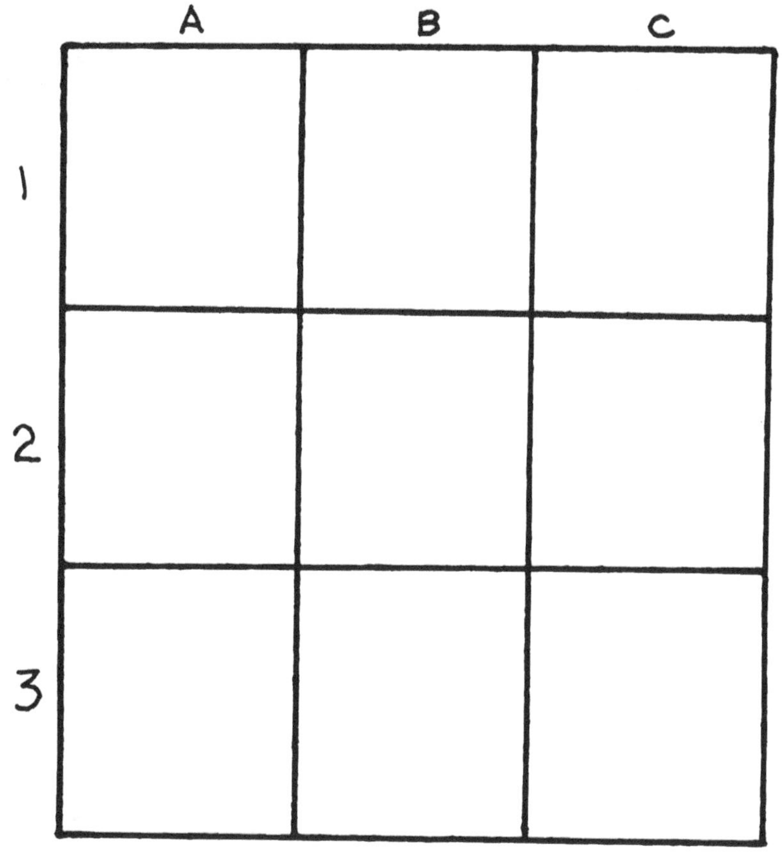

Whirlwind Words

Read about the whirlwind in 2 Kings 2:1–11. Then connect the words from the story to follow Elijah's path to heaven.

HEAVEN

VIDEO

SKATES

FIRE

BACKPACK

CLOAK

MUD

ELISHA

SNEAKERS

DOGFOOD

JORDAN

PROPHETS

JERICHO

PIZZA

MITTENS

LORD

WHIRLWIND

ELIJAH

What a Blessing!

To find out how Elisha helped a family, read 2 Kings 4:8–10, 17–22, and 32–37. Then read the sentences below. The picture in each sentence resembles a letter of the alphabet. Can you guess which letters? Then think of a word suggested by the pictures and fill in the blanks with the missing letters.

1. A well-to-do woman asked Elisha to stay for a ____ ____  (v. 8).

2. The woman and her husband made a room on the roof and put in it a bed, a table, a ____  ____ ____ ____, and a lamp for Elisha (v. 10).

3. The woman gave birth to a ____  ____ (v. 17).

4. The boy sat on his mother's lap until ____  ____ and then died (v. 20).

5. When Elisha reached the  ____ ____ ____, the boy was lying dead on his couch (v. 32).

6. Elisha laid on the boy, mouth to mouth,  ____  ____ to eyes, hands to hands (v. 34).

7. The boy ____ 

____ ____ ____ ____ ____ seven times and opened his eyes (v. 35).

8. Elisha said to Gehazi, "  ____ ____ ____ the Shunammite" (v. 36).

9. When Elisha told the woman to take her son, she fell at his  ____ ____ ____ (v. 37).

Who Said That?

Read 2 Kings 5:1–14. Then complete the printed letters by drawing straight lines between pairs of crosses and circles. Then match what is said with the person who said it.

_______________ "If only my master would see the prophet who is in Samaria!"

_______________ "Am I God? Can I kill and bring back to life?"

_______________ "Go, wash yourself seven times in the Jordan, and your flesh will be restored and you will be cleansed."

_______________ "Are not Abana and Pharpar, the rivers of Damascus, better than any of the waters of Israel?"

_______________ "By all means, go."

Bad Shape

Captured by their enemies, the Israelites were in bad shape. To learn why, match the shapes underneath each blank with the letter shapes above. Write the letters on the blanks. Read 2 Kings 17 to find out more about the story.

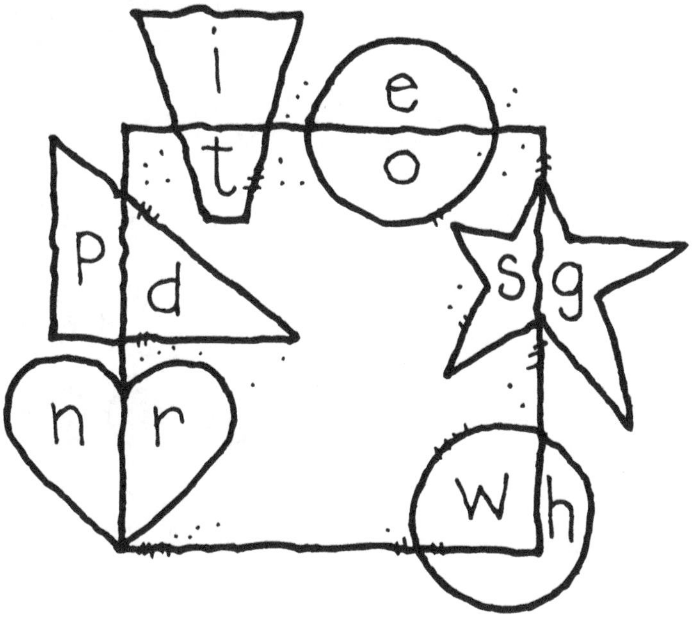

They ______ and

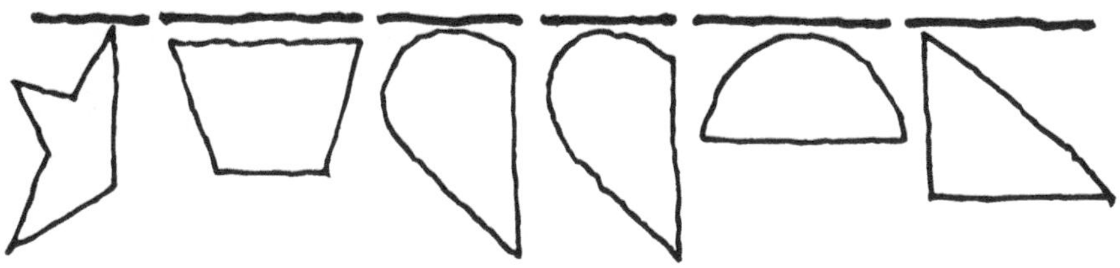

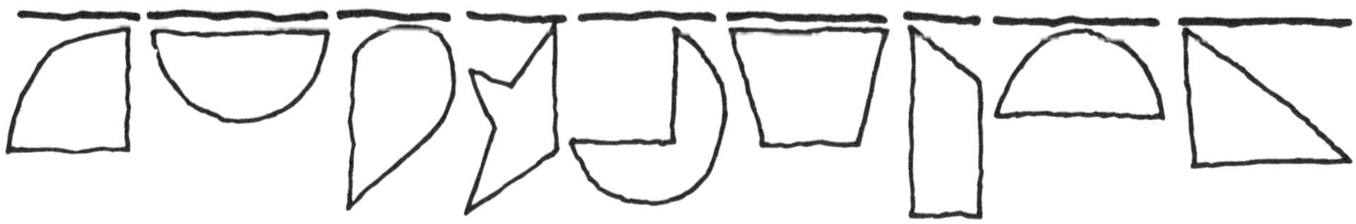

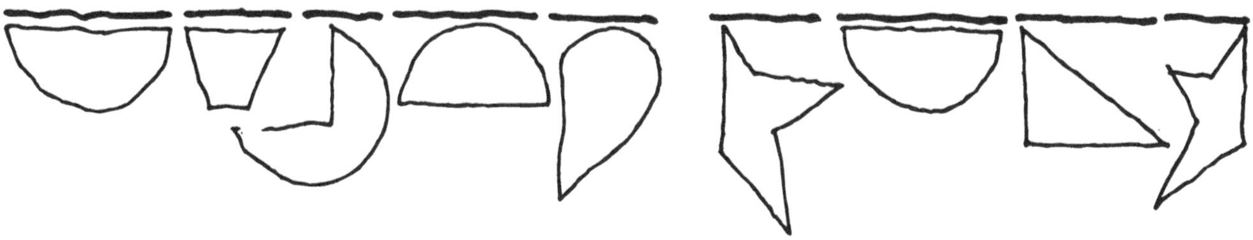

What Was Their Downfall?

Read 2 Kings 17:7–18. Start with the circle that is numbered the same as the sentence and follow the arrows to fill in the blanks. When completed, you will find out what Israel did to cause their downfall with God.

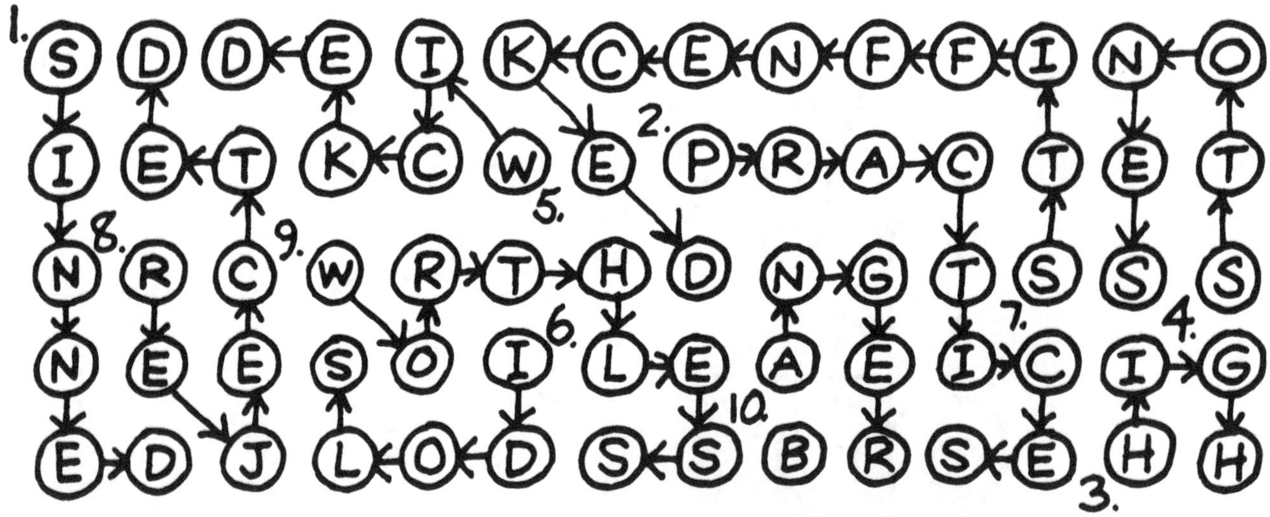

1. The Israelites had ___ ___ ___ ___ ___ ___ against the Lord their God.
2. They followed the ___ ___ ___ ___ ___ ___ ___ ___ ___ of the nations the Lord had driven out.
3. They built themselves ___ ___ ___ ___ places in all their towns.
4. They set up sacred ___ ___ ___ ___ ___ ___ and poles.
5. The did ___ ___ ___ ___ ___ ___ things that provoked the Lord to anger.
6. They worshipped ___ ___ ___ ___ ___.
7. They would not listen and were as ___ ___ ___ ___ ___ ___ ___ ___ ___ ___ ___ as their fathers.
8. They ___ ___ ___ ___ ___ ___ ___ ___ his decrees and covenant.
9. They became ___ ___ ___ ___ ___ ___ ___ ___ ___.
10. They provoked the Lord to ___ ___ ___ ___ ___.

Our God Is Greater

Read 2 Chronicles 2–7 to complete these statements. Use the numbered letters in your answers to fill in the missing words from 6:2 and 7:3.

Solomon gave orders to ___ ___(5) ___ ___ ___(6) a

___ ___ ___ ___ ___(1) ___(2) for the ___(10) ___ ___ ___ of the

Lord (2:1). The temple would be ___(3) ___(4) ___(2) ___ ___

because our God is greater than all others (2:5).

Solomon built the temple on Mount ___ ___(7) ___(4) ___(11) ___ ___(8) (3:1).

When the temple was finished, the trumpeters and singers gave

___ ___ ___ ___ ___(12) ___ and thanks to the Lord (5:13).

Solomon built the temple as a place for the Lord to dwell ___(13) ___(7) ___(4) ___(2) ___(9) ___(2) ___(4) (6:2).

They gave thanks to the Lord, saying, " ___(8) ___(2)   ___(11) ___(12)   ___(3) ___(7) ___(7) ___(6);

___(8) ___(11) ___(12)   ___(1) ___(7) ___(9) ___(2)   ___(2) ___(10) ___(6) ___(5) ___(4) ___(2) ___(12)

___(13) ___(7) ___(4) ___(2) ___(9) ___(2) ___(4) " (7:3).

Work Boxes

Fill in the work boxes by following the instructions below. See 2 Chronicles 24:1–14 (NLT) for help.

Boxes

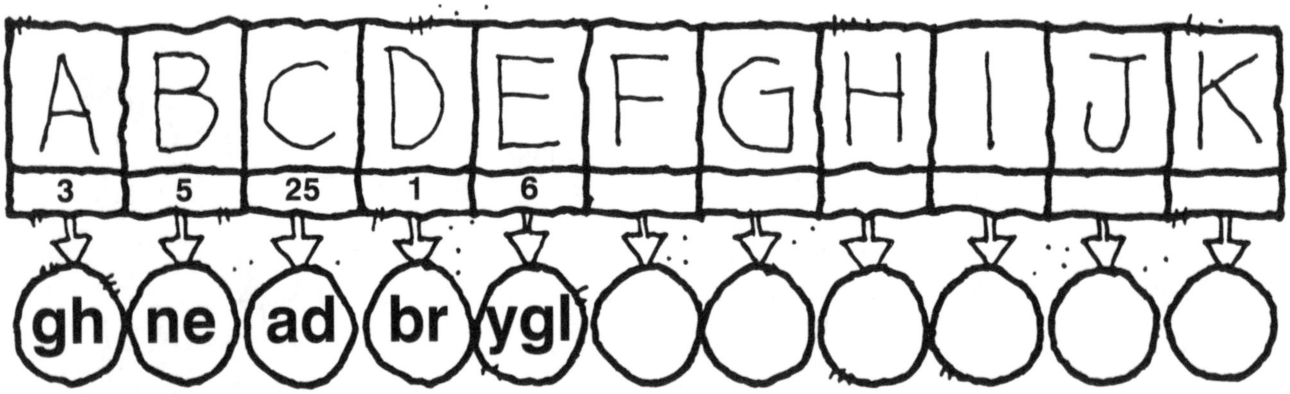

Solve the math puzzles below using the numbers in the rectangles above. Write your answers in the work boxes below.

1. Add boxes **A**, **B**, and **G**. Place the total in work box **E**.
2. Subtract box **B** from box **C**. Place the answer in work box **K**.
3. Add boxes **C** and **D**. Place the total in work box **B**.
4. Subtract box **A** from box **B**. Place the answer in work box **G**.
5. Add boxes **B** and **E**. Place the total in work box **F**.
6. Subtract box **G** from box **A**. Place the answer in work box **A**.
7. Subtract box **J** from box **H**. Place the answer in work box **D**.
8. Subtract box **B** from box **J**. Place the answer in work box **I** .
9. Add boxes **G** and **D**. Place the total in work box **C**.
10. Add boxes **B** and **I**. Place the total in work box **J**.
11. Subtract box **K** from box **I**. Place the answer in work box **H**.

To learn how God's people helped repair a temple, write the letters shown below the same number at the top of the page in the circles below each work box.

Work Boxes

The Secret of Success

Uzziah became king when he was 16 years old and was a successful and powerful ruler for many years. How did he do it? Use these charts to find out. At the top of each column, write the letter indicated by the black square in the box. See 2 Chronicles 26:1–5.

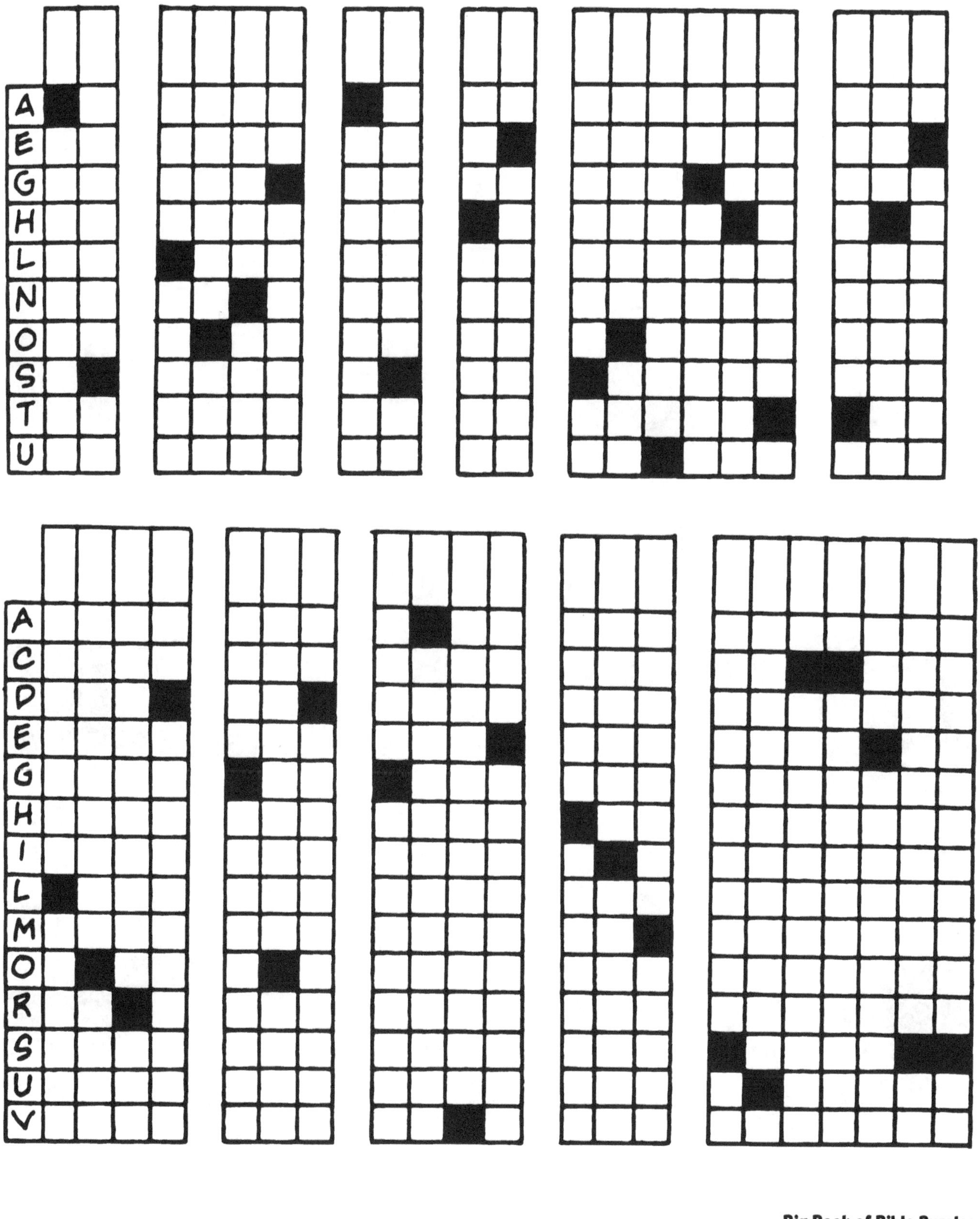

Construction Site

How did the Israelites rebuild a city wall? To find out, look at the wall below. Find the brick in the code key that exactly matches a blank brick in the wall. Write the letter in the matching blank brick. Read Nehemiah 6:15–16 if you need help.

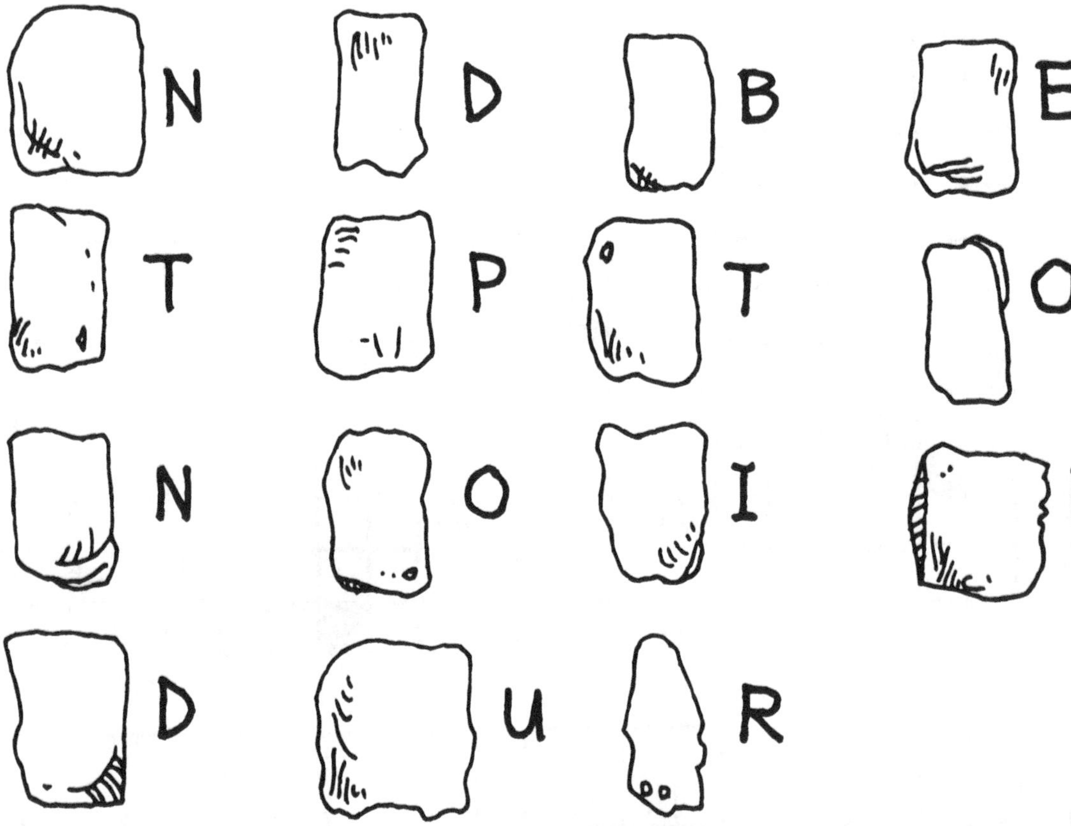

A Brave Queen

The Jews in Susa were in danger. If Queen Esther tried to save her people, she might be killed. To find out what Esther decided, decode the message below. Read more about what happened in Esther 4:1—8:8.

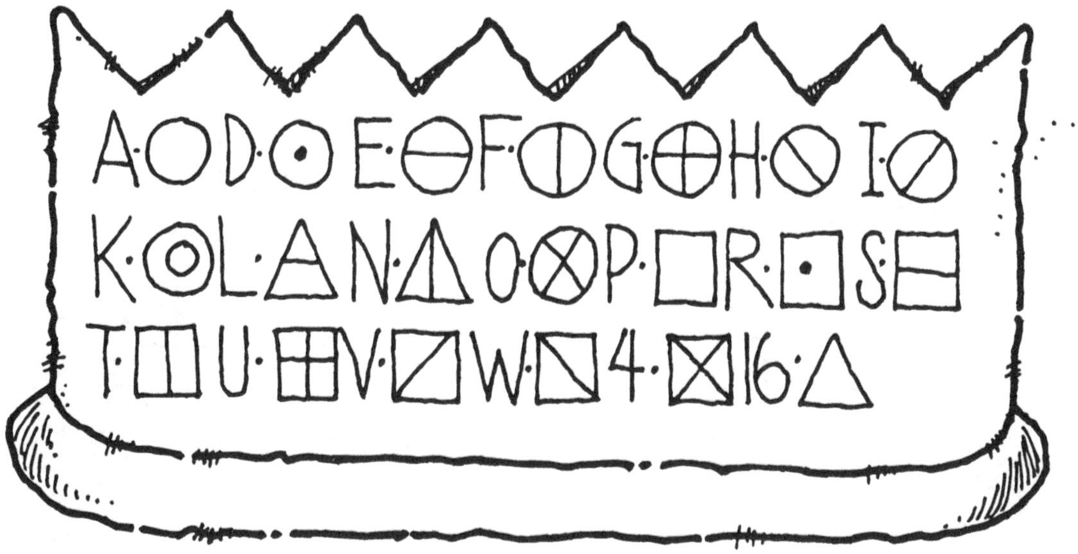

Why Me?

Read Job 38:1–11 and 42:1–3. God questioned Job to demonstrate His power. Color in each square that contains a question mark. When completed, you will find Job's answer to God.

Lost Sheep

Help the sheep find the shepherd. Find the wrong letter in each sheep's name. Read Psalm 23 for help. Put the correct letters in the blank below using the numbers from the sheep.

Who is our shepherd? ______ ______ ______ ______ ______ ______ ______

1 2 3 4 5 6 7

Wise Up!

Wise King Solomon had a very important job. Read Proverbs 23:19–21, 29; and 24:1–2 for clues to complete the picture. If a statement below is true, move the number of spaces given. If the statement is false, do not move. Use a marker or crayon to make a thick line as you follow the directions.

Begin at the large dot in the northwest corner.

1. If we are to listen, move **9** spaces south.
2. If we are to be wise, move **13** spaces east.
3. If we are to keep our hearts on the right path, move **2** spaces north.
4. If we are to join those who drink too much wine, move **3** spaces northeast.
5. If gluttons become poor, move **13** spaces west.
6. If there are six questions in verse **29**, move **7** spaces north.
7. If we are asked who has sorrow, move **3** spaces southeast.
8. If we are to envy wicked men, move **2** spaces southwest.
9. If we are not to desire wicked men's company, move **3½** spaces northeast.
10. If wicked men's hearts plot violence, move **3½** spaces southeast.
11. If wicked men's lips talk about making trouble, move **3** spaces northeast.
12. If Solomon is telling us to "Wise Up," move **9** spaces south.

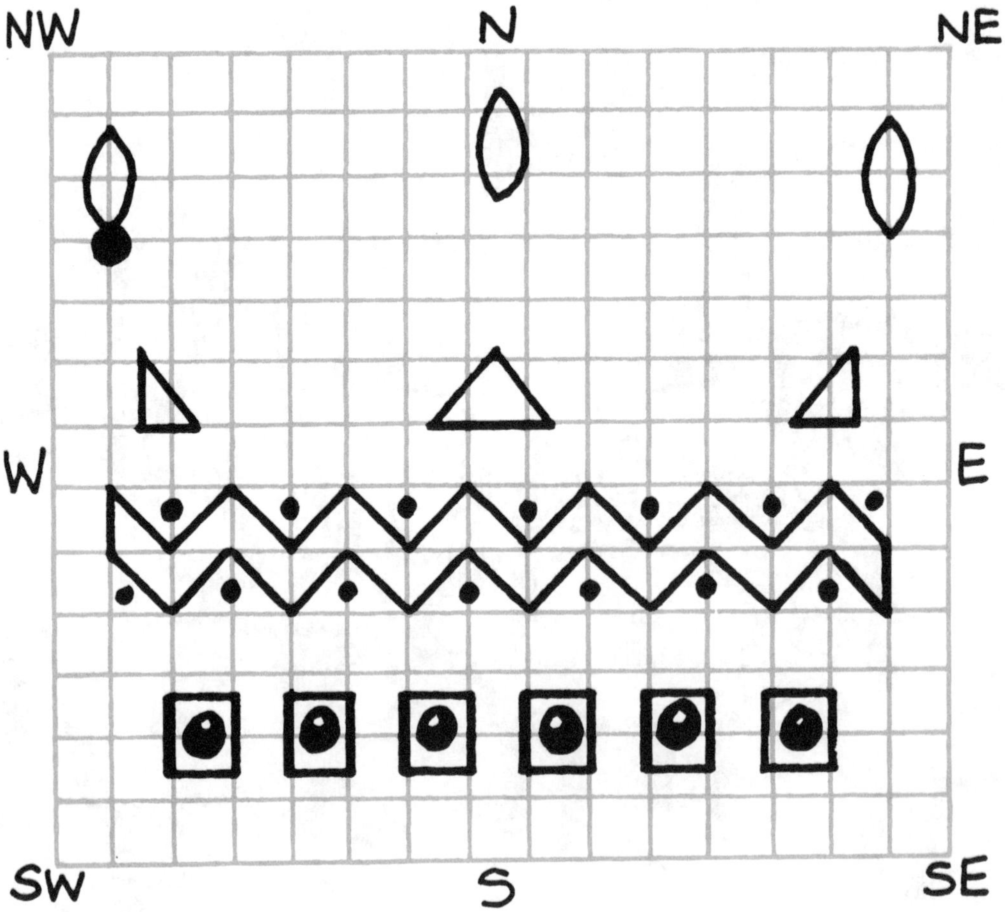

When the Lord Calls

What did Isaiah say when he heard the Lord calling for someone to do His work? Isaiah's answer, which should be our answer too, is hidden in this puzzle. Color all the spaces containing a dot to make the answer appear. Read Isaiah 6:8 (ICB).

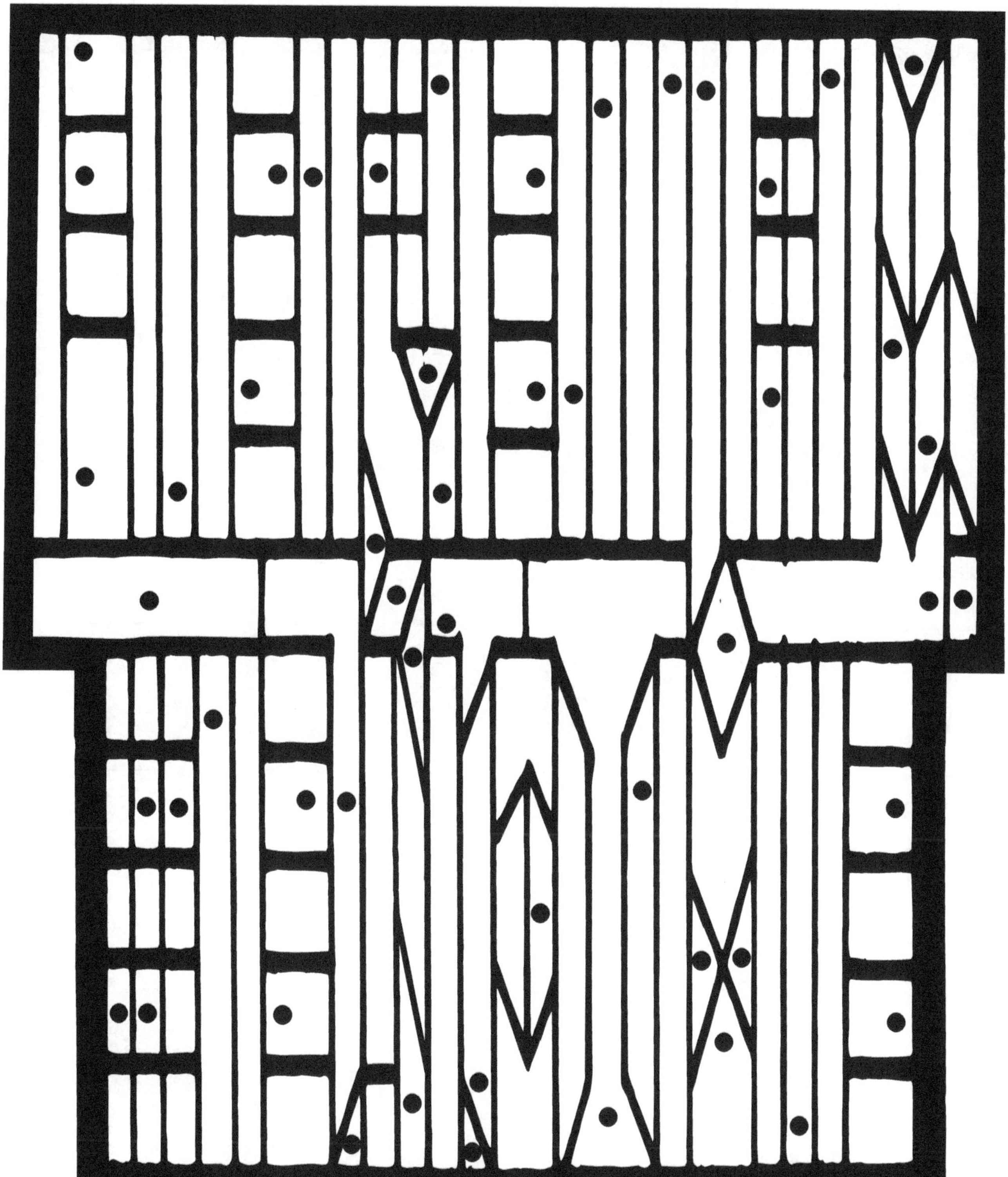

His Name Is ...

Cross out every B, J, K, Q, X, and Z to discover names for Jesus. Read Isaiah 9:6 and Luke 1:32–35 for help. Write the names below.

W	B	O	J	N	K	D	Q	E	X	R	Z	F
U	L	Z	C	X	O	U	K	N	Q	S	E	L
O	J	R	B	M	K	I	G	X	H	T	Z	Y
G	O	X	D	B	E	J	V	K	E	Q	R	L
A	S	Z	T	I	Q	N	B	G	J	F	K	A
T	Q	H	B	E	J	R	K	P	R	X	I	N
Z	C	E	O	X	F	P	E	X	A	C	Z	E
S	B	O	J	N	K	O	Q	F	T	Z	H	E
M	O	Z	S	J	T	B	H	K	I	Q	G	H
S	O	X	N	O	F	K	G	J	O	B	D	Q

Isaiah 9:6

1. __ __ __ __ __ __ __ __ __   __ __ __ __ __ __ __ __ __

2. __ __ __ __ __ __   __ __ __

3. __ __ __ __ __ __ __ __ __ __ __   __ __ __ __ __ __

4. __ __ __ __ __ __   __ __   __ __ __ __ __

Luke 1:32–35

5. __ __ __   __ __   __ __ __   __ __ __ __   __ __ __ __

6. __ __ __   __ __   __ __ __

Missing Alphabet

Discover which letter of the alphabet is missing from each line and write them in order on the spaces below. Then read Isaiah 40:25–26. The answer tells us of the greatness of God.

1. A B C D E F H I J K L M N O P Q R S T U V W X Y Z
2. A B C D E F G H I J K L M N P Q R S T U V W X Y Z
3. A B C E F G H I J K L M N O P Q R S T U V W X Y Z
4. A B C D E F G I J K L M N O P Q R S T U V W X Y Z
5. B C D E F G H I J K L M N O P Q R S T U V W X Y Z
6. A B C D E F G H I J K L M N O P Q R T U V W X Y Z
7. A B C D E F G H I J K L M O P Q R S T U V W X Y Z
8. A B C D E F G H I J K L M N P Q R S T U V W X Y Z
9. A B C D F G H I J K L M N O P Q R S T U V W X Y Z
10. A B C D E F G H I J K L M N O P R S T U V W X Y Z
11. A B C D E F G H I J K L M N O P Q R S T V W X Y Z
12. B C D E F G H I J K L M N O P Q R S T U V W X Y Z
13. A B C D E F G H I J K M N O P Q R S T U V W X Y Z

___ ___ ___   ___ ___ ___   ___ ___   ___ ___ ___ ___ ___!

The Prophet

A prophet foretold the coming of a suffering servant of God, one who would bear the sins of many and suffer for their salvation. The servant the prophet spoke of was Jesus. Do you know the name of the prophet? Trace the path through the maze. Then color in the path to find the answer. Read Isaiah 53.

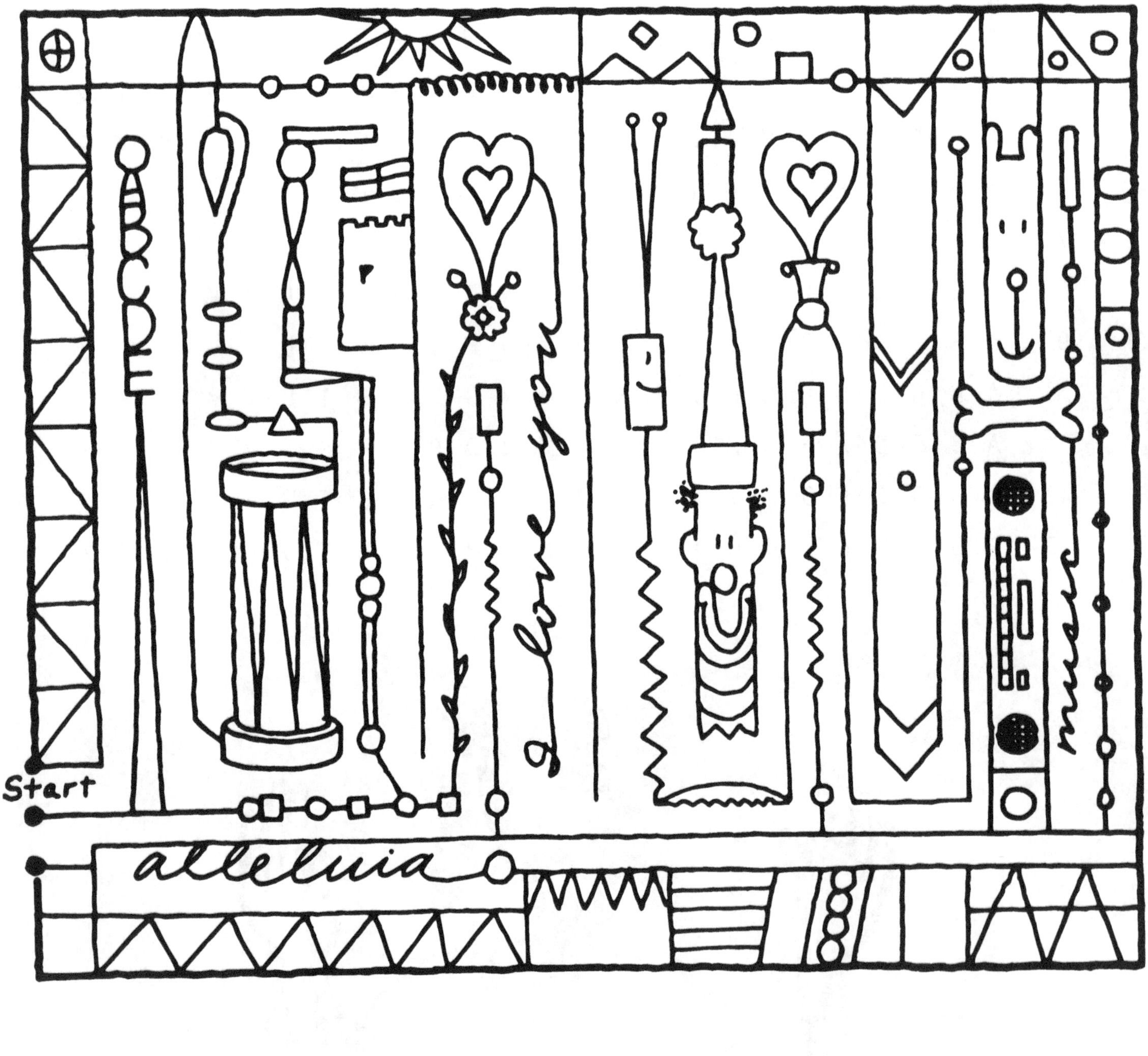

Taking Shape

God is the Creator who shapes each person in His image. The Lord used a special example to help Jeremiah understand this. To see what the Lord said, find the answers to the clues. Copy the letters of your answers into the puzzle boxes with matching numbers. Then read Jeremiah 18:1–6.

1	2	3	4	■	5	6	7	8	■	9	10	■	11	12	13	■	14	15	16	17
■	■	18	19	■	20	21	22	■	23	24	25	26	27	28	,	■	29	30	■	■
31	32	33	■	34	35	36	■	37	38	■	39	40	■	41	42	43	44	.	■	■

1. One who paints or draws ___ ___ ___ ___ ___ ___ (7 32 26 2 29 11)

2. Something around a picture ___ ___ ___ ___ ___ (19 28 15 39 27)

3. Item at the end of a fishing line ___ ___ ___ ___ (12 18 30 3)

4. Writing instrument ___ ___ ___ (23 13 10)

5. Contraction for you + would ___ ___ ___ ___ (8 24 36 44)

6. Easter flower ___ ___ ___ ___ (1 37 6 40)

7. What bees make ___ ___ ___ ___ ___ (14 35 43 22 34)

8. A good one is on your shoulders ___ ___ ___ ___ (21 4 31 17)

9. Camping need ___ ___ ___ ___ (20 33 38 25)

10. Fancy dishes or a country ___ ___ ___ ___ ___ (5 41 9 16 42)

Cistern Escape

The Israelites threw Jeremiah into a cistern. How did he get out? Find the book of Jeremiah in your Bible and read Jeremiah 38:3–10 to answer the questions below. Then take the letters from the circles and write them in the rocks.

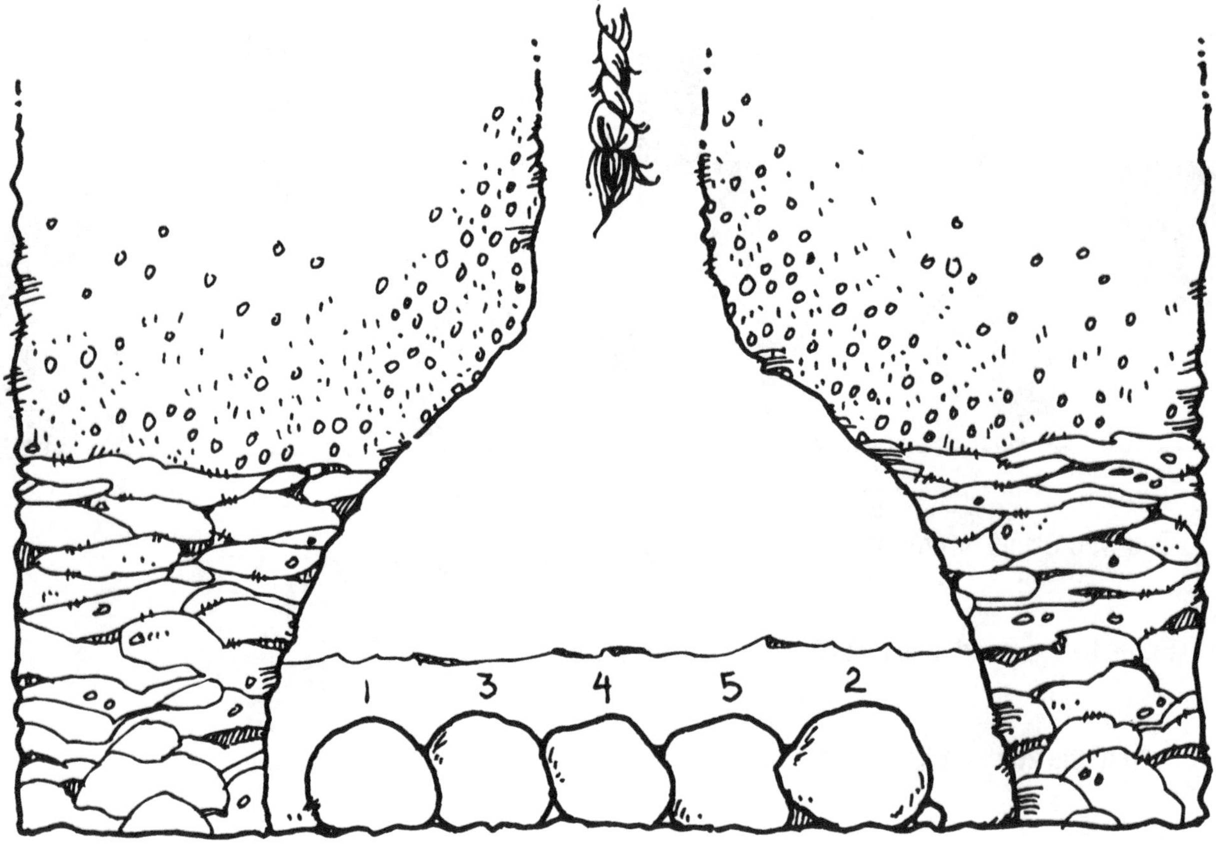

1. Jeremiah said the city would be handed over to the ___ ◯ ___ ___ of the king of Babylon (v. 3).

2. They put Jeremiah into a ___ ___ ◯ ___ ___ ___ ___ (v. 6).

3. The cistern was in the ___ ◯ ___ ___ ___ ___ ___ ___ ___ (v. 6).

4. Jeremiah was a ◯ ___ ___ ___ ___ ___ ___ ___ (v. 9).

5. The king said, "Lift Jeremiah out before he ___ ___ ◯ ___ " (v. 10).

Captured!

Read Jeremiah 39:1–12 and 40:1–4. Number the events in order 1 to 9. To find out why Jerusalem fell, fill in the blanks below by copying the letters from the top of each link in order.

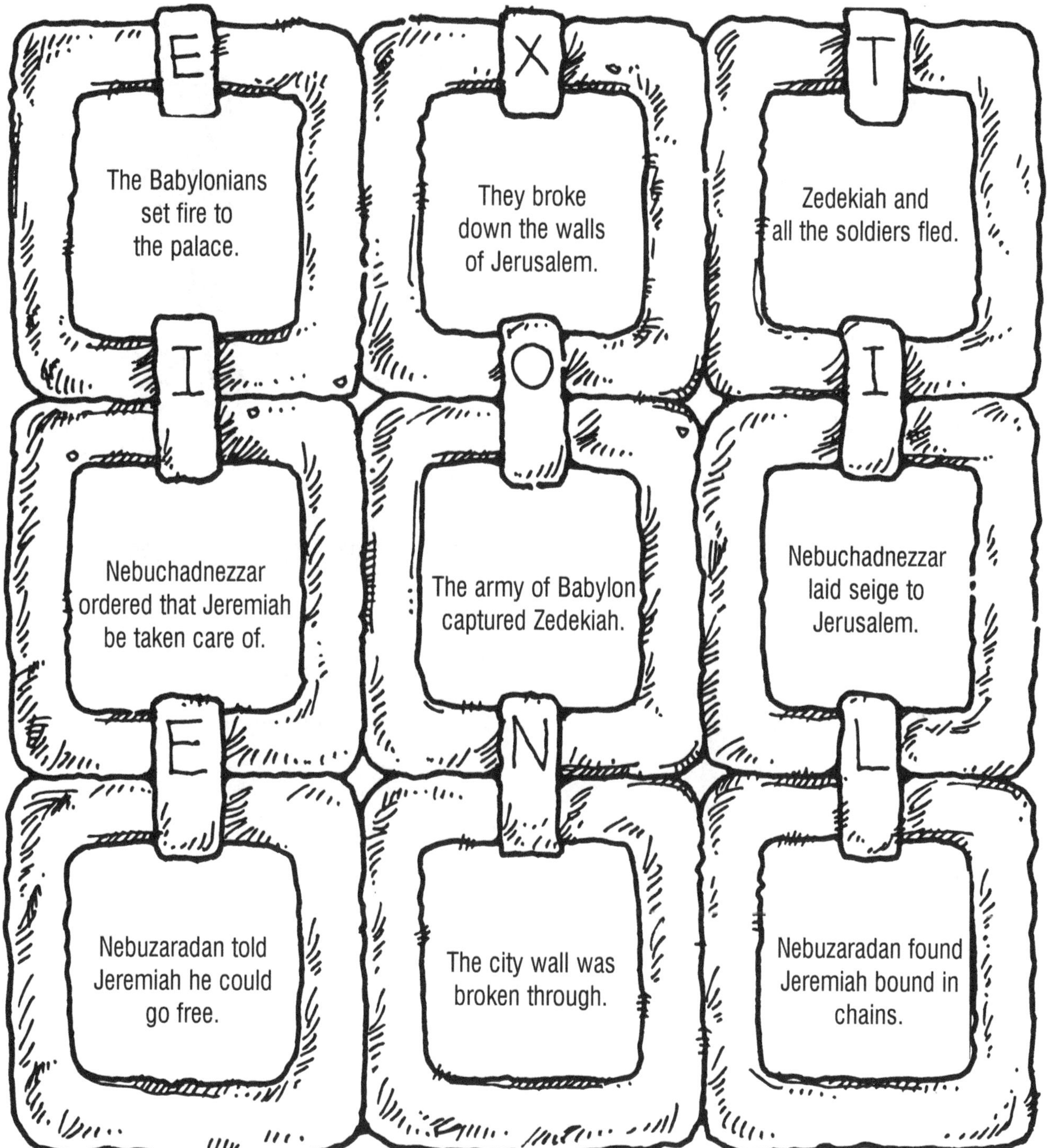

The captives from Jerusalem and Judah were carried ____ ____ ____ ____

____ ____ ____ ____ ____ to Babylon.

Follow Directions

Zedekiah did not follow the Lord's directions. See Jeremiah 52:1–11.Carefully follow these directions.

1. Cross out all words beginning with the letter Q.
2. Cross out all names of buildings.
3. Cross out all words with 12 or more letters.
4. Cross out all names of bodies of water.
5. Cross out all names of flowers.

Now read the leftover words from left to right in order to find out what happened when Zedekiah disobeyed God's laws.

ZEDEKIAH	QUEEN	PALACE	ROSE
SCHOOL	BECAME	KING	NEBUCHADNEZZAR
AND	TULIP	DID	EVIL.
DAISY	HE	TURNED	DAFFODIL
AWAY	FROM	HOUSE	QUIT
CREEK	QUIET	LAKE	GOD.
THE	ZINNIA	BABYLONIAN	PETUNIA
ARMY	QUIZ	SURROUNDED	SEA
FACTORY	THE	QUILT	CITY.
PEOPLE	STARVED.	SOON	THE
OCEAN	RIVER	ARMY	BROKE
IN	MARIGOLD	AND	OFFICE
BURNED	QUICK	LILY	EVERYTHING.

The Lord's Promise

Read Ezekiel 36:27. Follow the letters of the words in this verse to trace a path through the maze.

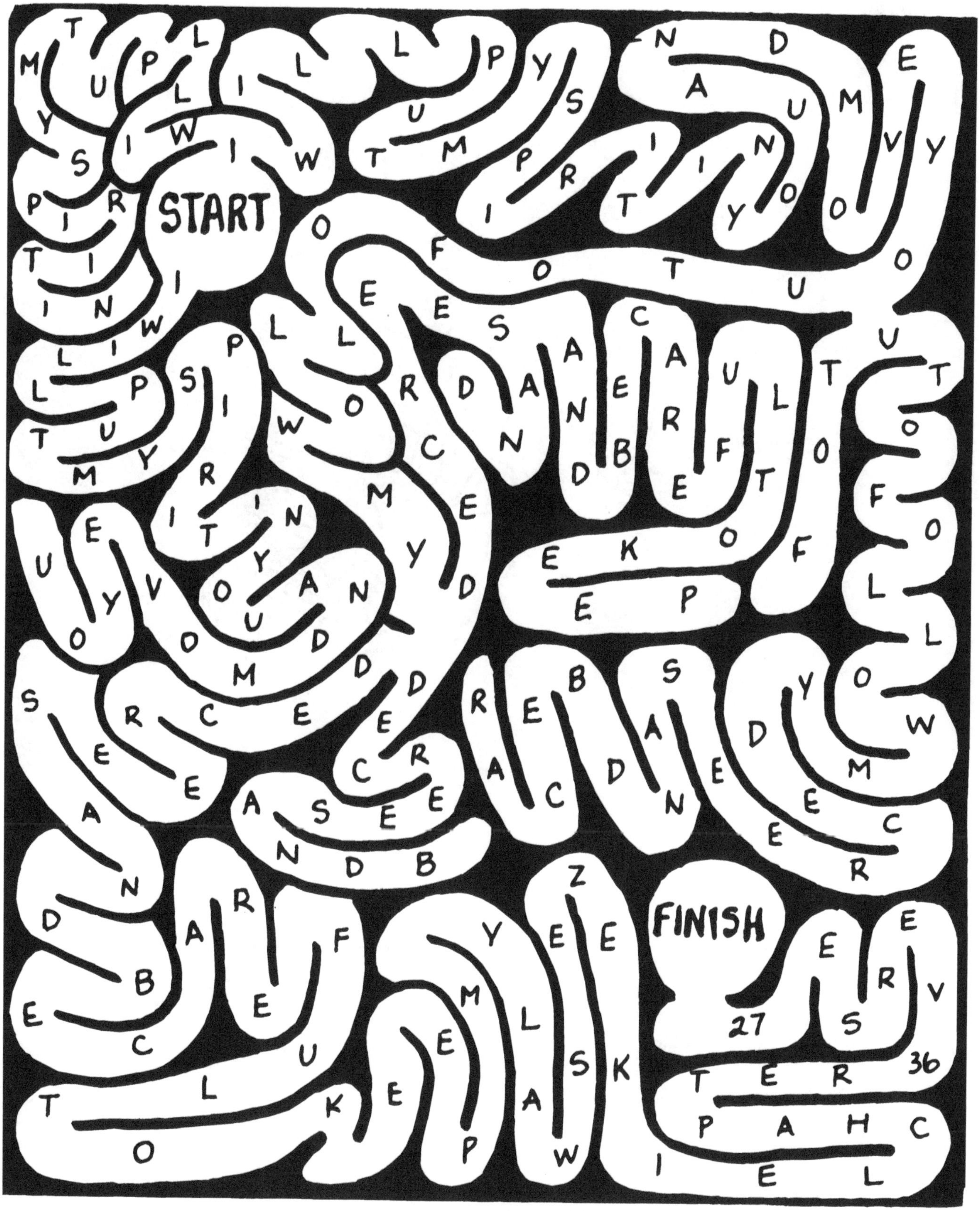

What's on the Menu?

In Daniel 1, Daniel and his friends chose their own meals. Follow the paths from the men on the left to the plates on the right. Write the letters in the blanks at the bottom in the order the men appear.

Daniel	able
Shadrach	ine
Meshach	roya
Abednego	sandw
king's court	dandw
king's court	ater
king's court	lfoo
king's court	veget

Daniel, Shadrach, Meshach, and Abednego ate

___ ___ ___ ___ ___ ___ ___ ___ ___ ___

___ ___ ___   ___ ___ ___ ___ ___ .

The men from the king's court ate

___ ___ ___ ___ ___   ___ ___ ___ ___

___ ___ ___   ___ ___ ___ ___ .

God Protects His Faithful

King Nebuchadnezzar declared that everyone had to worship a gold statue instead of God. A few Jews disobeyed this command, and this made the king very angry. These people were thrown into a blazing furnace. To find out what happened, begin with the letter S by the star. Use a light color to color in every other letter on the path around the flames. Write the colored letters and then the uncolored ones in the blanks below. See Daniel 3.

_ _ _ _ _ _ _ _ _, _ _ _ _ _ _ _ _, _ _ _

_ _ _ _ _ _ _ _ _ _ _ _ _ _ _ _ _

_ _ _ _ _ _ _ _ _ _ _ _

_ _ _ _ _ _ _ _ _ _ _ _ _ _ _ _ _ _ _ _

_ _ _ _ _ _ _ _ _ _ _ _ _ _.

The King Learns a Lesson

Read Daniel 4:30–37, then read each sentence below. If the sentence is true, color the circle in the TRUE column. If the sentence is not true, color the circle in the FALSE column. Copy the colored letters and then the uncolored ones onto the blanks below to find a message.

		TRUE	FALSE
1.	God said Nebuchadnezzar would lose his royal authority (v. 31).	O	L
2.	The king was driven away from the people (v. 33).	N	L
3.	He had to eat birds and fish (v. 33).	P	L
4.	His nails grew like bird claws (v. 33).	Y	O
5.	At the end of the time, he looked up to heaven (v. 34).	G	W
6.	He refused to honor and glorify God (v. 34).	E	O
7.	His honor as king was restored (v. 36).	D	R
8.	His advisers took over his throne (v. 36).	F	I
9.	He became greater than before (v. 36).	S	U
10.	He said that God's ways were not just (v. 37).	L	A

____ ____ ____ ____   ____ ____ ____   ____ ____

____ ____ ____-____ ____ ____ ____ ____ ____ ____ ____.

Handwriting on the Wall

King Belshazzar gave a party. He and his guests drank wine and praised false gods. Suddenly a hand appeared and wrote a message on the wall. The words below tell what the message meant. Use the numbered letters to fill in the puzzle. The finished puzzle will tell you what happened to King Belshazzar. See Daniel 5.

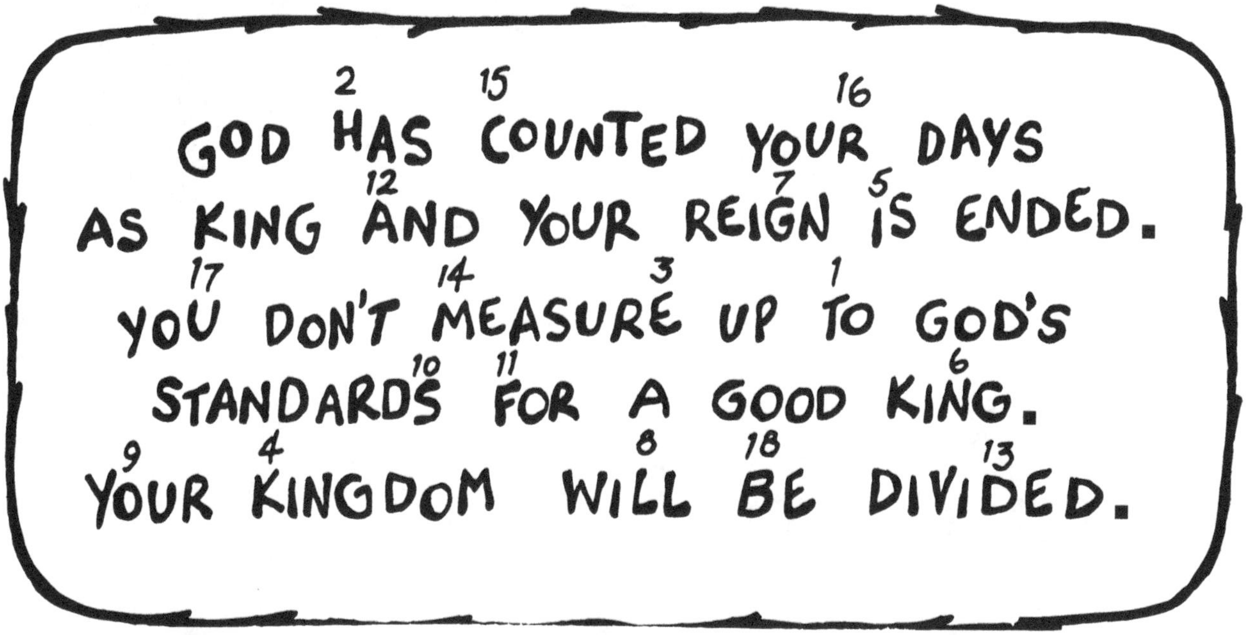

1 2 3 ■ 4 5 6 7 ■ 8 9 10 1 ■ 2 5 10

8 5 11 3 ■ 12 6 13 ■ 1 2 3

14 3 10 10 12 7 3 ■ 15 12 14 3 ■ 1 16 17 3

18 3 15 12 17 10 3 ■ 2 3 ■ 13 5 13

6 9 1 ■ 2 9 6 9 16 ■ 7 9 13

Lion Tamer

Using a ruler, draw a line from the letter under the lion on the top row to the left ear of the matching lion on the bottom row. Each line will go through letters in the middle of the page. Copy the letters in order at the bottom of the page. Read Daniel 6 to learn about Daniel in the lions' den.

G s g s t e o m t

e a o l h

l t n i h d s o n

h u u s

___ ___ ___'___ ___ ___ ___ ___ ___

___ ___ ___ ___ ___ ___ ___

___ ___ ___ ___ ___, ___ ___ ___ ___ ___ ___

A Straight Wall

A plumb line is used to help build a straight wall. Read Amos 1:1 and 7:7–16. Then make this wall tall and straight by finding the words with A in them and fitting them in the bricks.

1. ___________ was the shepherd who became a prophet (1:1).
2. He was a prophet when ________________ was king of Judah (1:1).
3. He was a prophet when Jeroboam son of Jehoash was king of _________________ (1:1).
4. Amos was among the shepherds of ___________________ (1:1).
5. Amos was a prophet two ____________ before the earthquake (1:1).
6. The Lord was standing by a wall with a plumb line in his ____________ (7:7).
7. The ________________________ of Israel will be ruined (7:9).
8. The Lord will rise against the house of______________________ with a sword (7:9).
9. ________________ was the priest of Bethel (7:10).
10. This priest thought Amos was raising a ________________ against Jeroboam (7:10).
11. Amaziah told Amos to get out and go back to the land of ___________ (7:12).

Crazy Clues

Choose a letter of the alphabet for each crazy clue below. Then fill in the same letter in all the boxes with the same number. For example, the letter for clue 1 goes in all the boxes with a 1. When all the letters are filled in, read what the people did in Haggai 1:2–14.

1. If you add this letter to *kit*, you have something you can fly with a string.
2. This letter is in both *tea* and *fist*.
3. The sound a cat makes has this letter in it. So does the sound an owl makes and the sound a cow makes.
4. If you add this letter to *sake*, you have something that's cool and frosty (and chocolate, vanilla, or strawberry).
5. This letter plus *nt* makes a small, crawling creature. This letter plus *rk* makes a big boat.
6. This letter sometimes sounds like *eeeee*. It's a crazy letter. It's also the next-to-last letter of the alphabet.

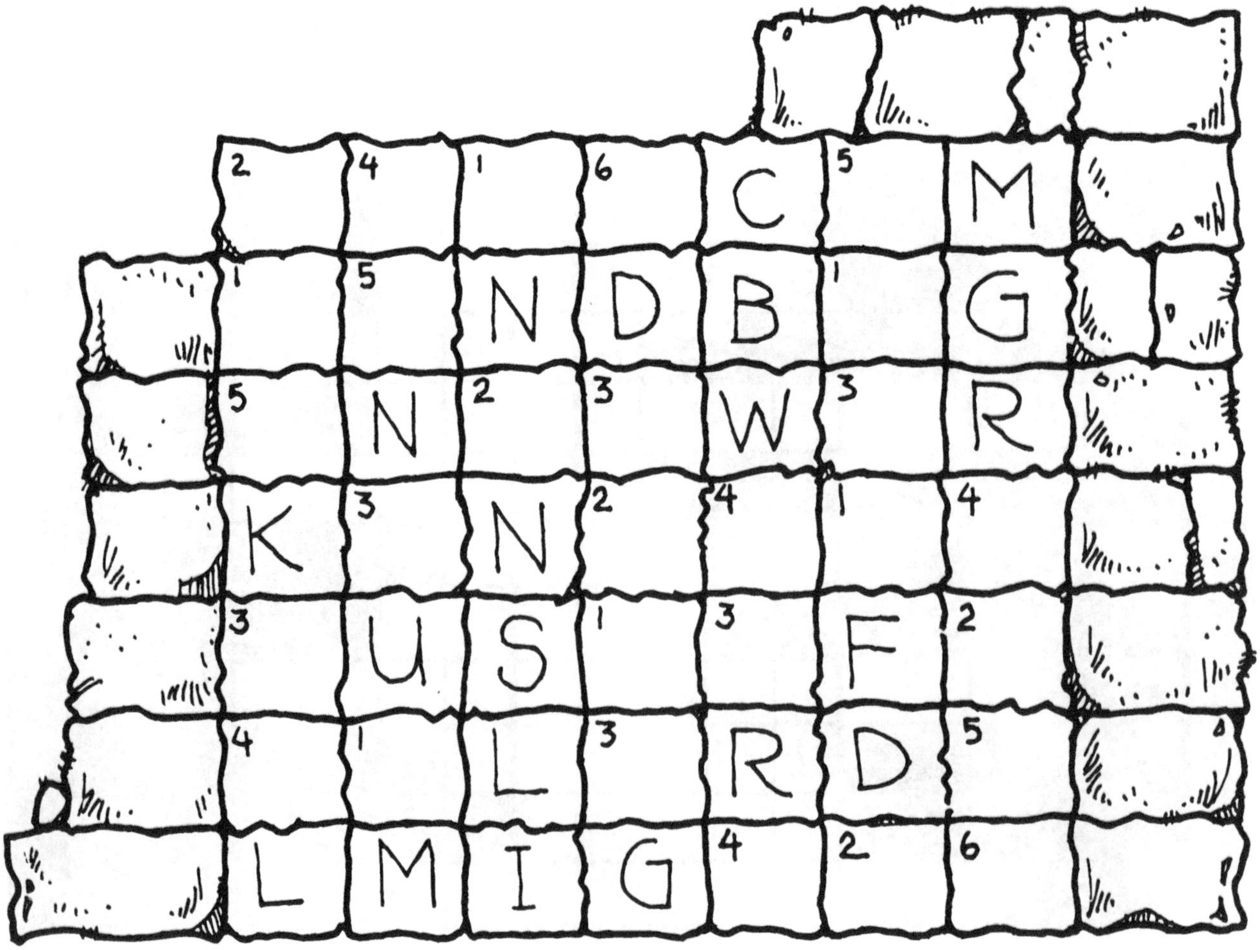

Give and Receive

Use these picture and letter clues to find the message from Malachi 3:8–12.

The Genealogy of Jesus

Read Matthew 1:1–17. Number the fathers in historical order. Write the son's name beside his father's name. Then write the letters that match the symbols on the lines below.

FATHERS	SONS
__ ABRAHAM	_ _ _ _ _ (☆ under 3rd)
__ JESSE	KING _ _ _ _ _ (△ under 4th)
__ JACOB	_ _ _ _ _ (/ under 5th)
__ KING DAVID	_ _ _ _ _ _ _ (♡ under 5th)
__ SALMON	_ _ _ _
__ OBED	_ _ _ _ _ (□ under 4th)
__ ISAAC	_ _ _ _ _ _ (∞ under 3rd)
__ BOAZ	_ _ _ _ (• under 2nd)

There were **30 + 12** generations from

___ ___ R ___ ___ ___ ___ TO ___ ___ R ___ ___ T.

☆ • ☆ / ☆ ♡   ∞ / △ □

A Gift for Me?

Finish the sentence from Matthew 1:21 by going through the maze. Pick up the letters as you go and put them on the lines below. There is only one correct path. When completed, you will know why God gave us this gift.

"You are to give him the name ____

____

____."

Come and Worship!

Matthew 2:1–11 (ICB) tells the story of the wise men. Read the Scripture, then fill in the puzzle using the clues given. The shaded squares will spell the name of an important city.

1. When they found the child, they ____________ down (v. 11).
2. Wise men from the ______________ came to Jerusalem (v. 1).
3. "We saw his ____________" (v. 2).
4. Herod asked them where the ______________ was to be born (v. 4).
5. They presented Him with gifts of _____________ (v. 11).
6. The child's name was ____________ (v. 1).
7. The child was born during the time of King _____________ (v. 1).
8. Jesus was born in a town in ________________ (v. 1).
9. The wise men saw the child with His mother, ______________ (v. 1).

Star Search

Draw a line from the first part of each word on the top line to the last part of the word in the second line. Start and end your lines on the dots. The words are names of people and places in Matthew 2:1–2 and 11–23. After you have connected all the names, write the letters crossed by the lines in order from left to right in the blanks at the bottom of the page. You will find out what the Magi did when they saw Jesus.

___ ___ ___ ___ ___ ___ ___ ___ ___   ___ ___ ___!

Jesus Is Baptized

Matthew 3:13–17 tells us of the baptism of Jesus. But what happened when Jesus was baptized? Use the code to find the answer.

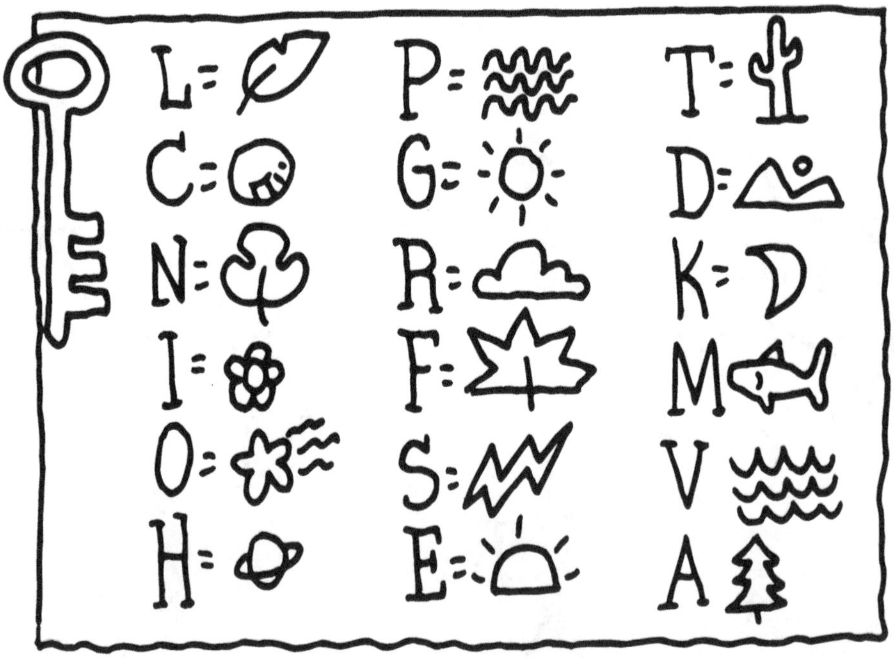

The Spirit

Read Matthew 3:16–17. Follow the connected letters and write them in order on the lines below. Then break the letters into words.

GOD SAID, "________________________________

____

__________________________." MATTHEW 3:17

Yield Not to Temptation

Follow the traffic signs to find a message that helped Jesus steer away from the Devil. Each sign stands for a letter. Learn which letter from the partly decoded message below. Read Matthew 4:1–11 for help. Then decode the message.

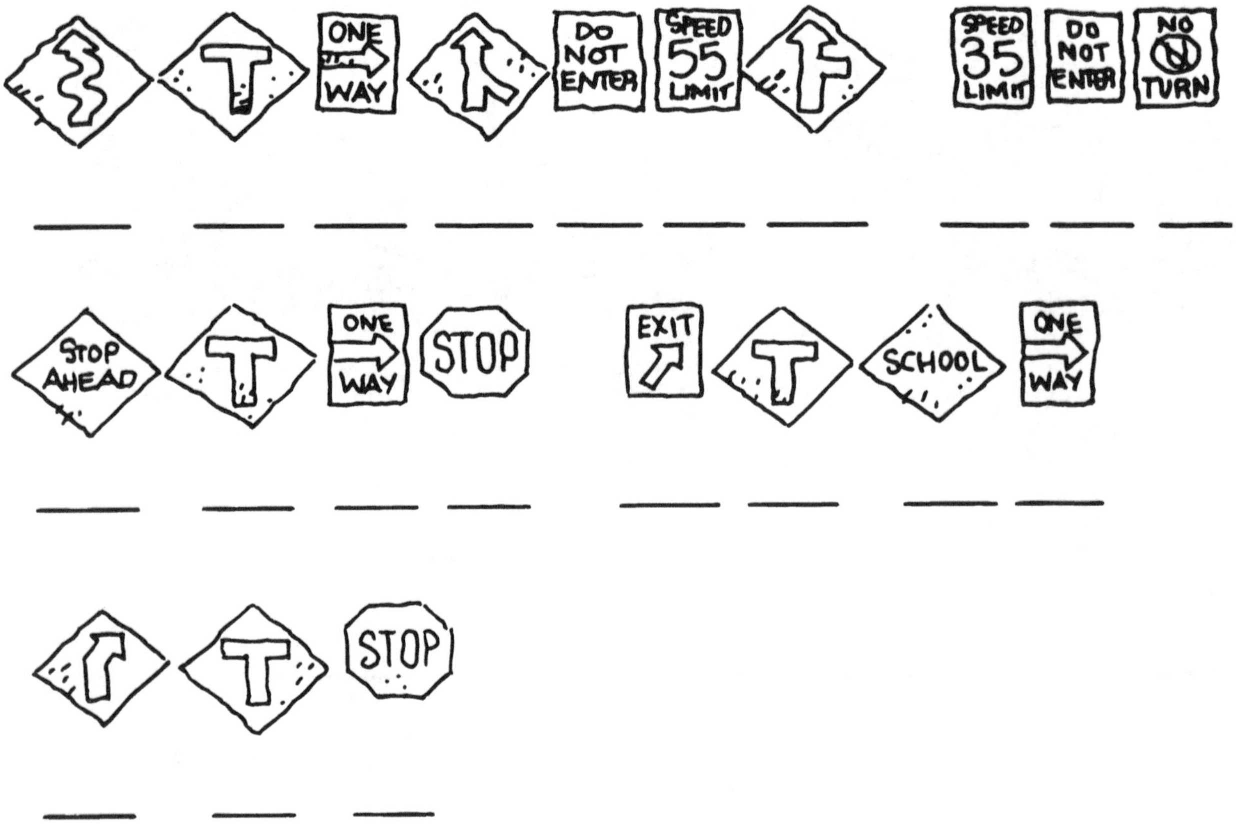

Calling Followers

Read Matthew 4:18–22; 9:9; and Mark 3:13–19. Unscramble the names on the lines provided. Then finish the sentence with the letters that you figured out really belong with symbols.

P EETR

M TTWEAH

J SMEA

T MOHSA

J NOH

J SEMA

A DWRNE

S MOTIN

J DAUS

T HADEUSDA

B ARTHMEWOLO

P LITPH

These men were Jesus'

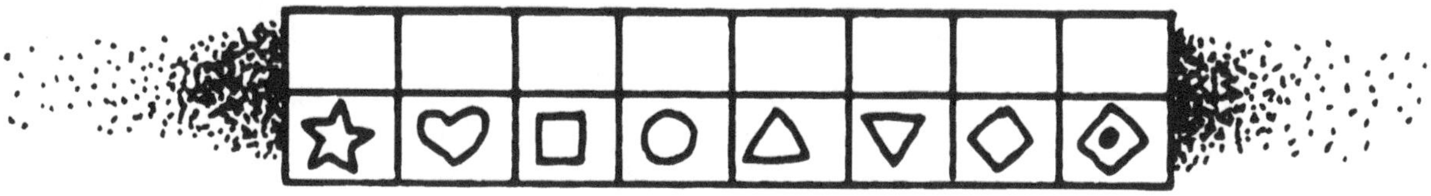

Who Is Blessed?

Read Matthew 5:1–12. Then color in the spaces below that name the people who Jesus said would be blessed. You will find out where Jesus was teaching.

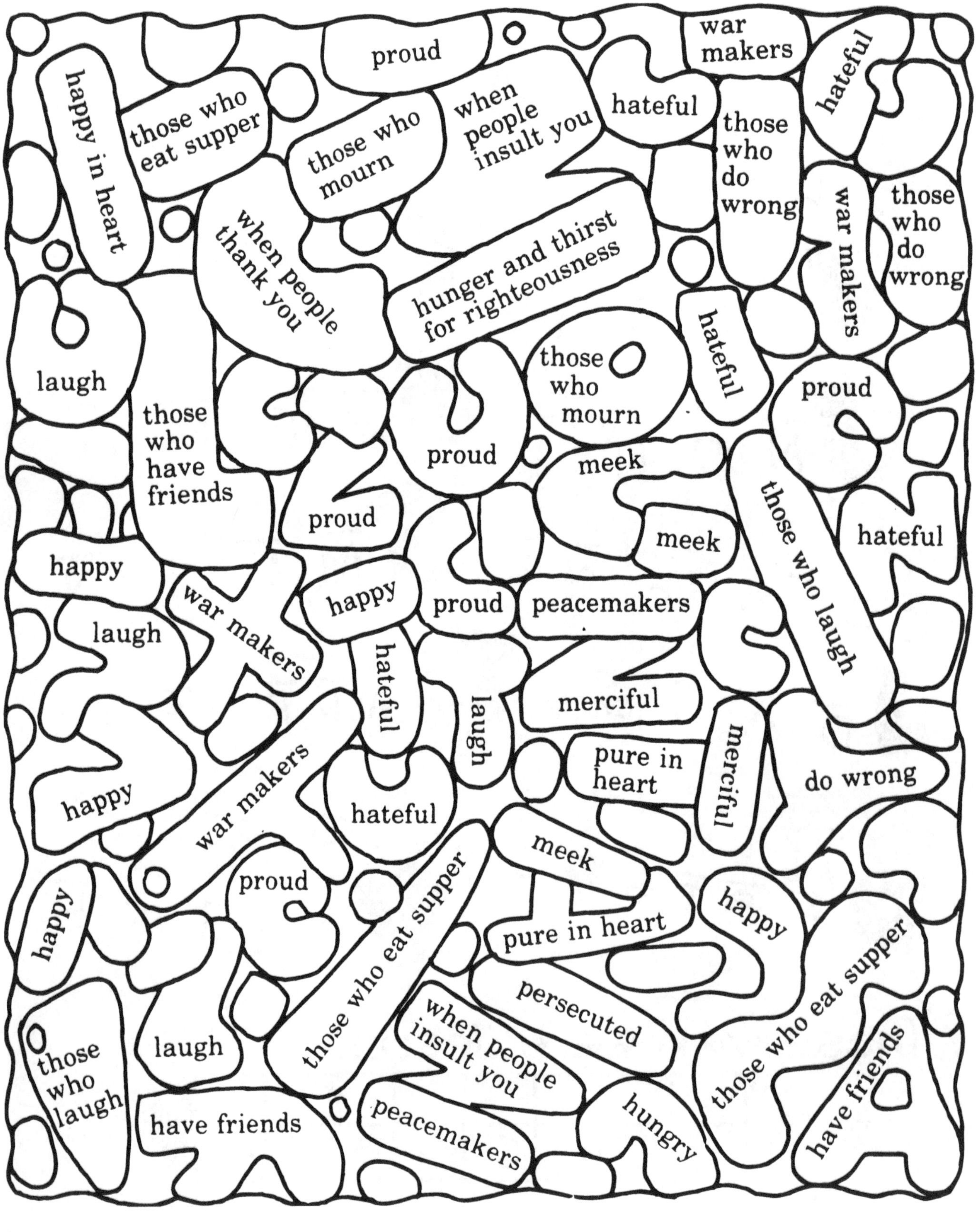

What Am I?

Read the story below by changing the letters and pictures into words. Then read Matthew 5:13–16.

A Wise Builder

People use many different things to build their houses. Jesus talked about how to build wisely or foolishly. Choose the right materials to solve the code below and learn who is a wise builder. Read Matthew 7:24–29 to find out more.

A wise builder is one who …

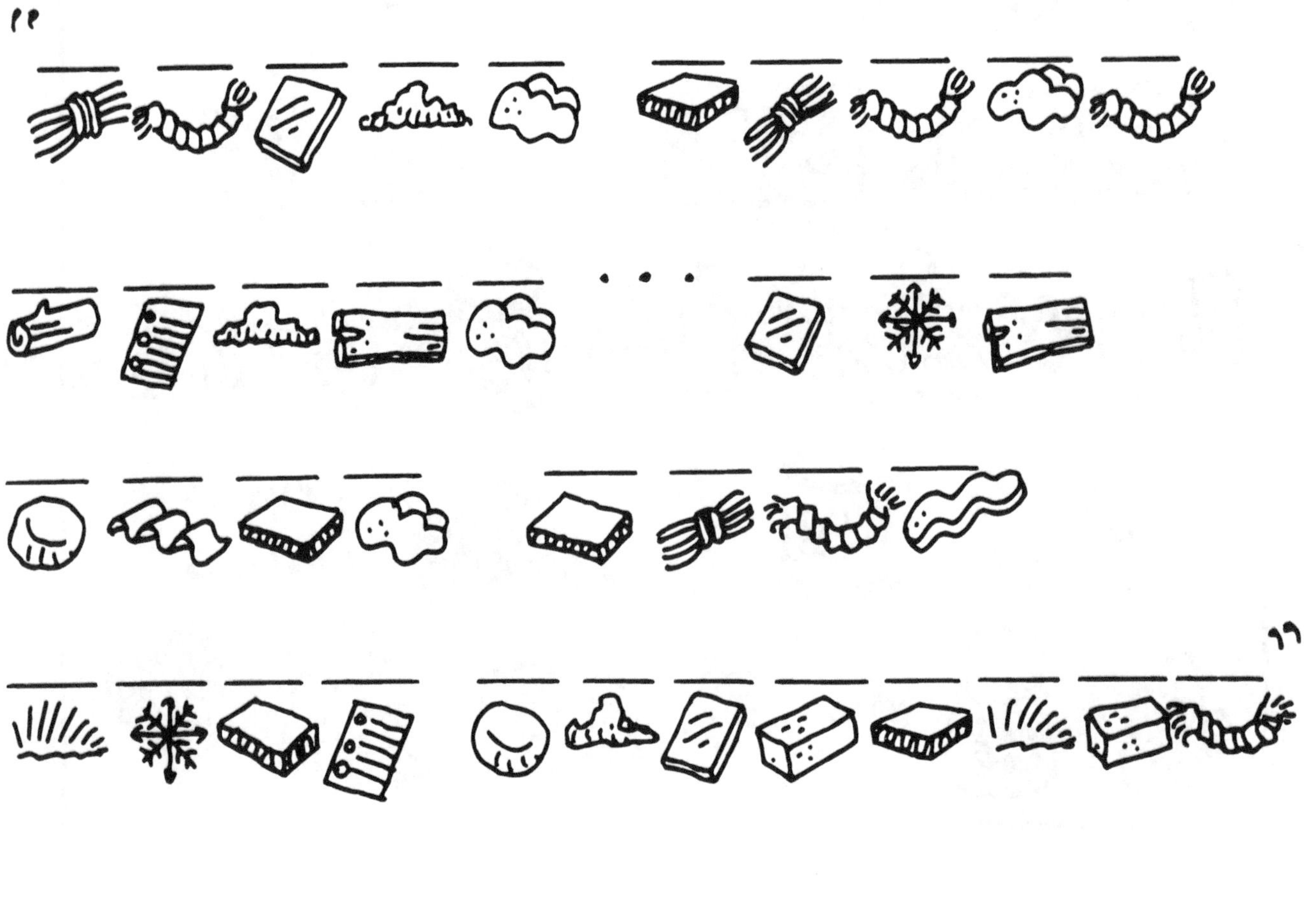

12 Men

Use the letters of the word DISCIPLES to place the names of nine disciples in the grid below. You will find them mentioned in Matthew 10:2–4 and John 1:35–45.

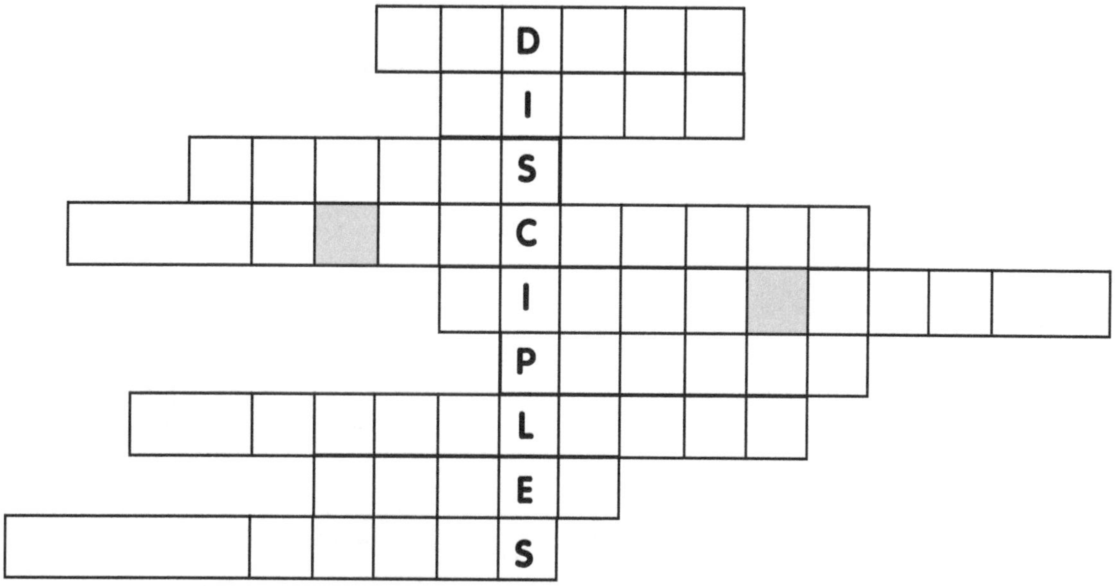

1. Simon Peter's brother
2. The zealot
3. Listed just before the tax collector
4. The betrayer
5. Andrew's brother
6. Listed before Bartholomew
7. Listed after Philip in Matthew; John calls him Nathanael
8. Son of Alphaeus
9. Named before Simon, he is also known as Judas

Now, can you name the other three?

______________________, ______________________, and ______________________.

Find the Treasure

Find the missing words of Matthew 13:44–46 hidden on the treasure chest. A number is included with each word. Place the word in the blank with the same number.

(v. 44) The kingdom of heaven is like a ______________ (1) hidden in a ______________ (2) .

When a ______________ (3) found it, he hid it again, and then in his ______________ (4) went

and sold all he had and bought that ______________ (2) .

(v. 45) Again, the kingdom of heaven is like a ______________ (5) looking for fine ______________ (6) .

(v. 46) When he found one of great ______________ (7) , he went away and sold everything he had

and bought it.

Cross It Out

Read Matthew 14:1–12 and follow the directions below.

1. Cross out one brother.
2. Cross out one wife.
3. Cross out one girl.
4. Cross out two words about John.
5. Cross out three things the daughter did.
6. Cross out one word for jail.
7. Cross out three groups of people.
8. Cross out a word telling how John was killed.
9. Cross out two titles for Herod.
10. Circle the words from Exodus 20:14.
11. Read the remaining words to learn how Herod reacted to John's message from God (Matt. 14:5).

PHILIP	YOU	HEROD	DAUGHTER
SHALL	WANTED	PROPHET	PLEASED
BEHEADED	KING	NOT	TO
DISCIPLES	DANCED	BAPTIST	KILL
HERODIAS	ADULTERY	JOHN	TETRARCH

Jesus Walked on Water

Read Matthew 14:22–33. Unscramble the large letters to find a name, then write them in the correct order in the top of the empty grid. Copy the columns under each bold letter in the correct order. Now read from left to right to find a message from verse 33.

E	**U**	**J**	**S**	**S**
those	were	Then	who	in
boat	him	the	worshipped	saying
you	the	Truly	are	Son
God	✿	of	✿	✿

Peter's Confession Hourglass

Read Matthew 16:13–17. Write the missing words from the story on the lines by the correct number.

When **12** came to the **4** of Caesarea **2**, he asked his **1**, "**7 8** people say the Son of Man **9**?"
They replied, "**6** say **11** the **14**; others say Elijah; and still others, **15** or one of the prophets."
"But what about **10**?" he asked. "Who do you say I am?" Simon Peter answered, "You are the **13**, the Son of the **16**."Jesus replied, "**3** are you, Simon son of **5**, for this was not revealed to you by man, but by my Father in heaven."

1. ___ ___ ___ ___ ___ ___ ___ ___ ___

2. ___ ___ ___ ___ ___ ___ ___ ___

3. ___ ___ ___ ___ ___ ___ ___

4. ___ ___ ___ ___ ___ ___

5. ___ ___ ___ ___ ___

6. ___ ___ ___ ___

7. ___ ___ ___

8. ___ ___

9. ___ ___

10. ___ ___ ___

11. ___ ___ ___ ___

12. ___ ___ ___ ___ ___

13. ___ ___ ___ ___ ___ ___ ___

14. ___ ___ ___ ___ ___ ___ ___

15. ___ ___ ___ ___ ___ ___ ___ ___

16. ___ ___ ___ ___ ___ ___   ___ ___ ___

Forgive

Peter asked Jesus if he should forgive his brother seven times. What was Jesus' answer? Put the words from the shapes in the matching shapes in the heart. Then read Matthew 18:21–35 to find out more about forgiveness.

Two Sons

Read Matthew 21:28–32 (ICB) and check the right answers. Copy the letter from each correct box onto the first line. Then copy the letters from the wrong answer boxes onto the second line.

There was a man who had [one[E] | two[C]] sons.

He went to the [first[H] | second[N]] son and said, ["Daughter[T] | Son[A],]

go and [work[N] | play[E]] today in my [vineyard[G] | barn[R]]."

The son answered, "I [will[T] | will not[E]] go."

But later the [son[A] | daughter[H]] decided he [should[N] | should not[E]] go, and he went.

Then the [mother[K] | father[D]] went to the other [son[B] | daughter[I]] and said,

"Son, go and [work[E] | play[N]] today in my [vineyard[L] | barn[G]]."

The son answered, "[No[D] | Yes[I]], sir, I [will[E] | will not[O]] go and work."

But he did not go. Which of the [two[V] | three[M]] sons obeyed his father?

The priests and leaders answered, "The [first[E] | second] son."

__ __ __ __ __ __   __ __ __   __ __ __ __ __ __ __

__ __ __ __ __ __   __ __ __   __ __ __ __ __ __ __

When Will Jesus Come?

Follow the lines from the lanterns to the blank spaces and put the letters that are in the lanterns on the spaces. You will learn what we know about when Jesus will return. Read Matthew 25:1–13 to find out more.

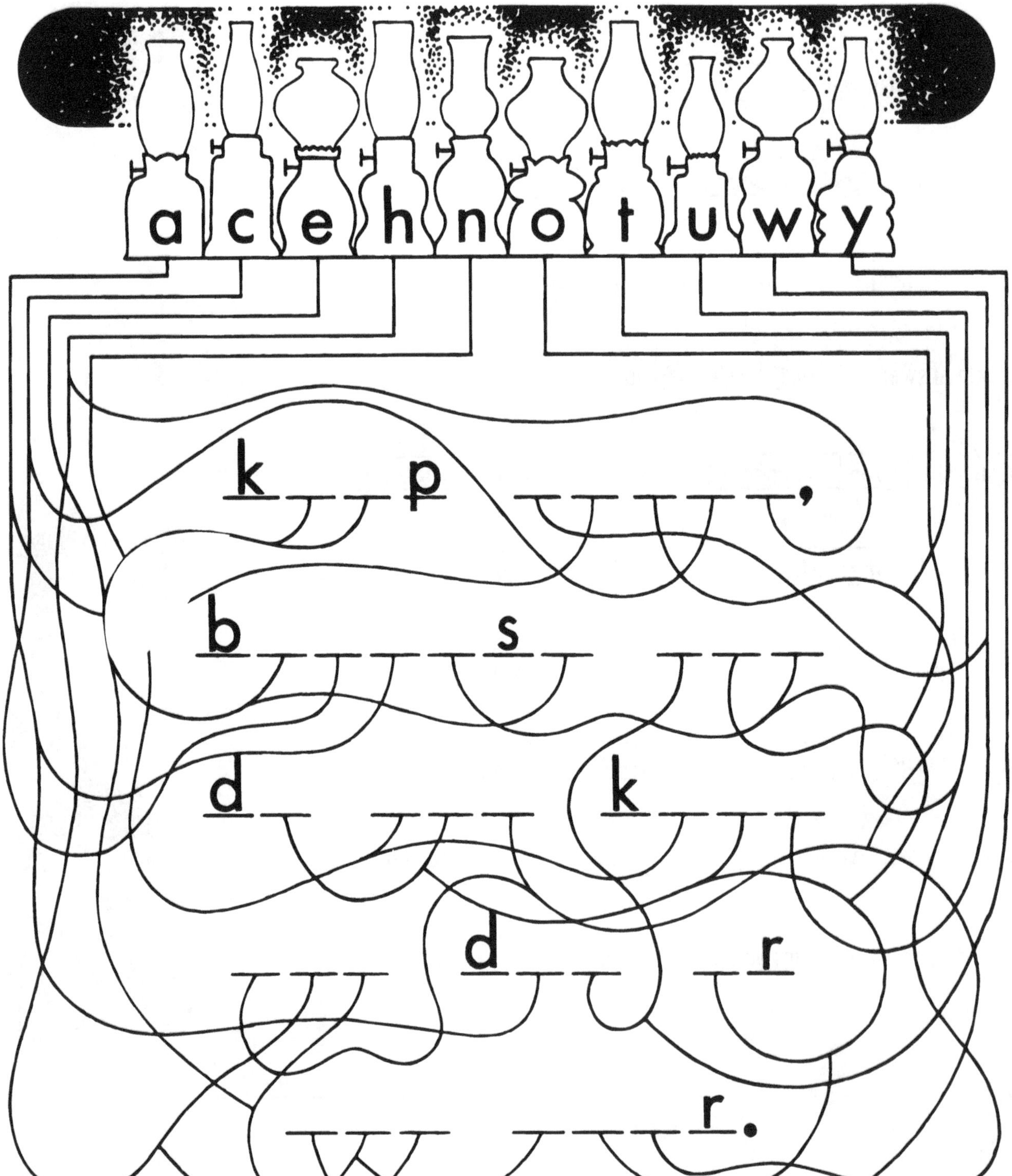

One Talent

Follow the directions below.

1. Subtract box **C** from box **F**. Place the answer in work box **A**.
2. Subtract box **D** from box **A**. Place the answer in work box **B**.
3. Add boxes **C** and **D**. Place the total in work box **C**.
4. Add boxes **E** and **F**. Place the total in work box **D**.
5. Subtract box **D** from box **E**. Place the answer in work box **E**.
6. Add boxes **C**, **D**, and **F**. Place the total in work box **F**.
7. Subtract box **A** from box **G**. Place the answer in work box **G**.
8. Add boxes **B** and **F**. Place the total in work box **H**.

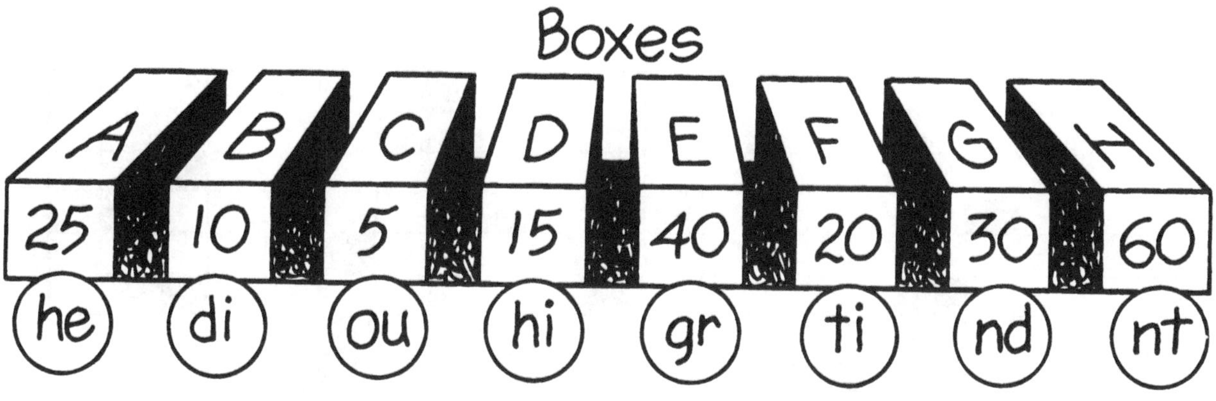

In the circles below each work box, write the letters that appear below the same number at the top of the page. Read Matthew 25:24–30 to find out more.

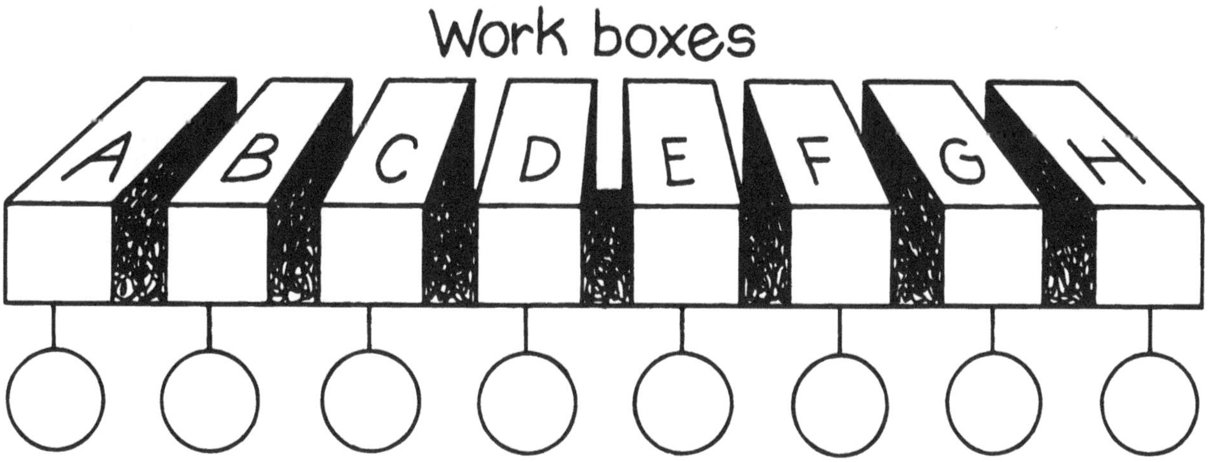

What did the servant with one talent do with his money?

What's the Question?

Read Matthew 25:31–46 and then color in the coded squares to read the question from the Scripture. Some of the squares have been filled in for you.

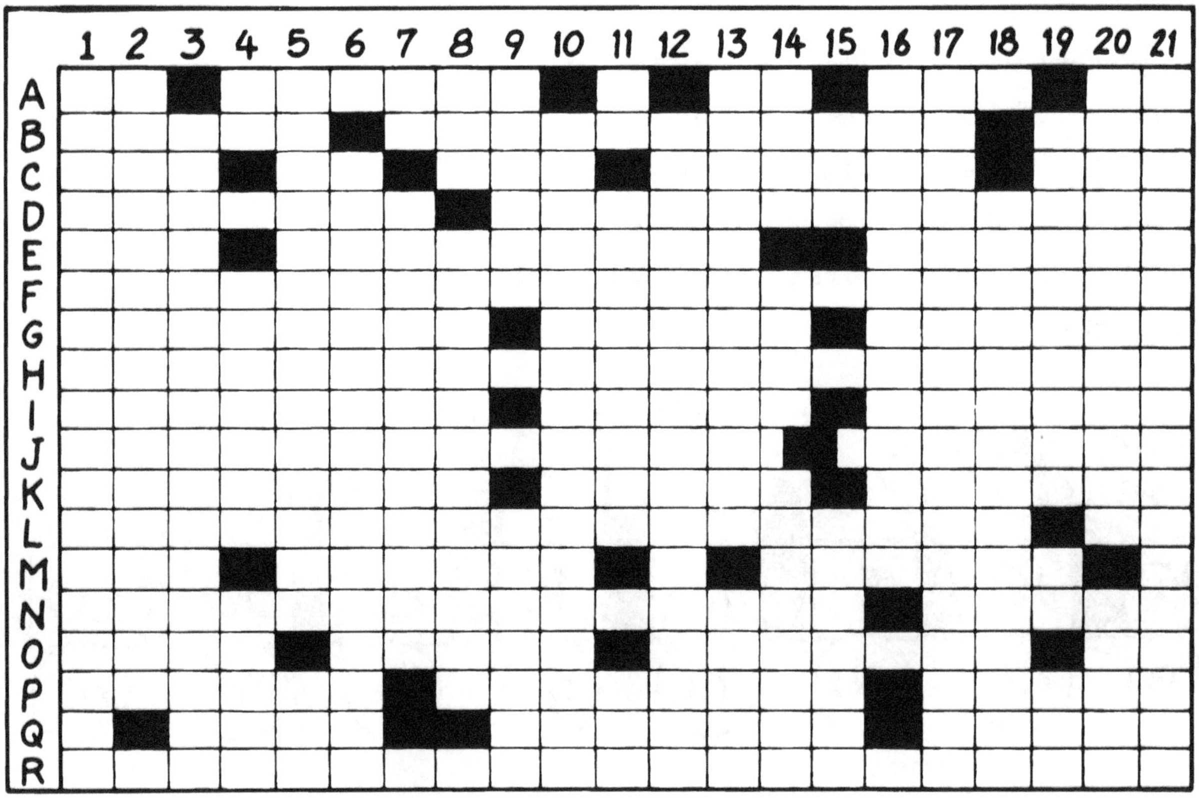

C–6	I–11	P–19	G–11	A–20	C–14	K–10
P–2	H–15	A–8	I–14	O–2	K–13	O–7
M–7	E–18	D–18	C–19	M–12	N–11	C–3
L–20	P–4	Q–4	Q–3	D–14	P–11	C–8
Q–9	G–13	E–2	O–12	A–18	E–8	J–11
C–20	A–11	A–14	H–13	M–15	B–10	P–9
M–2	N–20	A–16	C–2	J–13	C–10	M–9
Q–13	O–13	E–3	Q–11	N–7	N–9	D–6
E–12	M–16	B–8	M–17	I–13	M–3	O–9
A–4	H–11	C–15	A–6	B–14	E–6	K–11
P–13	G–14	N–19	O–4	G–10	D–4	D–10
R–19	A–2	O–16	M–8	N–2	E–10	J–9
E–16	E–11	B–2	B–20	N–13	H–9	

See the Stone?

A message from Matthew 28:1–10 is hidden in the stones of this puzzle. Color all the spaces where the stones overlap, then read the uncolored words to find the message.

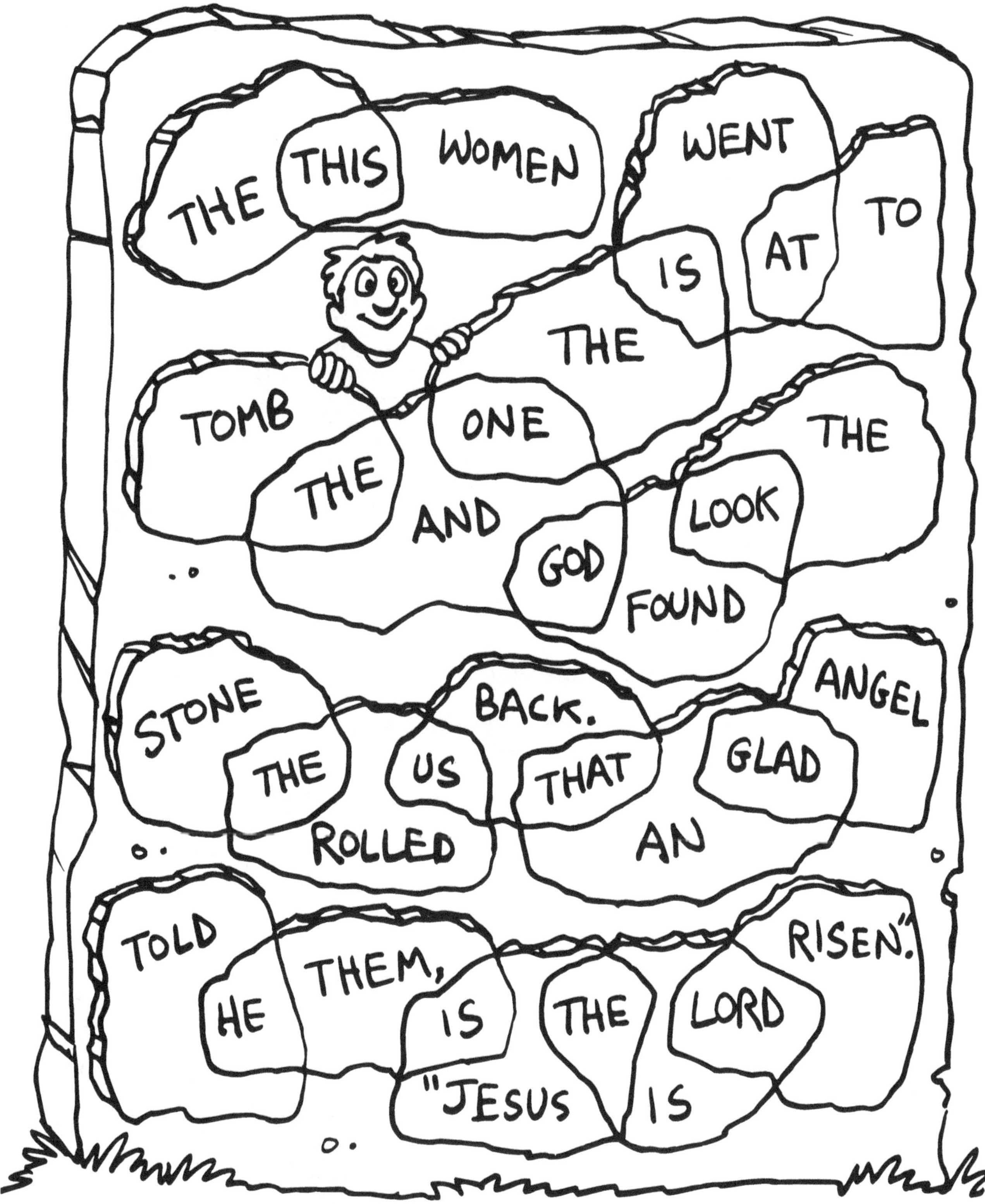

A Final Message

What did Jesus say to His disciples before He returned to heaven? To find out, turn the letters below into words by adding vowels. Read Matthew 28:16–20 for help.

J_S_S S__D,

"G_ _ND M_K_

D_SC_PL_S _F _LL

N_T__NS, B_PT_Z_NG

TH_M _N TH_ N_M_ _F

TH_ F_TH_R _ND

_F TH_ S_N _ND _F TH_

H_LY SP_R_T, _ND

T__CH_NG TH_M T_ _B_Y

_V_RYTH_NG _ H_V_

C_MM_ND_D Y__."

Forgiven!

What is the first thing Jesus said to the paralyzed man? To find out, go down the line of boxes below each number on the graph and find the colored squares. Do numbers 1 through 10 in order. Write the letters from beside the colored squares in order in the blanks of the message. Read Mark 2:1–12 to find out more.

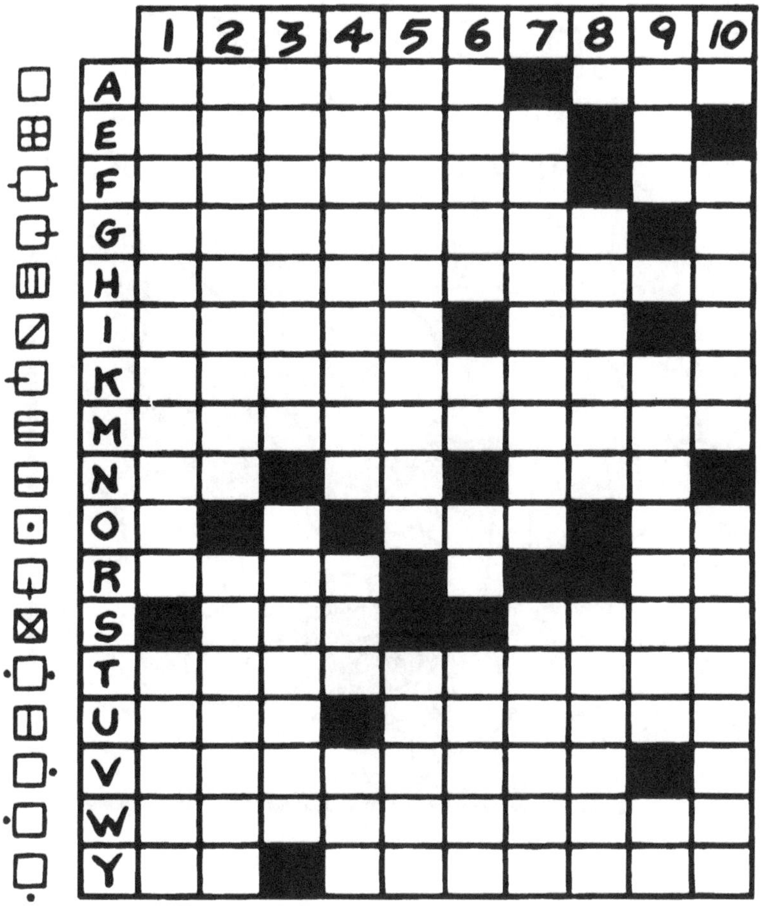

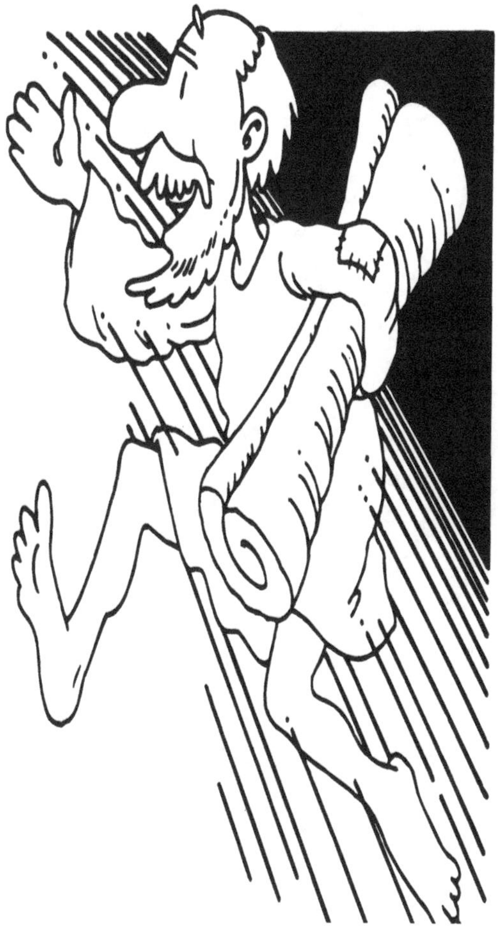

“___, ____ ____ ___ ________.”

Why did Jesus tell the paralyzed man to get up, take up his mat, and go home? To find out, put each letter that has a symbol beside it on the line above the same symbol.

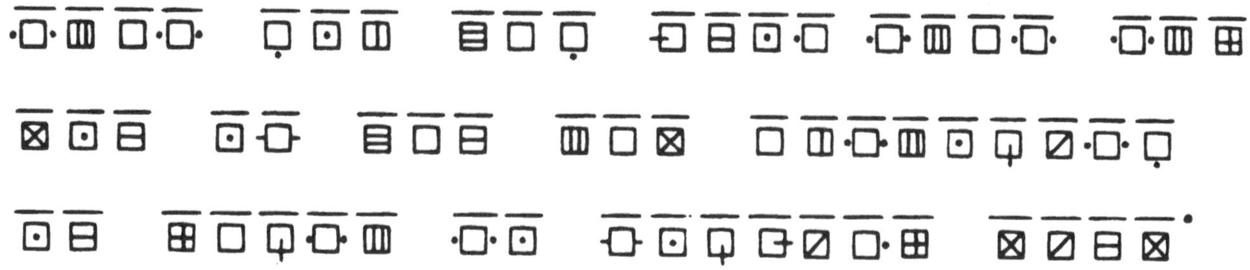

Healing of the Demon-Possessed Man

Read Mark 5:1–20. Then read each statement below and follow the directions. When completed, you will find something from the Scripture you just read.

1. If Jesus went to the Gerasenes, color the 2s black and the 9s yellow.
2. If a man who lived in the tombs had never been chained, color the 4s blue and the 3s green.
3. If the man's name was Larry, color the 8s red and the 5s black.
4. If the demons begged to be sent into a herd of pigs, color the 5s orange and the 6s black.
5. If the evil spirits came out of the man and into the pigs, color the 4s black and the 7s green.
6. If there were about 200 pigs, color the 8s yellow and the 1s purple.
7. If the pigs drowned, color the 3s red and the 8s black.
8. If the people were afraid, color the 1s blue.

A Rich Man's Mistake

Jesus told a rich young man to sell everything he had and follow Him. What did the rich man do? Work these math problems to learn the code. Then fill in the blanks below to find out. Read Mark 10:17–22 to check your answer.

9 + 5 = A	16 + 15 = C	12 + 7 = L	24 + 3 = N	24 + 13 = S
34 + 14 = U	24 + 15 = Y	37 − 12 = D	34 − 17 = E	15 − 11 = R
48 − 19 = T	3 x 2 = B	3 x 3 = G	3 x 4 = H	7 x 3 = W

12 17   21 17 27 29   14 21 14 39   37 14 25

6 17 31 14 48 37 17   12 17   12 14 25

9 4 17 14 29   21 17 14 19 29 12

A Slave

Read Mark 10:35–38 and 40–45. Beginning with column number 1, go down each column until you come to a dot. Copy the letter at the left of the dot onto the first blank.

	1	2	3	4	5	6	7	8	9	10	11	12	13	14	15	16	17
A					•								•			•	
B								•			•						
E			•	•				•			•			•			
F								•							•		
H		•															
I								•									
L												•				•	•
M									•								
N					•												
O		•					•							•			
R				•				•									
S						•		•		•	•						
T					•	•		•		•							
U									•								
V			•										•				
W	•			•													

___ ___ ___ ___ ___ ___ ___ ___   ___ ___ ___ ___ ___   ___ ___

___ ___   ___ ___ ___ ___ ___   ___ ___ ___ ___   ___ ___

___ ___ ___ ___ ___   ___ ___   ___ ___ ___. Mark 10:44

Important Phone Call

Use the telephone dial to find out which commandments Jesus considered most important. Each pair of numbers has a dial number and a letter number. For example, 53 is dial number 5 and the third letter on that dial, L. After you have finished, check your answer by reading Mark 12:30–31.

________ 53–63–83–32 ________ 81–42–32 ________ 53–63–72–31 ________ 93–63–82–72

________ 41–63–31 ________ 91–43–81–42 ________ 21–53–53 ________ 93–63–82–72

________. 42–32–21–72–81 ________ 53–63–83–32 ________ 93–63–82–72

________ 62–32–43–41–42–22–63–72 ________ 21–73 ________. 93–63–82–72–73–32–53–33

The Widow's Offering

Find out what the widow put in the offering by placing the correct letter in the blank. Check your answer by reading Mark 12:41–44.

1. _____ You'll find me once in *snake* and twice in *elephant*.

2. _____ You'll find me in *vanilla*, but not in *chocolate* or *lemon lime*.

3. _____ I'm once in *ears* and twice in *eyes*.

4. _____ I'm a consonant in *treasure* but not in *stadium*.

5. _____ You'll see me in *yard*, but not in *lard*.

6. _____ Look for me twice in *tight* and *little*.

7. _____ I'm a consonant in *house* and also in *heart.*

8. _____ I'm a vowel in *Illinois* but not in *Oregon*.

9. _____ I'm a consonant found once in *bean* and twice in *banana*.

10. _____ I'm a consonant in *green*, but not in *brown*.

The widow put in ___ ___ ___ ___ ___ ___ ___ ___ ___ ___ .

Missing Word ABCs

Turn to Mark 15:21–28 and 33–39 (ESV) to locate the missing words in this list of ABCs.

A ___ ___ ___ ___ ___ ___ ___ ___ Simon was his father (v. 21).

B ___ ___ ___ ___ ___ It ripped from top to ____________ (v. 38).

C ___ ___ ___ ___ ___ ___ This ripped (v. 38).

D ___ ___ ___ ___ ___ ___ ___ What came at the sixth hour (v. 33)?

E ___ ___ ___ ___ ___ They thought He called ____________ (v. 35).

F ___ ___ ___ ___ ___ ___ ___ Jesus thought God had ____________ Him (v. 34).

G ___ ___ ___ ___ ___ ___ ___ Where was Jesus taken (v. 22)?

H ___ ___ ___ ___ The centurion ____________ His cry (vv. 37, 39).

I ___ Simon was on his way ______ from the country (v. 21).

J ___ ___ ___ Group of people mentioned (v. 26).

K ___ ___ ___ The inscription said He was a ____________ (v. 26).

L ___ ___ ___ They cast ____________ (v. 24).

M ___ ___ ___ ___ The wine was mixed with ________________ (v. 23).

N ___ ___ ___ ___ The hour mentioned (v. 34).

O ___ ___ ___ ___ ___ ___ Then they ____________ Him wine (v. 23).

P ___ ___ ___ ___ ___ ___ ___ Simon was a ____________ (v. 21).

R ___ ___ ___ ___ ___ ___ The others crucified were ____________ (v. 27).

S ___ ___ ___ ___ ___ What they filled (v. 36).

T ___ ___ ___ ___ The hour mentioned (v. 25).

U ___ ___ ___ ___ Darkness covered the land ____________ the ninth hour (v. 33).

Alleluia!

Write the words missing from this part of Mark's gospel in the puzzle boxes. The chapter and verse where the answers are found are at the end of each sentence.

Joseph of (**1**) ________________ went boldly to (**2**) __________and asked for Jesus' (**3**) __________ (15:43).

Joseph (**4**) __________ the body in linen and placed it (**5**) __________ a tomb and rolled a (**6**) __________ against the (**7**) ________________ (15:46).

Three women brought (**8**) __________ to anoint (**9**) __________ body (16:1).

They saw a young (**10**) __________ dressed in a white (**11**) ___________ sitting on the (**12**) __________ side, and they were (**13**) ___________ (16:5).

Now read the circled letters in numerical order to find out what the young man said to the women.

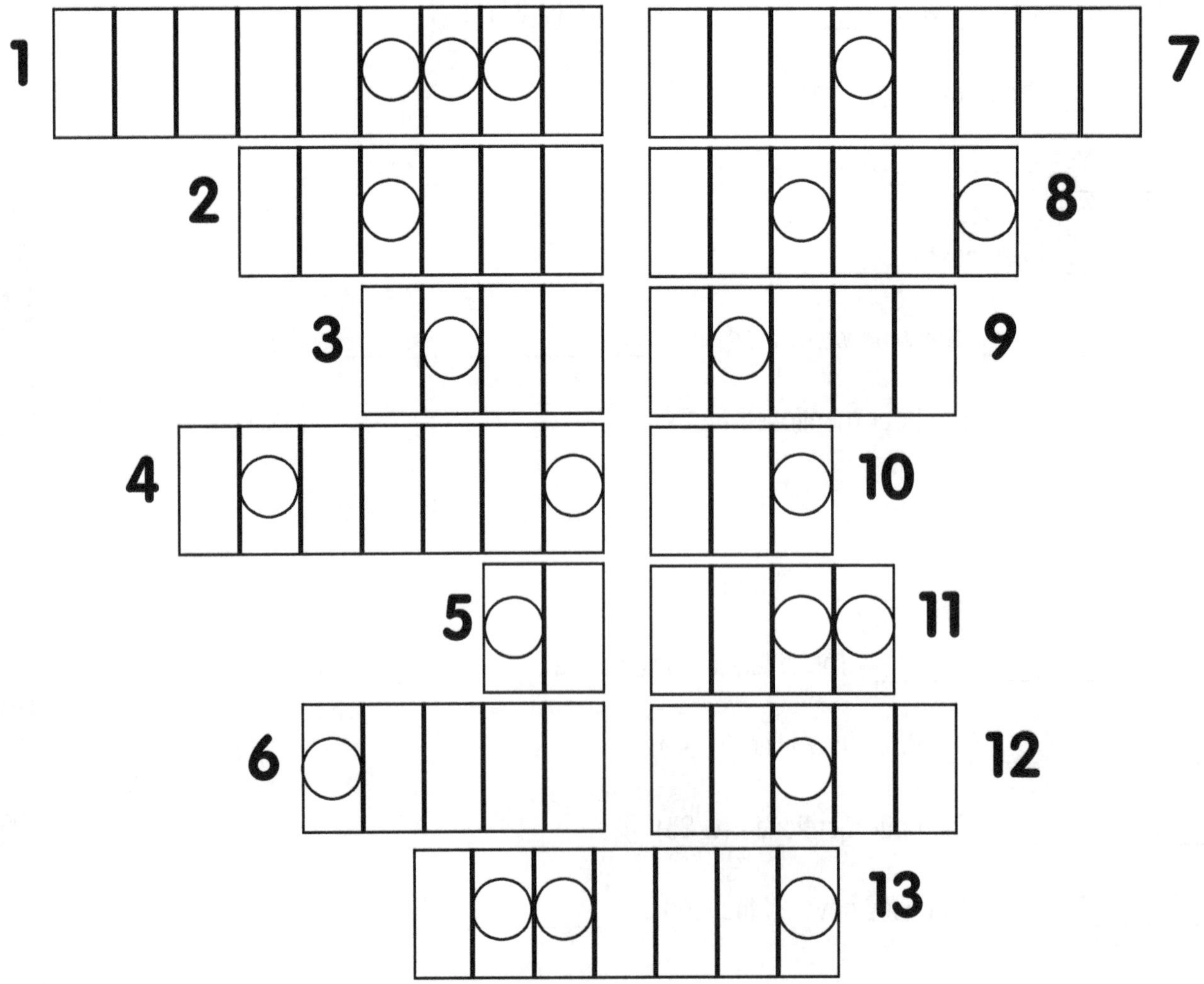

Chrono-Code

Read Luke 1:8–25. Number the sentences below in the order they happened. Then write the letters next to each number on the blanks at the bottom of the page. You will find out what the angel said to Zechariah.

___ **U** The worshippers at the temple prayed outside.

___ **A** Elizabeth said, "The Lord has done this for me."

___ **B** Zechariah returned home.

___ **O** The angel said John was not to drink any wine.

___ **H** Gabriel said Zechariah would not be able to speak.

___ **R** Zechariah was afraid.

___ **Y** Zechariah was chosen to burn incense.

___ **P** The angel promised the birth of John.

___ **D** Zechariah made signs to the people but couldn't speak.

___ **E** The people wondered why Zechariah was taking so long.

___ **N** Zechariah asked, "How can I be sure of this?"

___ **S** An angel appeared in the temple.

___ ___ ___ ___   ___ ___ ___ ___ ___ ___   ___ ___ ___
1 6 2 4   5 4 12 1 9 4   8 12 3

___ ___ ___ ___   ___ ___ ___ ___ ___.
11 9 9 7   8 9 12 4 10

The News

Read Luke 1:26–28, 30–33, 38–42, and 46–47. Use the code to fill in the missing words.

It's a Boy!

Use the code to find out what Zechariah wrote on his tablet. Read Luke 1:57–67 if you need help.

A Savior

Read Luke 2:1–20. Find the angel's message by going through the maze. Then write the letters on the lines below, using only the letters on the correct path to Jesus.

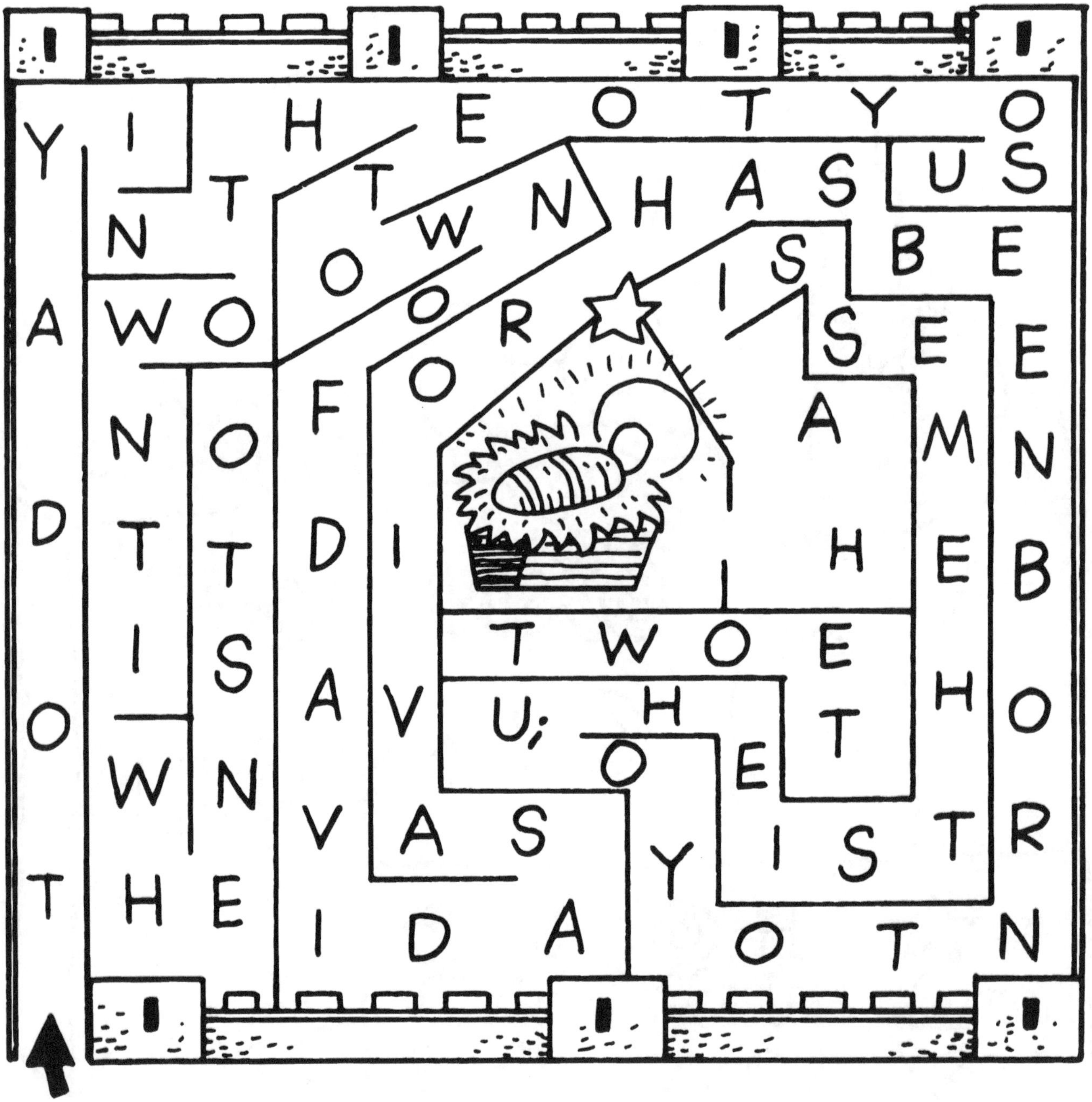

____

____

____

Scrambled Rulers

Unscramble the names and titles of rulers below. Read Luke 2:1–20 if you need help. Then write the letters over numbers in the blanks with matching numbers at the bottom of the page to find an important message.

NIRISIQUU	___	___	___	___	___	___	___	___	___
				11		20			6

RACASE	___	___	___	___	___	___
		4	15		7	

VADID	___	___	___	___	___
		13	8		3

GUTSUSUA	___	___	___	___	___	___	___	___
	5				1		14	

VOGORNER	___	___	___	___	___	___	___	___
		2		16		17	18	

STRICH	___	___	___	___	___	___
		12		9		

DORL	___	___	___	___
		10	19	

___	___	___	___	Y		___		___	___	___	___	___	___
1	2	3	4			5		6	7	8	9	10	11

___	___	___		B	___	___	___		B	___	___	___ !
12	13	14			15	16	17			18	19	20

Jumble John

Unscramble these persons or groups in Luke 3:2–3 and 10–18. Write the letters in the matching shapes at the bottom of the page to find what John preached.

OXATELOTSRCLC

LOSIDERS

LEEPPO

DOWRC

GDO

SNANA

PHAISAAC

HAZEIARCH

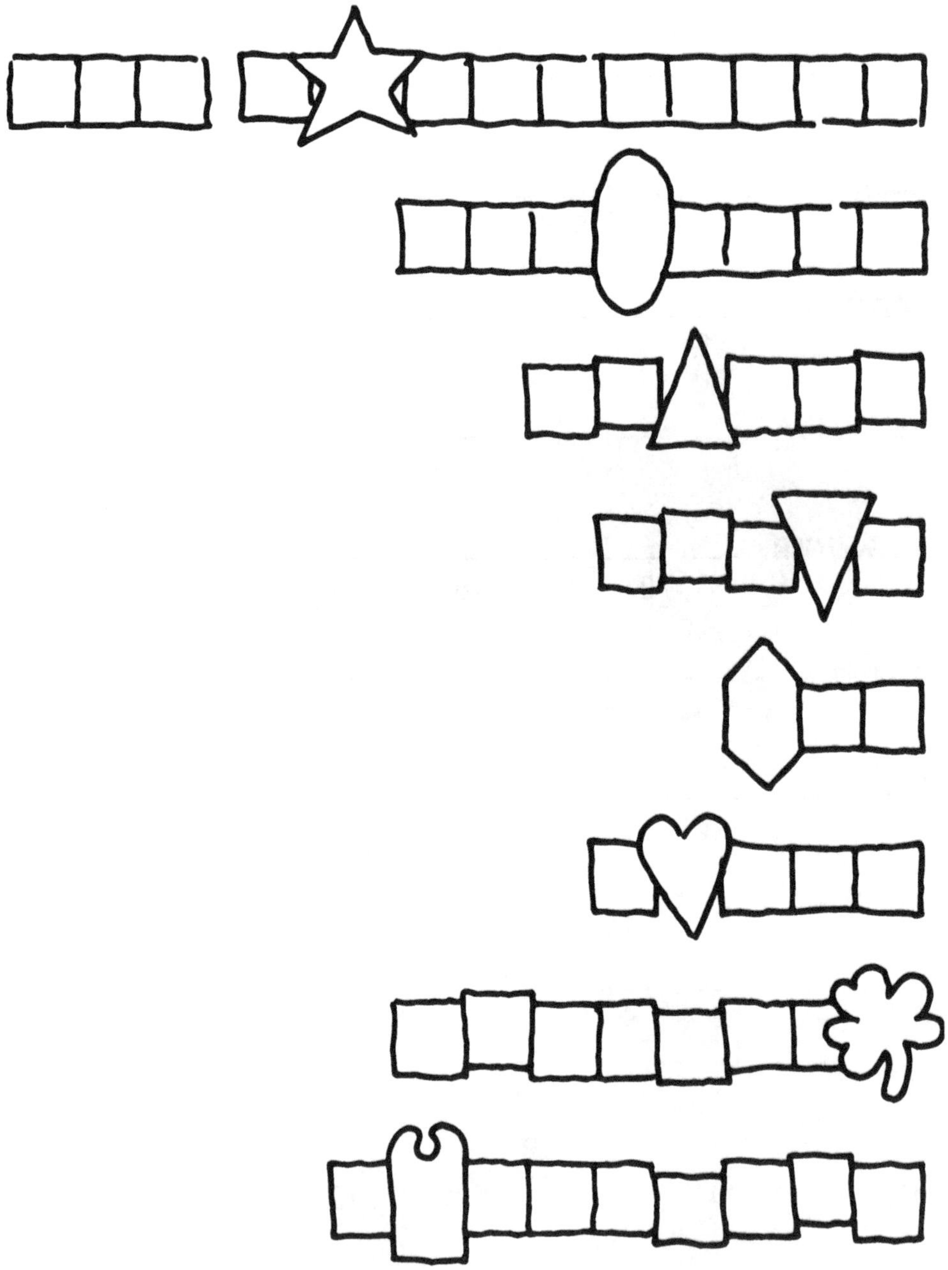

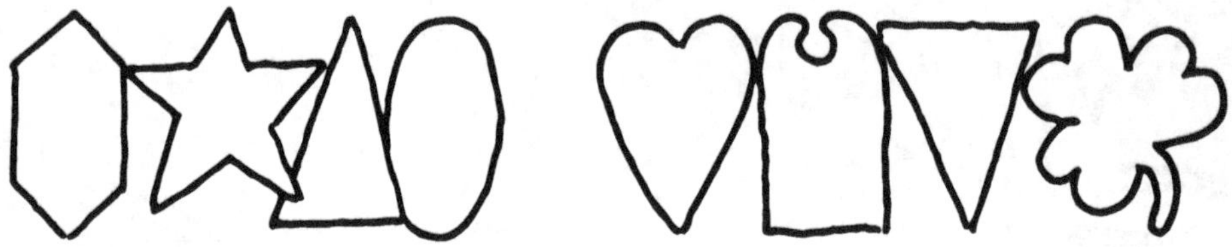

Fishers of Men

Read the Bible story from Luke 5:1–11. This tells the exciting story of Jesus calling His first disciples. Then fill in the puzzle using the clues given.

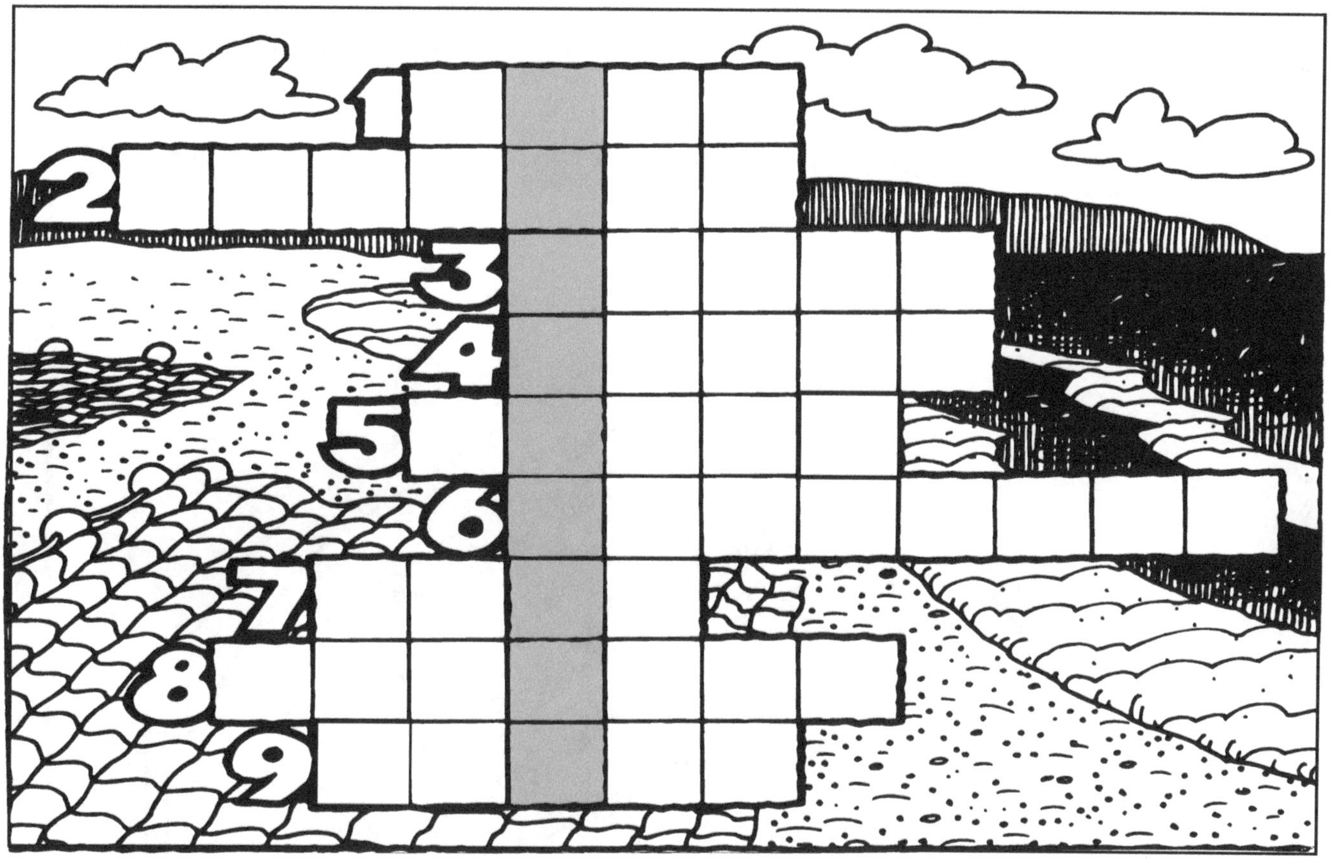

1. Two boats were at the water's ______________________________ (v. 2).

2. The fishermen were ______________________________ their nets (v. 2).

3. One of the boats belonged to ______________________________ (v. 3).

4. Jesus wanted them to put down their nets for a ______________________________ (v. 4).

5. The fishermen had worked all ______________________________ (v. 5).

6. They caught so many fish that they signaled for their ______________________________ (v. 7).

7. Simon ______________________________ at Jesus' knees (v. 8).

8. James and John were sons of ______________________________ (v. 10).

9. ______________________________ told Simon he would catch men (v. 10).

The Alabaster Jar

Read Luke 7:36–50. In the puzzle, cross out the 12 words from the story listed below. There will be several letters left over but only eight different kinds. Write down each letter once. Then put these eight letters in the correct order to make a word that tells about the woman's sins.

Words: Pharisee, Simon, perfume, feet, tears, hair, sinful, prophet, money, pay, debts, table

The woman's sins were ____ ____ ____ ____ ____ ____ ____ ____.

Good Soil

Read Luke 8:4–8 and 11–15. Finish the verse by matching the shapes at the top of the page with the same shapes below.

The ______ on ______ ______

stands for those with a

______ and ______ ______,

who hear the ______,

retain it, and by

______, ______

a ______.

Jesus Calms a Stormy Sea

What did the disciples say about Jesus after He calmed a storm? To find out, follow the line from each letter to the empty circle and write the same letter in the circle. Read Luke 8:22–25 for help.

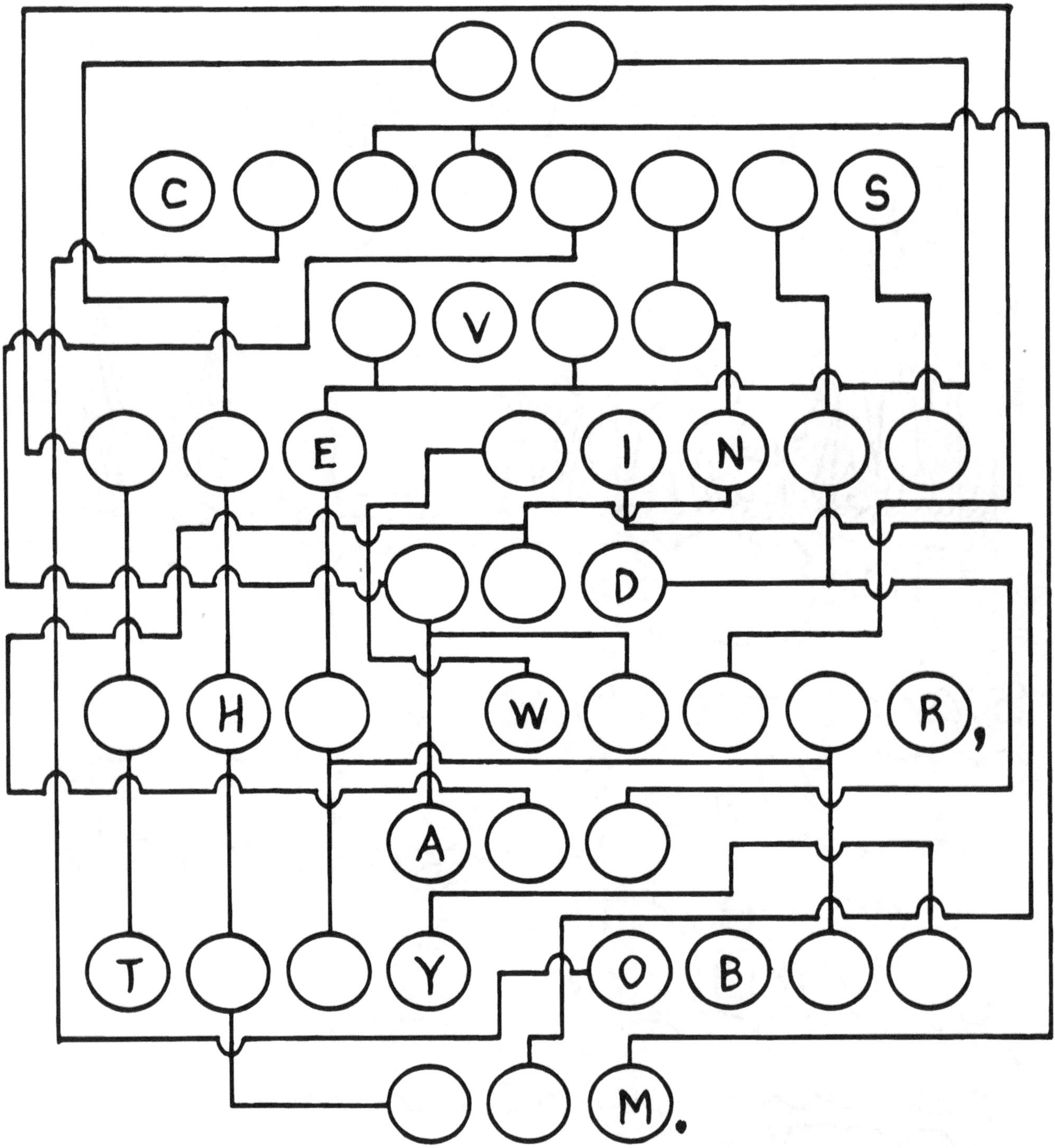

Just Believe

Read Luke 8:41–55. Starting with column 1, go down each column until you find a dot. Copy the letter to the left of the dot onto the first blank. Fill in the blanks in order.

	1	2	3	4	5	6	7	8	9	10	11	12	13	14	15	16
C		●														
D			●													●
E				●			●					●			●	
G			●													
H		●				●										
I		●							●	●						
L		●														
M	●															
N														●		
P					●			●								
R							●		●		●		●			
S							●									
T				●						●		●				
U				●								●				
Y	●															

“___ ___ ___ ___ ___ ___ ___, ___ ___ ___

___ ___!” ___ ___ ___ ___ ___ ___ ___ ___ ___

___ ___ ___ ___ ___ ___ ___ ___.

The Glory of the Lord

Play detective and see if you can spot mistakes in the following statements about Luke 9:28–36. Put a line through the word(s) that are wrong. Above these mistakes, write the correct word(s).

1. About seven days later, Jesus took three men with Him into the mountains.
2. The three men were Peter, Andrew, and James.
3. Jesus took these men to the mountains to fast.
4. While Jesus was praying, His hands changed.
5. Jesus' hair became as bright as a flash of lightning.
6. Three people from the time of the Old Testament appeared with Jesus.
7. Peter and the others were not sleepy.
8. While Peter was speaking, a thunderstorm came.
9. They heard a voice speak from the ground.
10. The voice told them Jesus was His Son and that they were to obey Him.
11. When they came down from the mountain, they told everyone what they had seen.

A Good Neighbor

Read Luke 10:29–37 and answer the questions. Circle the letter of each correct answer. Find the spaces in section 1 that contain the same letter as the answer to the question 1, and color them in. Do the same with the other three sections.

1. A man was going to Jericho when he fell into whose hands?

a. hermits **b.** robbers **c.** soldiers

2. A priest passed by the man. Who else passed by?

a. a merchant **b.** a Jew **c.** a Levite

3. Who took pity on the man?

a. a Samaritan **b.** an innkeeper **c.** the governor

4. Which of the three was a neighbor to the hurt man?

a. the priest **b.** the Levite **c.** the Samaritan

What Did Martha Open?

Read Luke 10:38–42; Romans 10:17; and 15:4. Answer the questions below with the most correct word from the list.

1. At whose feet did Mary sit? ______________________
2. Martha was worried and ______________________.
3. Mary ______________________ to Jesus.
4. Faith comes from ______________________ the message.
5. Everything that was written in the past was written to ______________________ us.
6. Who did the better thing: Martha, Mary, or the disciples? ______________________

Mary	Teach	Listened
Help	Upset	Talked
Hearing	The Lord's	Martha's

Now complete the picture by drawing a line from the first circled letter in answer 1 to the following circled letter and so on through answer 6. The picture you draw is the answer to the title question.

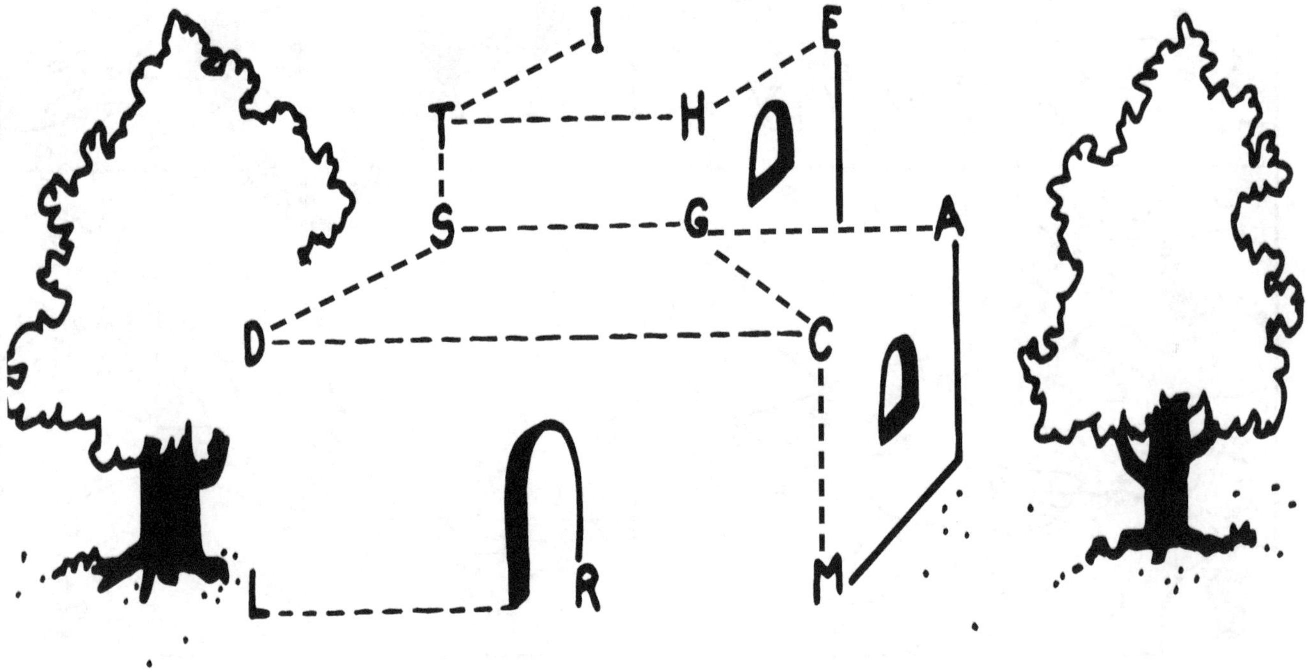

Decode the Prayer

Use the code to fill in the missing words and find out what Jesus tells us about prayer. Read Luke 11:1–10 to check your answers.

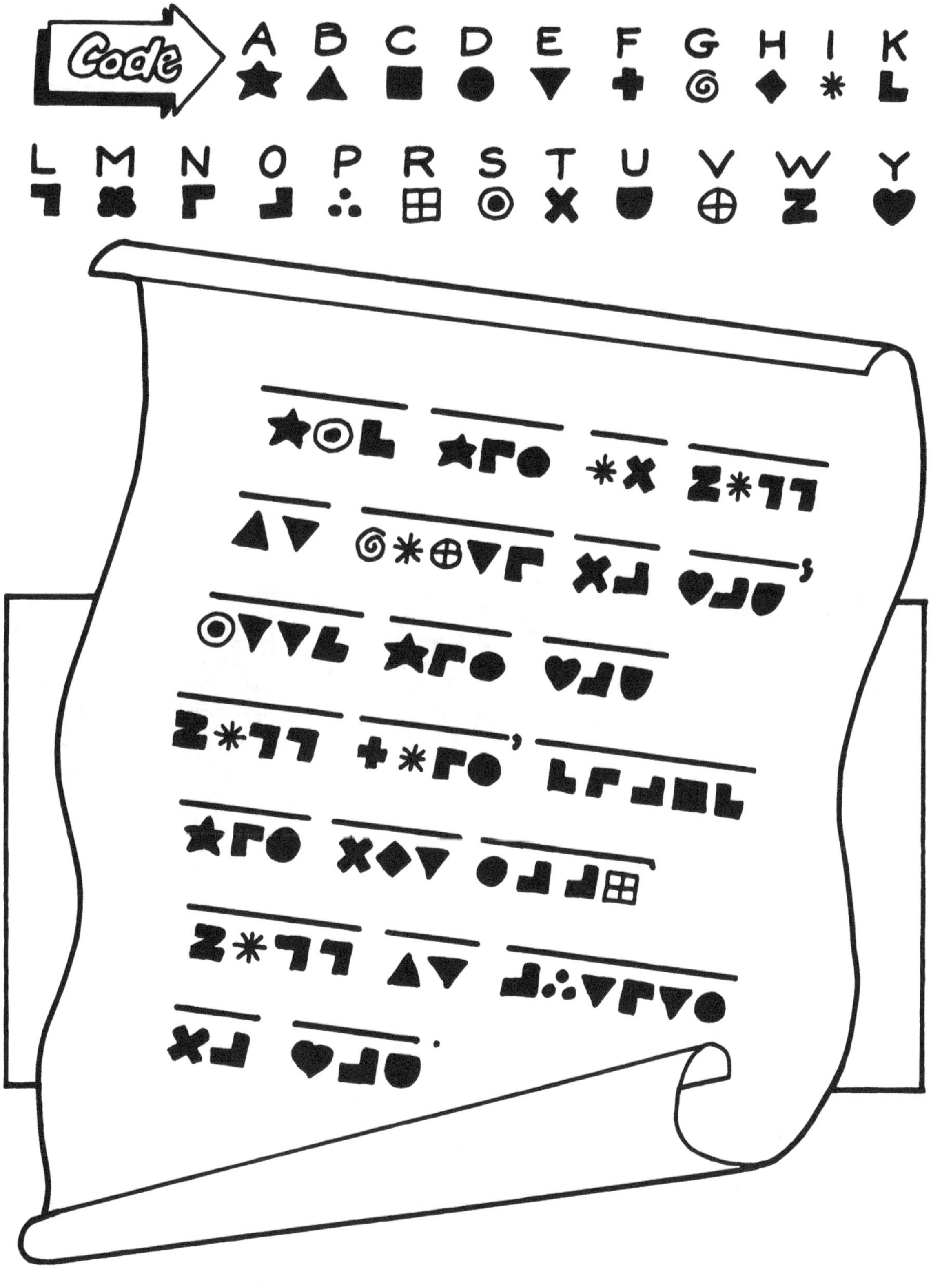

Rich Man

Read Luke 12:16–21. Start with chain 1 and follow the line of letters to find the first word. Write the word in the first blank. Fill in the other words to find out what happened to the rich man.

"But God said to him, 'You ____________ (1) ! This very ____________ (2) your ____________ (3) will be ____________________ (4) from you. Then ____________ (5) will ____________ (6) what you have ____________ (7) for ____________ (8)?' This is how it will be with anyone who ____________ (9) up things for ____________ (10) but is not ____________ (11) ____________ (12) ____________ (13)." Luke 12:20–21

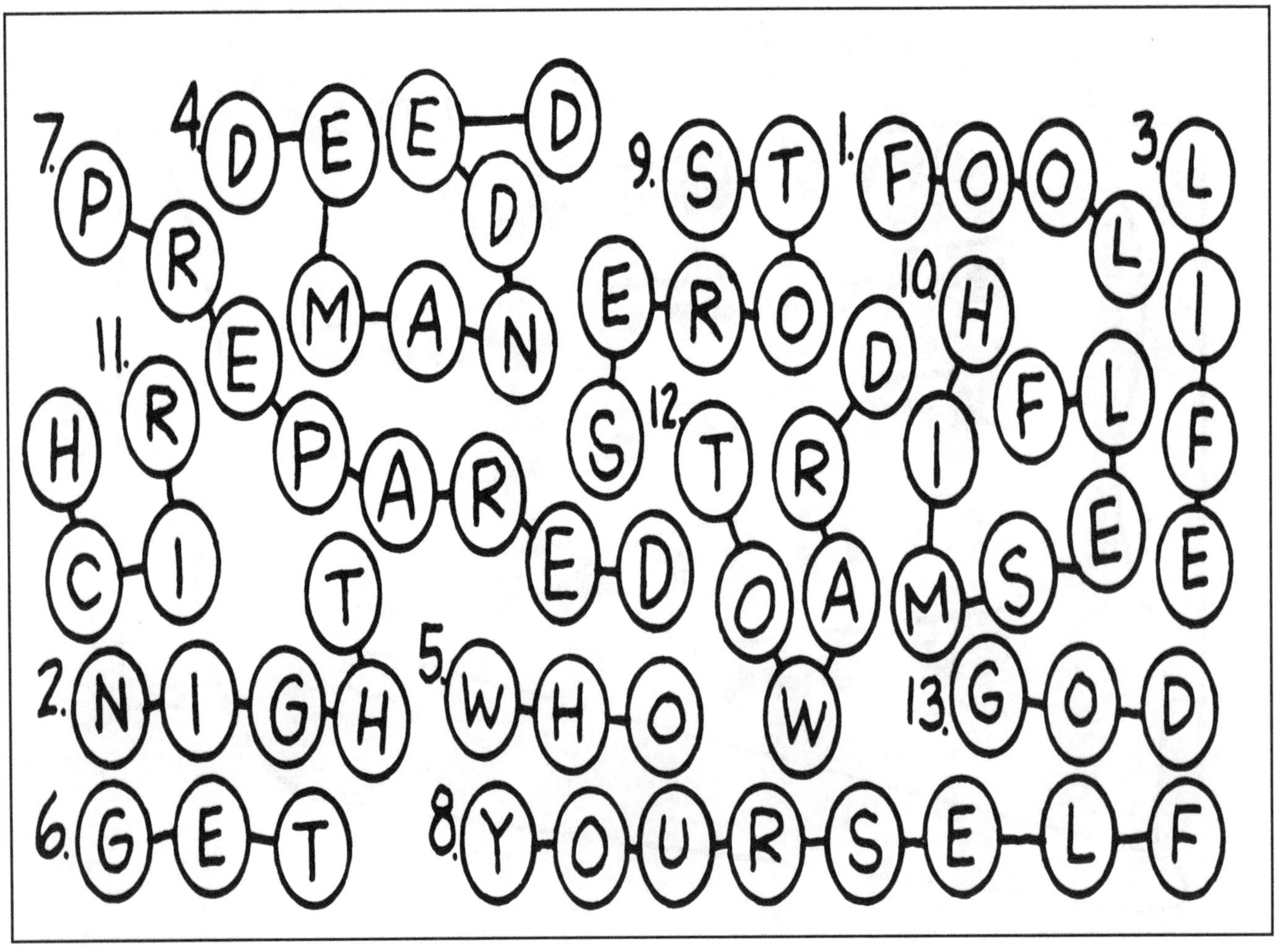

Repent!

Read Luke 15:4–7. Decode the pictures to fill in the blanks and complete the verse about repentance.

There will be more rejoicing in heaven over one

___ ___ ___ ___ ___ ___

who

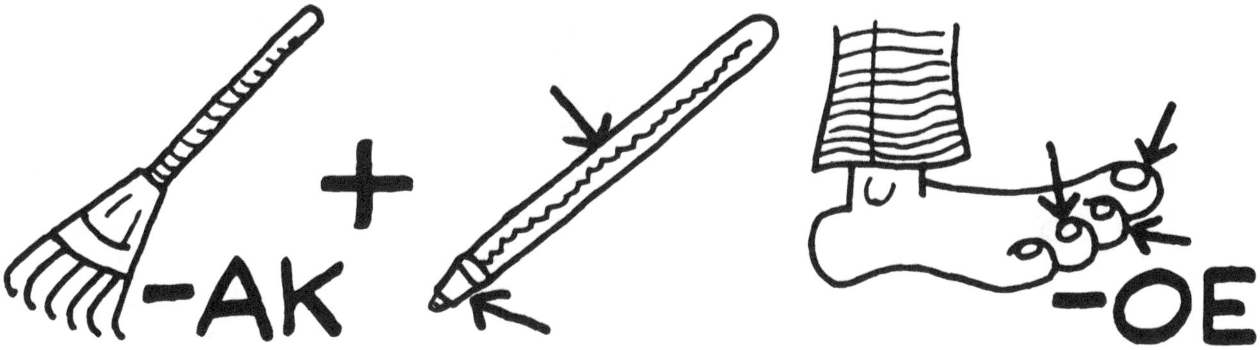

___ ___ ___ ___ ___ ___ ___

than over 99

___ ___ ___ ___ ___ ___ ___ ___ ___

persons who do not need to repent.

Lost and Found

Figure out each clue and write what it is on the blanks beneath the picture. Then, starting with the picture labeled 1, take the first and last letters of your word and write them on the blanks at the bottom. Read Luke 15:11–32 to find out more.

__ __ __ __ __ __ __ __ __ __ __ __ __

__ __ __ __ __ __ __.

The Rich Man and Lazarus

Read Luke 16:19–31. Use the clues to unscramble the words. Then write the circled letters in order in the spaces at the bottom of the page to find the rich man's request.

(v. 24) the rich man called to _______________

MAAHBAR ___ ___ ___ ___ ◯ ___ ___

(v. 20) a beggar named _______________

ZARALUS ___ ___ ___ ◯ ___ ___ ___

(v. 28) number of rich man's brothers _______________

IFEV ___ ___ ◯ ◯

(v. 19) rich man dressed in _______________

ELURPP ◯ ___ ___ ___ ___ ___

(v. 31) _______________ to Moses and the Prophets

TINSEL ___ ◯ ___ ◯ ___ ___

(v. 19) rich man lived in _______________

RXULUY ___ ___ ___ ___ ___ ◯

(v. 20) Lazarus was covered with _______________

ROESS ___ ◯ ___ ___ ___

(v. 31) they will not be _______________

CDCNNVIOE ___ ___ ___ ___ ___ ◯ ___ ___ ___

(v. 28) this place of _______________

TTREMON ___ ___ ___ ◯ ◯ ___ ___

___ ___ ___ ___   ___ ___ ___ ___   ___ ___   ___ ___ .

Amazingly Healed

Find the answers to the questions by completing the maze. For help, read Luke 17:11–19.

1. Now on his way to ____________________, Jesus traveled along the border between Samaria and Galilee (v. 11).
2. As he was going into a village, ____________ ____________ who had leprosy met him (v. 12).
3. They called out in a loud voice, "____________________, ____________________, have pity on us!" (v. 13).
4. When he saw them, he said, "Go, show yourselves to the priests." And as they went, they were ____________________ (v. 14).
5. One of them, when he saw he was healed, came back, ____________________ God in a loud voice (v. 15).
6. He threw himself at Jesus' feet and thanked him—and he was a ____________________ (v. 16).
7. Jesus asked, "Were not all ____________________ cleansed?" (v. 17).
8. Then he said to him, "Rise and go; your faith has made you ____________________" (v. 19).

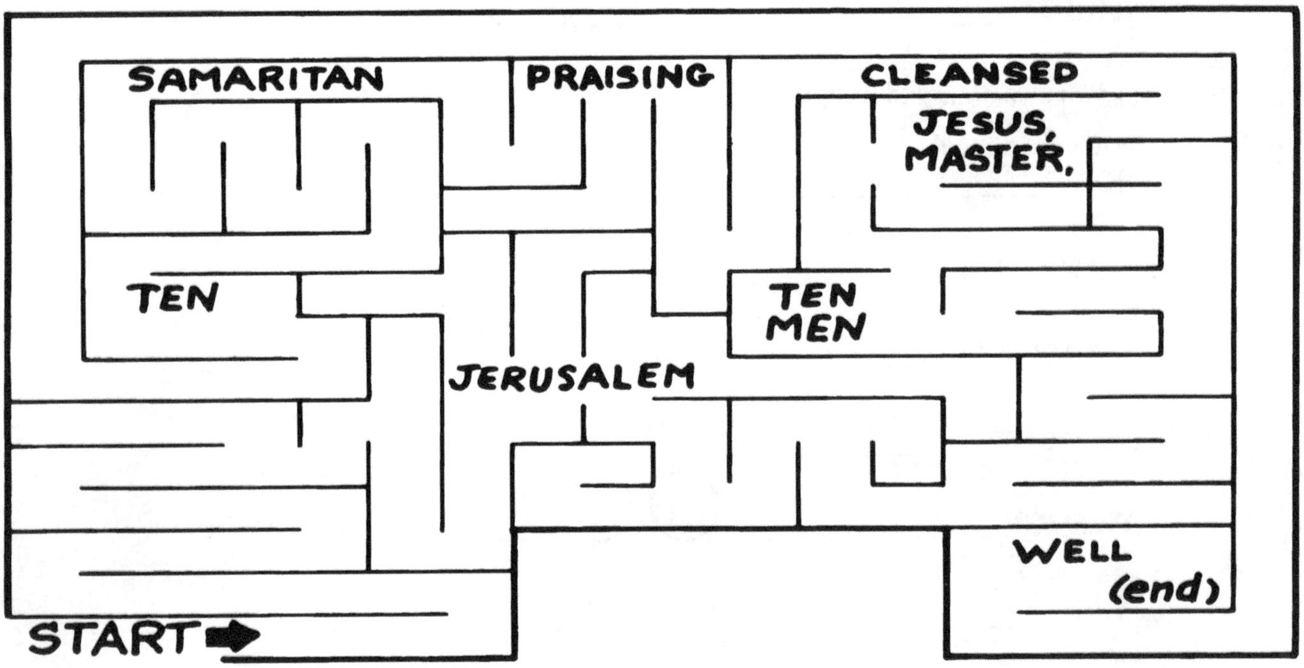

The Pharisee and the Tax Collector

Trace the letters of each maze in order to find what the Pharisee and tax collector said when they prayed to God. Read Luke 18:9–14 to find out more.

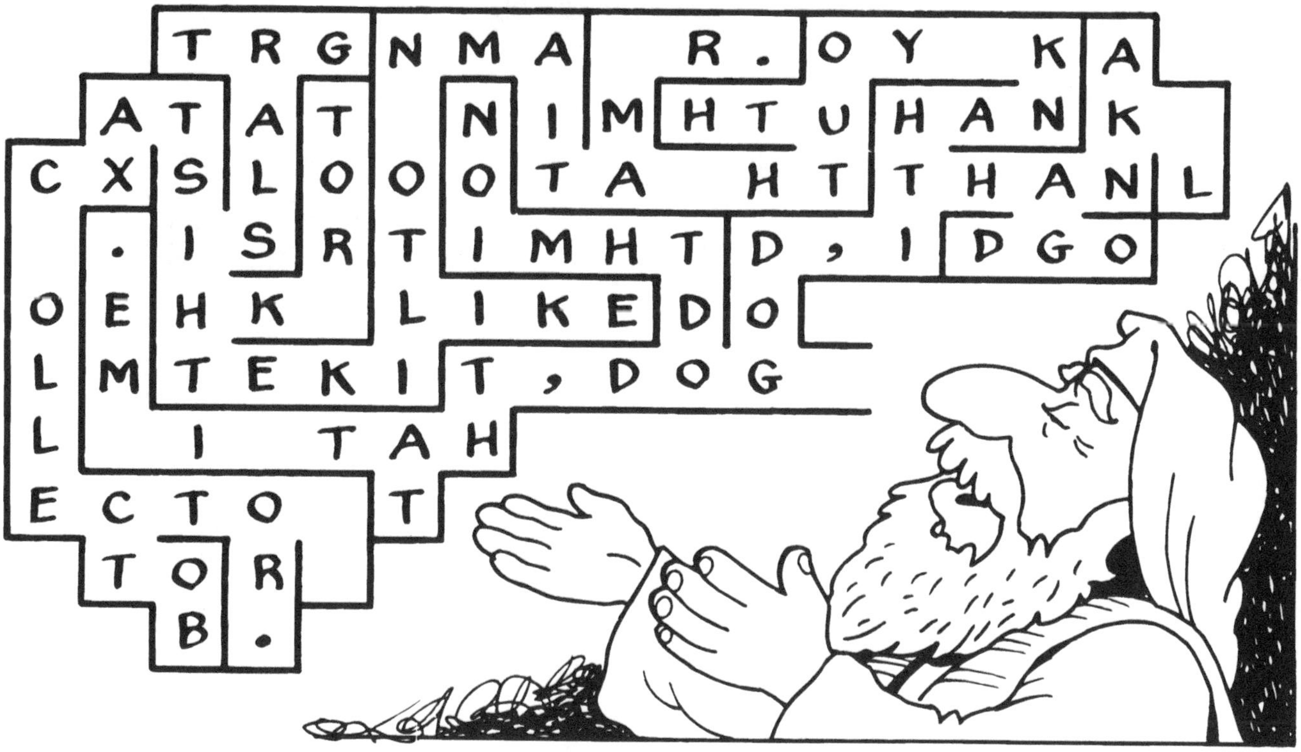

A Short Story

Read Luke 19:1–10. Use the clues to unscramble words. Then write the circled letters in order on the spaces at the bottom to learn God's commandment from Exodus 20:15.

(v. 4) A short man climbed this tree.

MYOSRCEA ___ ◯ ___ ___ ___ ◯ ___ ___

(v. 2) This man wanted to see Jesus.

SCAAZECHU ___ ___ ___ ___ ___ ___ ___ ◯ ◯

(v. 8) Zacchaeus said if he had done this, he would repay people.

DEECATH ___ ◯ ___ ◯ ___ ___ ___

(v. 2) He was wealthy because of his job as a …

ATX ELCORTOLC ___ ___ ___   ___ ___ ◯ ◯ ___ ___ ___ ___ ___

(v. 5) Jesus told Zacchaeus to …

MOEC WODN ___ ___ ___ ___   ___ ___ ___ ◯

(v. 8) He promised to pay back this much.

UROF SMEIT ___ ◯ ___ ___ ◯   ___ ___ ___ ___

(v. 5) Jesus wanted to ___________ at Zacchaeus's house.

YTAS ◯ ◯ ___ ___

(v. 1). Jesus entered this city.

CROHIEJ ___ ◯ ___ ___ ___ ___ ___

(v. 9) Zacchaeus received this.

NAITVOASL ___ ◯ ◯ ___ ___ ___ ___ ___ ___

___ ___ ___   ___ ___ ___ ___ ___   ___ ___ ___   ___ ___ ___ ___ ___.

Praise God!

Read Luke 19:28–40 about Jesus' ride into Jerusalem. Then solve the code to find out what the crowd said.

Amazing Love

John 3:16–21 tells about God's amazing love. To solve the puzzle, first work the math problems. Then beginning with the answer that is 1, write the words in order on the lines below.

11 + 11 = perish	5 + 6 = one	0 + 3 = so	28 − 20 = he	19 + 1 = shall	4 + 2 = world
98 − 85 = only	21 − 5 = whoever	25 − 2 = but	13 + 13 = life	13 − 3 = his	3 + 1 = loved
11 − 10 = for	45 − 30 = that	9 + 8 = believes	36 − 15 = not	23 − 21 = God	49 − 42 = that
	30 − 18 = and	38 − 20 = in	75 − 50 = eternal	10 − 5 = the	
		40 − 21 = him	6 + 8 = Son	4 + 5 = gave	
			8 + 16 = have		

Worship

Read John 4:19–26. Beginning at one of the lettered boxes, follow the line that leads from it to an empty box and put that letter in the empty box. Fill in the other boxes the same way.

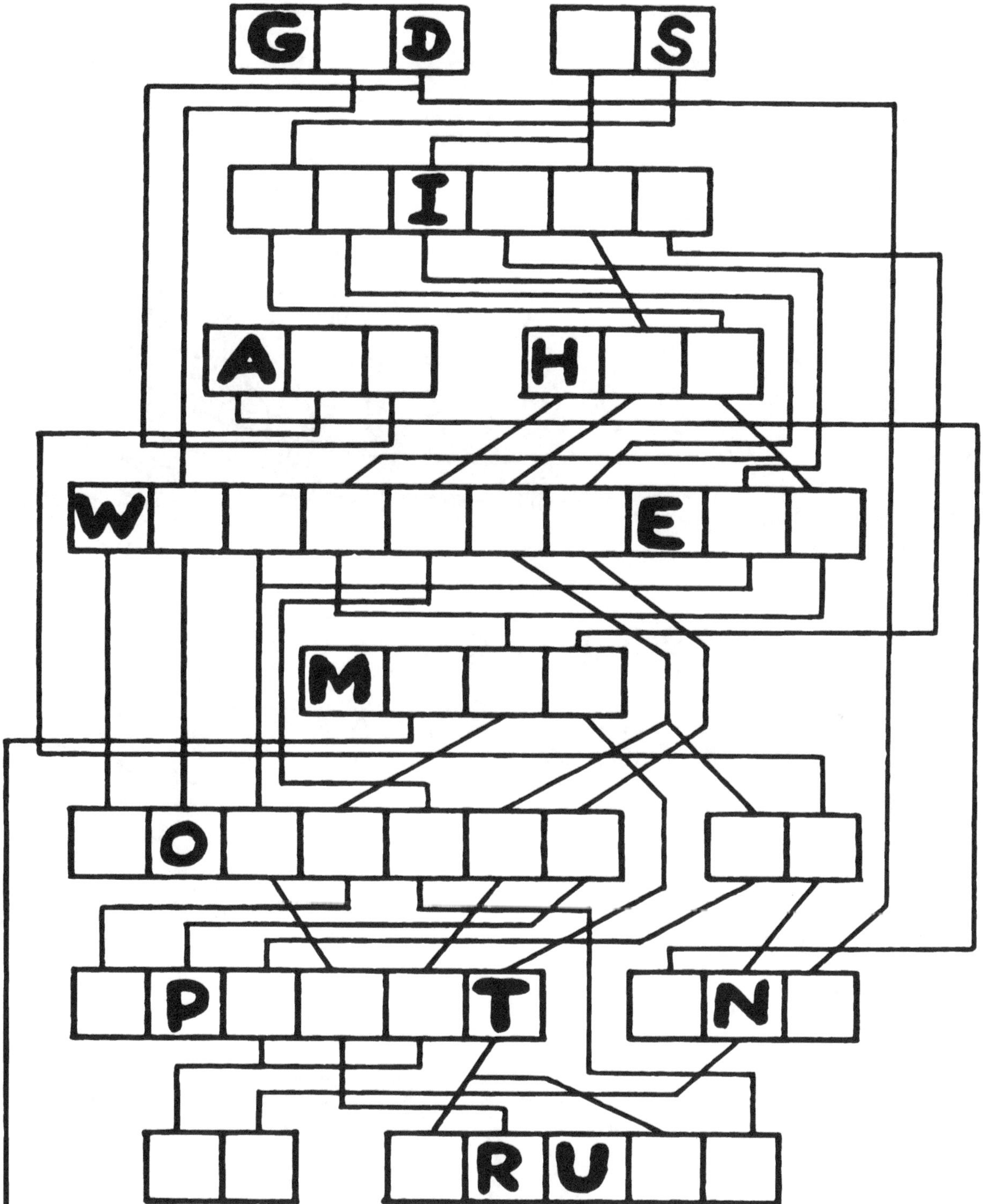

John 4:24

One Lunch That Fed More Than 5,000

What did Andrew ask Jesus about using five loaves and two fish to feed more than 5,000 people? How was Andrew's question answered? Use the code below to find out. Read John 6:1–13 to find out more.

Lazarus, Come Out!

What happened when Jesus raised Lazarus from the dead? To find the answer, write the words above in the matching shapes below. See John 11:32–45.

Jesus Is Risen

Answer the questions below.

1

Why did the Jews say Jesus must die (John 19:4–7)?

1. He was from Nazareth.
2. He was a king.
3. He claimed to be the Son of God.

2

The numbers below stand for letters of the alphabet. Which message tells what the notice Pilate wrote about Jesus said (John 19:16–19)?

4. 10, 5, 19, 21, 19, 15, 6 14, 1, 26, 1, 18, 5, 20, 8 11, 9, 14, 7 15, 6 20, 8, 5 18, 15, 13, 1, 14, 19
5. 10, 5, 19, 21, 19 15, 6 14, 1, 26,1, 18, 5, 20, 8 11, 9, 14, 7 15, 6 20, 8, 5 10, 5, 23, 19
6. 10, 5, 19, 21, 19 15, 6, 7, 1, 12, 9, 12, 5, 5 11, 9, 14, 7 15, 6 20, 8, 5, 10, 5, 23, 19

3

Which picture shows how Jesus was given a drink while He was on the cross (John 19:28–30)?

1. 

2. 

3. 

Write the answer number to each puzzle on the spaces below.

1 ________ 2 ________ 3 ________

Change the numbers into these groups of letters and write them on the bottom line.

1 = hewillc	3 = heisnot	5 = hereheha
2 = srisen	4 = ntothe	6 = goseewh

Separate these letters into words to find out what the angel said to the women at the tomb (Luke 24:1–7).

____

Easter Morning

Circle the letter in the true column if the sentence is true. Circle the letter in the false column if the sentence is false. Write the circled letters from top to bottom on the lines below for an Easter message. Then read John 20:1–18.

	True	False
1. Mary went to the tomb at sunset.	O	J
2. Mary found the stone rolled away.	E	S
3. The other disciple could run faster than Peter.	S	P
4. The burial clothes were all wrinkled.	N	U
5. Two angels in white were in the tomb.	S	L
6. Peter let the other disciple enter the tomb first.	B	A
7. Mary wept outside the tomb.	R	M
8. Someone told Mary to stop crying.	C	O
9. Mary thought Jesus was a gardener.	S	Q
10. Jesus wanted Mary to hug Him.	D	E

___ ___ ___ ___ ___   ___ ___ ___ ___ ___

Miraculous Catch of Fish

Find the answers for this maze in John 21:1–14.

1 across	"__________ going out to fish" (v. 3).
2 down	As soon as Simon Peter heard __________ say (v. 7).
3 across	"We'll go __________ you" (v. 3).
3 down	What Peter jumped into (v. 7).
4 across	He was __________ from the dead (v. 14).
5 down	Simon Peter __________ the net ashore (v. 11).
6 across	"No," they __________ (v. 5).
6 down	__________ Jesus appeared again (v. 1).
7 across	Then the __________ whom Jesus loved (v. 7).

Seek the Truth

Read Acts 1:1–12. Then read each sentence below. If a sentence is true, follow that number's trail in the puzzle from the T. If it is false, follow the trail from the F. Write the word at the end of each trail on the blanks below to spell a message.

		True	False
1.	After His suffering, Jesus showed himself to the apostles and gave proof that He was alive.	T	F
2.	Jesus appeared to them over a period of 20 days.	T	F
3.	Jesus told the apostles to wait for the gift His Father promised.	T	F
4.	Jesus was taken up before their eyes, and the sun hid Him from them.	T	F
5.	Two women dressed in blue suddenly appeared.	T	F
6.	Jesus will come back someday in the same way the apostles saw Him go to heaven.	T	F

_ _ _ _ _ _ _   _ _ _

_ _ _ _ _   _ _   _ _ _   _ _ _ _ _ _

Cross It Out

Read Acts 2:1–4, 14, and 36–41. Follow the directions below.

1. Cross out 4 words describing the Holy Spirit.
2. Cross out 1 preacher.
3. Cross out 1 feast.
4. Cross out 1 city.
5. Cross out 3 things Peter asked the crowd to do.
6. Cross out 1 number.
7. Cross out 1 nation.
8. Cross out 2 words for the disciples.
9. Cross out 3 things the crowd did.
10. Cross out 1 group of people.

Read the leftover words from left to right and top to bottom to learn Peter's message.

WIND	GOD	REPENT	ELEVEN	MADE
BE BAPTIZED	JESUS	FIRE	SAVE YOURSELVES	PETER
APOSTLES	PENTECOST	SOUND	BOTH	ISRAEL
LORD	TONGUES	JERUSALEM	HEARD	JEWS
ACCEPTED	AND	3000	MESSIAH	WERE BAPTIZED

Finding Words

The answers to the clues below all end with -ING. Use the word clues in the puzzle to fill in the squares with words from Acts 2:42–47.

BREAD

DEVOTED TO APOSTLES'

THEIR POSSESSIONS

SAVED

IN COMMON

THE FAVOR OF ALL PEOPLE

GOD

Write the letters from the shaded squares in order to learn who the phrases describe.

What Did the People Think?

Find out what the people thought about a miracle by filling in the missing words from Acts 3:1–10. Then write the letters on the blanks below with the same numbers.

1. ___ ___ ___ ___ ___ and ___ ___ ___ ___ were going to the temple.
   16 1 2

2. They were going to the temple to ___ ___ ___ ___ .
   13 4

3. A man crippled from birth was being carried to the temple gate called

   ___ ___ ___ ___ ___ ___ ___ ___ ___ .
   3 7

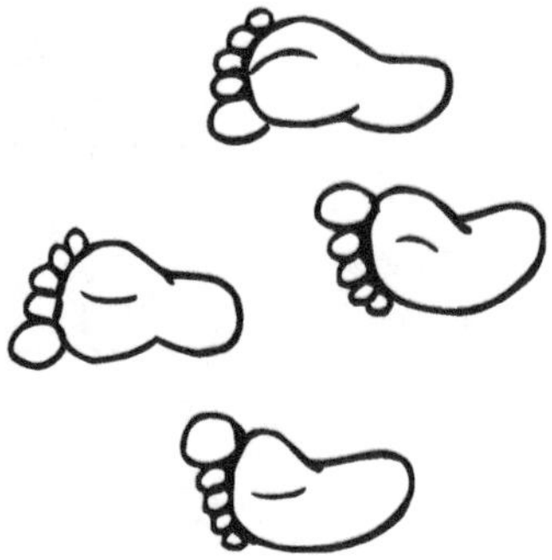

4. The man gave them his attention, expecting to get

   ___ ___ ___ ___ ___ ___ ___ ___ ___ from them.
   10 8

5. Peter said, "Silver or ___ ___ ___ ___ I do not have."
   9

6. "In the name of Jesus Christ of ___ ___ ___ ___ ___ ___ ___ ___, walk."
   11 15 6

7. He ___ ___ ___ ___ ___ ___ to his feet and began to ___ ___ ___ ___ .
   14 12 5

___ ___ ___ ___   ___ ___ ___ ___   ___ ___ ___ ___ ___ ___   ___ ___ ___ ___
1 2 3 4   5 3 6 3   7 8 9 9 3 12   5 8 1 2

___ ___ ___ ___ ___ ___   ___ ___ ___   ___ ___ ___ ___ ___ ___ ___ ___ ___
5 10 11 12 3 6   13 11 12   13 14 13 15 3 14 3 11 1

___ ___   ___ ___ ___ ___   ___ ___ ___   ___ ___ ___ ___ ___ ___ ___ ___
13 1   5 2 13 1   2 13 12   2 13 16 16 3 11 3 12

___ ___   ___ ___ ___ .
1 10   2 8 14

On Trial

During a trial, the jury looks at all the evidence and doesn't use information that doesn't affect the problem. Cross out from this list of evidence the following words:

1. Names of Old Testament books of the Bible.
2. Names of cities found in the Bible.
3. Names of animals found in the Bible.
4. Names of women found in the Bible.

Genesis	Peter	Esther	and
John	Proverbs	were	arrested
Jerusalem	for	talking	Jericho
sheep	about	Daniel	Jesus.
Mary	Peter	Bethany	said
the	people	had	crucified
Psalms	Jesus.	The	rulers
were	lion	donkey	astonished
Bethlehem	at	the	Martha
courage	Peter	and	John
showed	but	warned	goat
them	not	Jonah	to
Ruth	speak	of	Jesus.

The leftover words reading from left to right tell about a problem Peter and John faced in Acts 4:1–20.

What's in a Name?

The clues for this puzzle come from Acts 4:32–36. Rearrange the circled letters to find what the name of Barnabas means.

1. These were of one heart and mind (v. 32).

2. What they did with their things (v. 32).

3. The kind of power they had (v. 33).

4. The apostles continued to do this (v. 33).

5. What special thing they told about Jesus (v. 33).

6. They didn't have any person like this (v. 34).

7. The two things people sold (v. 34).

8. What people brought to apostles from selling lands and houses (vv. 34–35).

SON OF

Stephen's Last Stand

Read Acts 6:8–11 and 7:54–60. Find the listed words in the puzzle. When you find a word, color the letter squares blue if the word relates to Stephen. Color them red if the word relates to the members of the synagogue.

A	R	X	T	D	E	H	S	U	R	E	C	D
G	M	I	R	A	C	U	L	O	U	S	A	N
O	B	D	H	R	U	A	S	P	B	C	D	E
D	E	E	O	G	T	G	H	P	I	J	K	V
S	L	H	L	U	M	N	O	O	P	Q	R	A
G	S	S	Y	E	T	W	I	S	D	O	M	E
R	U	A	S	W	E	V	X	I	A	D	B	H
A	E	N	P	R	E	N	O	T	S	C	J	F
C	G	G	I	Y	H	G	N	I	L	L	E	Y
E	F	U	R	I	O	U	S	O	I	J	S	K
P	L	Z	I	S	R	E	D	N	O	W	U	O
N	R	M	T	D	E	G	G	A	R	D	S	Q

- WISDOM
- GOD'S GRACE
- ARGUE
- RUSHED
- POWER
- JESUS
- STONE
- OPPOSITION
- WONDERS
- MIRACULOUS
- DRAGGED
- HEAVEN
- FURIOUS
- HOLY SPIRIT
- YELLING
- GNASHED

The Ethiopian's Question

Cross out every C, F, G, J, Q, V, and X. Write the remaining letters in order on the blanks below to find the question the Ethiopian asked Philip. See Acts 8:36.

L	C	V	F	Q	O	J	C	X	O
V	K	V	J	C	H	F	J	Q	E
R	V	X	E	X	C	F	I	G	S
V	X	W	J	A	G	J	T	C	Q
E	G	F	R	V	J	Q	W	C	H
J	G	F	Y	Q	J	C	S	V	J
H	X	C	O	C	G	U	F	G	V
L	C	X	D	F	Q	N	J	C	J
T	V	Q	I	J	C	F	B	C	Q
E	X	F	B	G	F	V	A	J	P
G	T	C	I	J	C	Z	V	E	J
C	V	X	D	Q	V	J	C	G	F

___ ___ ___ ___, ___ ___ ___ ___ ___ ___ ___ ___ ___ ___ ___ ___ ___.

___ ___ ___ ___ ___ ___ ___ ___ ___ ___' ___ ___ ___ ___

___ ___ ___ ___ ___ ___ ___ ___?

Saul's Conversion

Remember, before his conversion, Paul was called Saul. Saul was blinded by a light during his conversion. Use the braille chart to decode the missing words. See Acts 9:1–19.

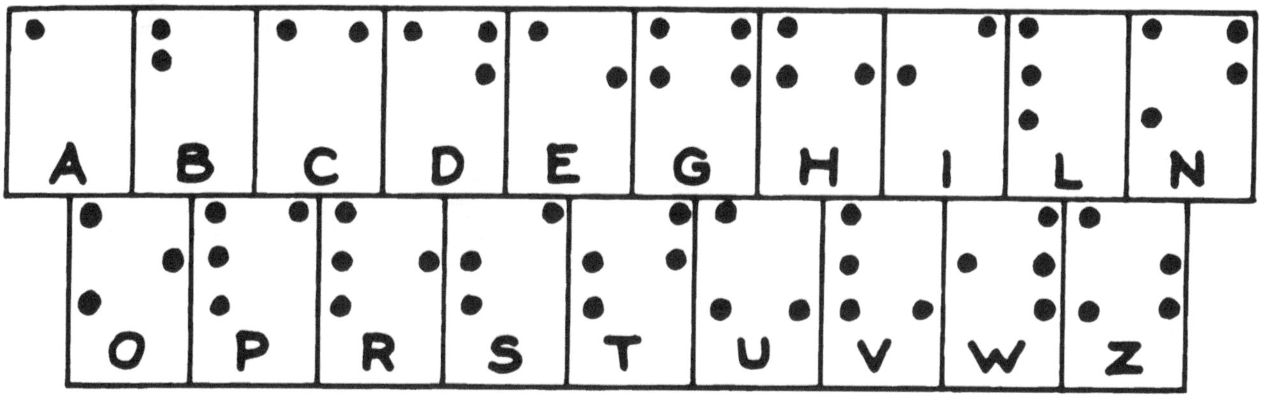

Saul was a 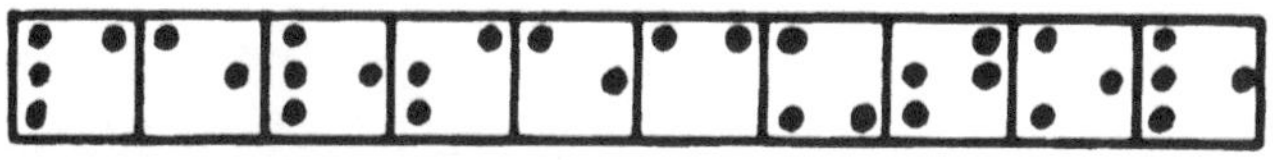 of Christians.

He became a 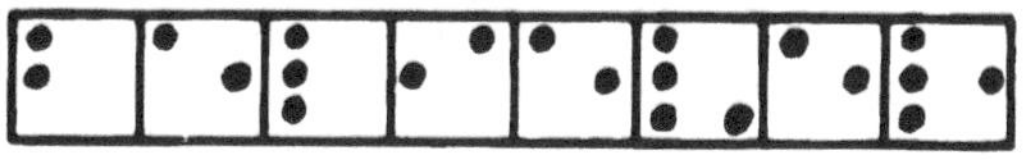 when Jesus came to him in

a 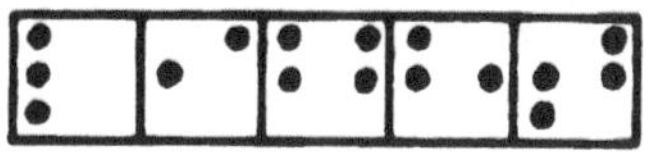. The light  Saul.

So, Jesus worked through  to restore Saul's

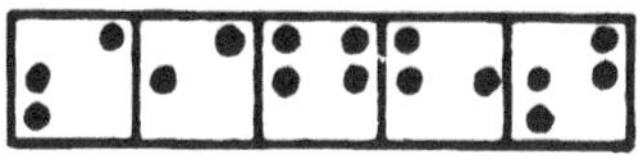, and to let Saul know that he, Saul, had been

 to be a  for Christ.

Then Saul was 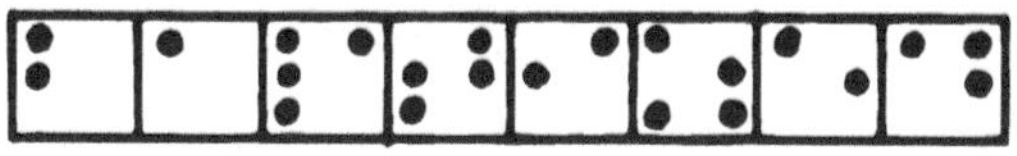.

Saul became a .

Joy in Joppa

Read Acts 9:36–42. Use the code and the word clues to fill in the boxes.

(tall box) = b, d, f, h, k, l, t
(box below line) = g, j, p, q, y
(square box) = c, m, n, r, s, v, w, x, z
(square box) = a, e, i, o, u

1. a town
2. a woman
3. another name for #2
4. a town
5. an apostle
6. Jesus' followers
7. two males
8. women whose husbands have died
9. people who believed in Jesus
10. who believed

Read Acts 9:42. Use the code to learn the result of God's miracle in Joppa.

Right or Wrong?

Read Acts 10:9–20 and 24–28. Then read the sentences. If the sentence is true, circle the word in the Right column. If the sentence is false, circle the word in the Wrong column. Then write the circled words in order at the bottom of the page to learn what God taught Peter.

	Right	Wrong
1. Peter went down in the basement to pray.	Simon	Peter
2. Peter fell into a trance and saw heaven open.	learned	taught
3. Peter saw a large sheet full of four-footed animals, reptiles, and birds.	not	people
4. A voice told Peter to get up and look at the animals.	about	to
5. After the vision, four men came looking for Peter.	names	call
6. The men came from Simon the soldier.	and	any
7. Peter went with the men to Caesarea to meet Cornelius.	man	sang
8. Cornelius saw Peter and bowed before him.	sad	impure
9. Peter talked with Cornelius and a large group of people in his house.	or	songs
10. It was against the Jewish law for Peter to visit a Gentile.	unclean	always

____

Christians Scatter

Put the first letter of the name of each picture below the picture. Work the map as the directions are given to you. Read Acts 11:19–30.

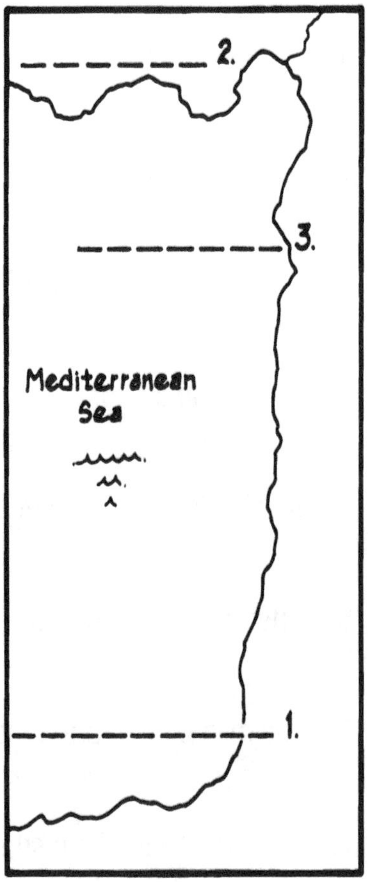

The Christians scattered from Jerusalem because of the stoning of

(Put Jerusalem on the map at point 1.)

went to Tarsus to look for Saul. (Put Tarsus at point 2.)
Barnabas and Saul worked one year at

The disciples were first called

at Antioch. (Put Antioch at point 3.)
Because of a famine the

at Antioch provided help for the brothers in Judea.

Good News!

Read Acts 13:1–3, 14–16, and 26–33. Use the food code to fill in the blanks.

1. The church at Antioch set apart Barnabas and corn–apple–cantaloupe–cauliflower.

   ____

2. The church worshipped and nectarine–apple–corn–watermelon–grapefruit–kiwi.

   ____

3. At Pisidian Antioch, Paul and Barnabas were asked to corn–spinach–grapefruit–apple–pea.

   ____

4. Paul told the men in the synagogue about bean–grapefruit–corn–cantaloupe–corn.

   ____

5. Paul told them that God raised Jesus from kiwi–grapefruit–apple–watermelon–cherry.

   ____

Now use the code to tell a friend what Paul and Barnabas told the people.

____	____	____	____
peach	cabbage	cabbage	kiwi

____	____	____	____
lettuce	grapefruit	zucchini	corn

CODE:

A	apple
D	kiwi
E	grapefruit
F	nectarine
G	peach
H	cherry
J	bean
K	pea
L	cauliflower
N	lettuce
O	cabbage
P	spinach
S	corn
T	watermelon
U	cantaloupe
W	zucchini

Paul and Barnabas

Read Acts 14:8–20. Go through the maze and put the letters from the path on the line provided. Then use the code to find out what Paul and Barnabas told the people.

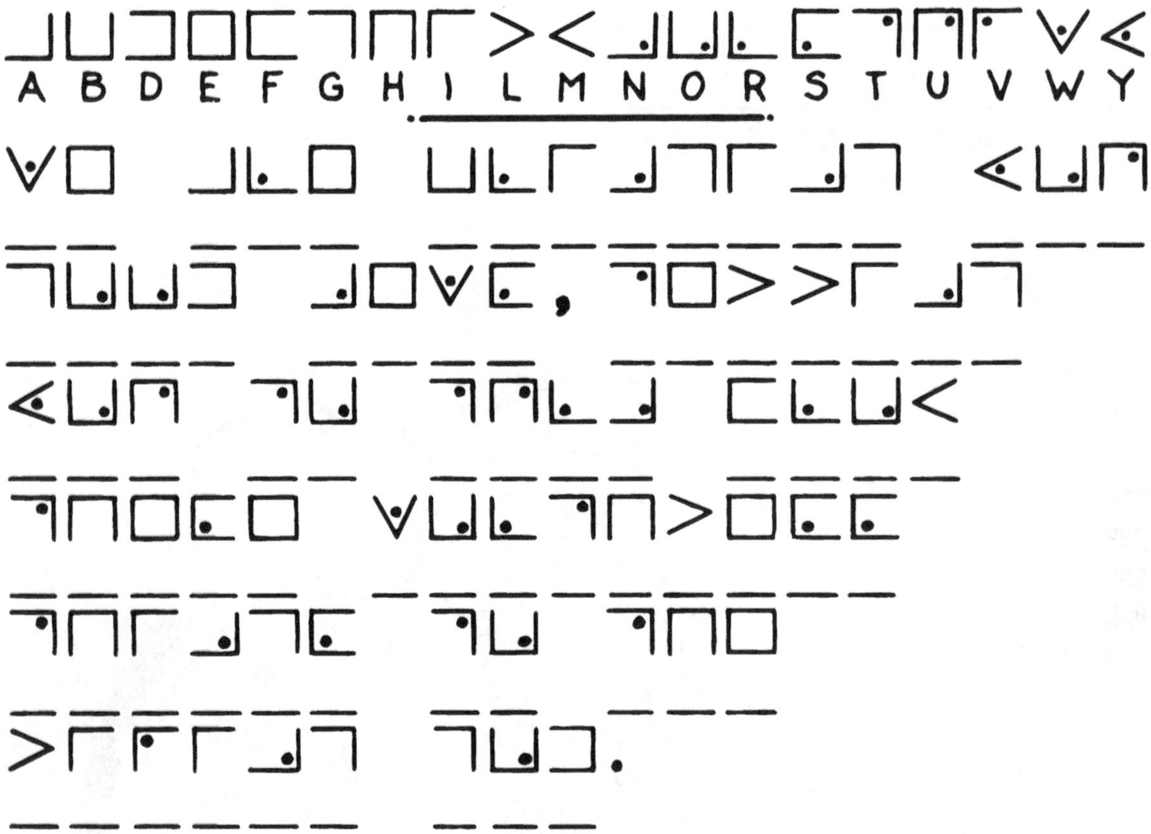

Prison

Read Acts 16:25–34 about Paul and Silas in prison. To find the good that came out of their being in jail, take the letters from the jailhouse and put them in the empty space below the boxes with the same numbers.

9	10	14		2	3	1	11	14	8		3	6	15		10	1	5

4	3	16	1	11	12		7	14	8	14		5	3	17	14	15

The Unknown God

Read Acts 17:22–31. To find out what Paul told the people in Athens, write the letter of the alphabet that comes before the letter shown in the box above each letter.

Paul told the people about these things:

1. How God raised Jesus

G	S	P	N

U	I	F

E	F	B	E

2. How God made the whole

X	P	S	M	E

3. How God is Lord of

I	F	B	W	F	O

and

F	B	S	U	I

4. How God made every

O	B	U	J	P	O

from one

N	B	O

5. How in God we live and move and

I	B	W	F

P	V	S

C	F	J	O	H

Spreading the Word

Read Acts 19:13–20. Decode the first two sentences by matching the symbols in the sentences to the symbols on the chart. Write the letter that matches the symbol.

The sons of Sceva were 

The evil-spirited man did this to the sons of Sceva.

To find the rest of the message, begin with column 1. Go down the column until you come to a shaded box. Copy the letter that is found to the left of the shaded box on the first blank. Do this for each column. Some columns will have more than one letter.

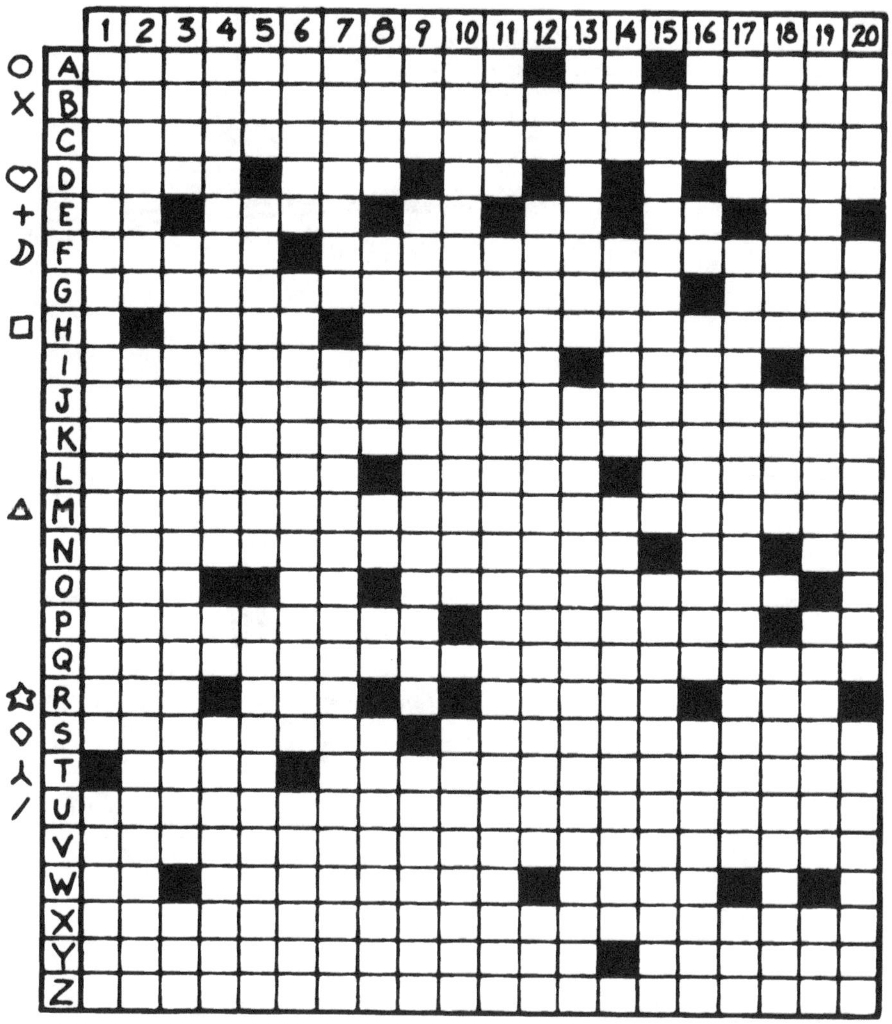

Paul's Mission

Read Acts 20:17–32. Use the word clues to unscramble the answers. Then write the circled letters in order in the spaces at the bottom of the page to learn Paul's mission.

(v. 17) Paul traveled from this city.

LEIUMTS ___ ___ ___ ___ ◯ ___ ___

(v. 17) Paul talked to these men.

EEDLRS ◯ ◯ ___ ___ ___ ___

(v. 19) Paul served the Lord with this.

TILMIHUY ___ ___ ___ ___ ___ ◯ ___ ◯ ___

(v. 23) Paul was warned by Him.

LOYH RIITSP ◯ ___ ___ ___   ___ ___ ___ ___ ___ ___

(v. 21) Paul preached to these people.

SEWJ, KREEGS ___ ◯ ___ ___, ◯ ___ ___ ___ ___ ___

(v. 23) Paul faced this problem.

NOSIRP ___ ___ ___ ___ ◯ ___

(v. 21) Paul wanted everyone to turn to Him.

OGD ___ ◯ ◯

(v. 24) Paul considered his life this.

GITHONN ___ ___ ___ ___ ___ ◯ ___

(v. 28) Paul told the elders to be these.

REDHEPSSH ___ ___ ◯ ___ ___ ___ ___ ___ ___

(v. 28) Paul told the elders to keep this.

CHATW ◯ ___ ___ ___ ___

(v. 31) Paul warned them with these.

REATS ___ ___ ___ ___ ◯

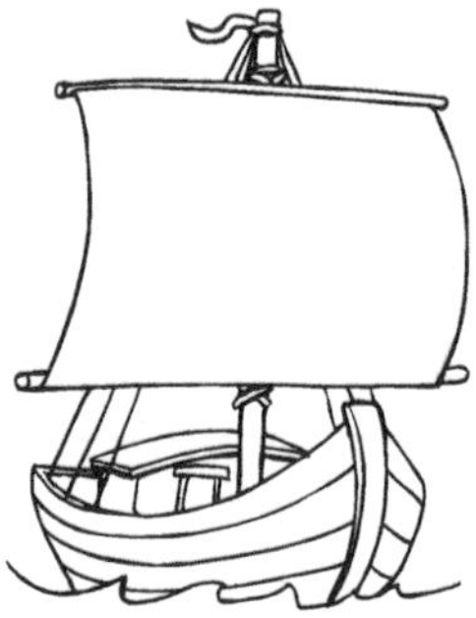

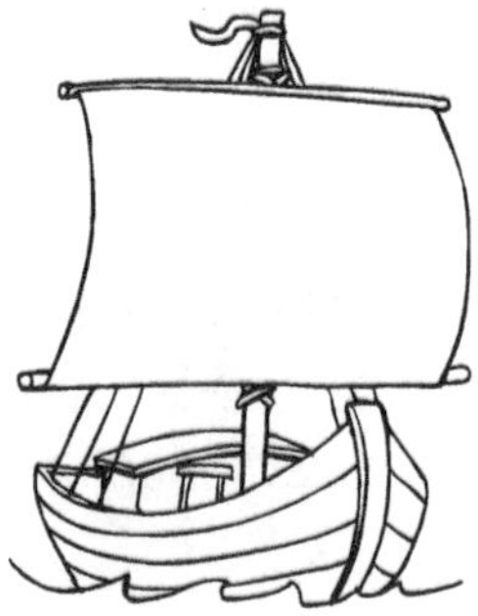

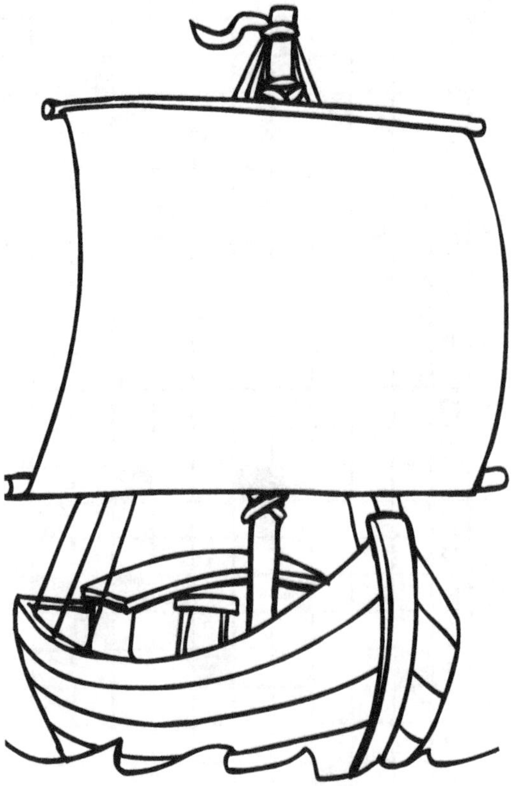

___ ___ ___ ___   ___ ___ ___   ___ ___ ___ ___   ___ ___ ___ ___

Shipwreck

To find out what Paul told the others on the boat before the shipwreck, color in the empty spaces. Read Acts 27:13–25 and 41–44.

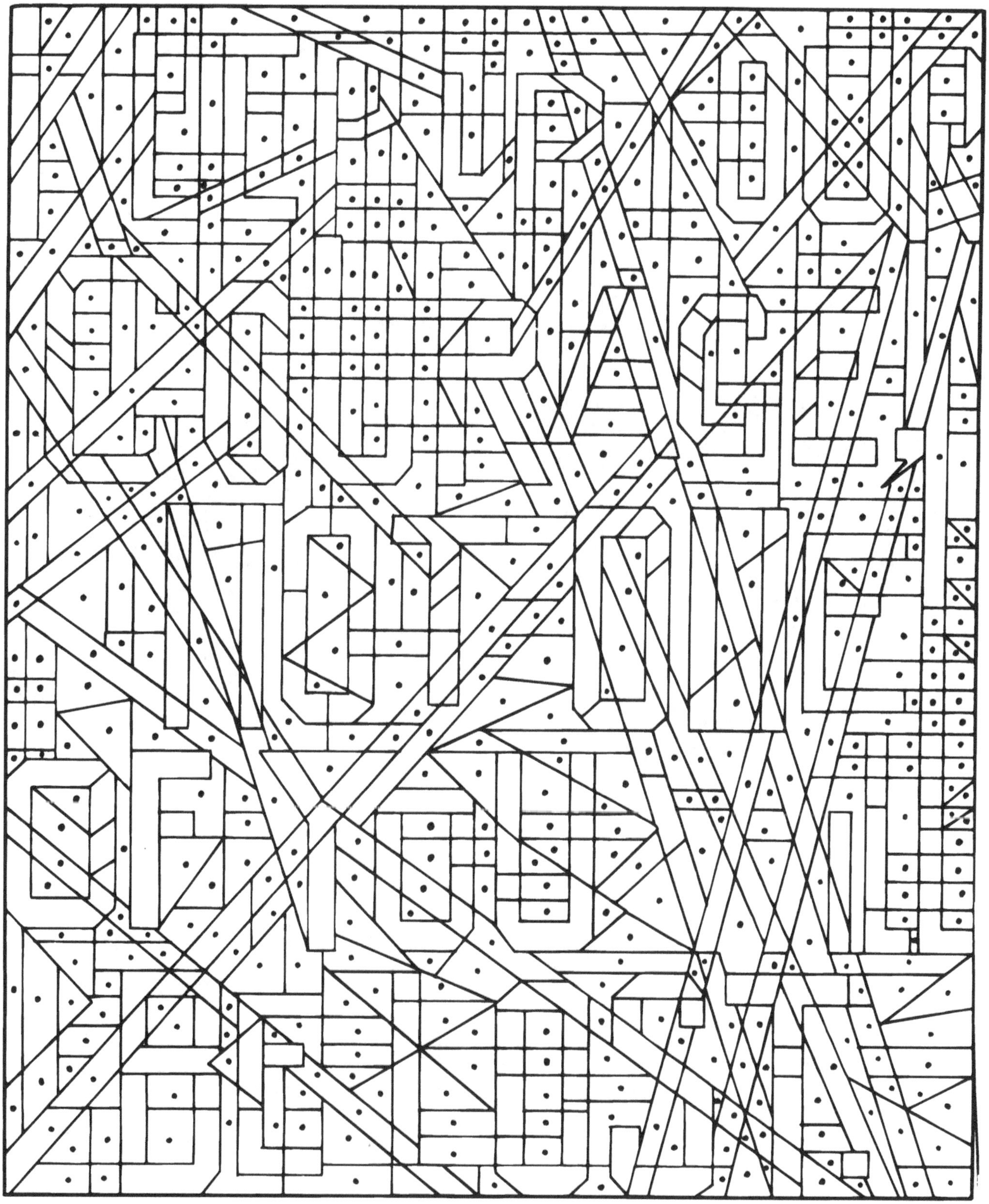

Love, Love, Love

Read Romans 12:9–19. Match the words or phrases in the flowers to the correct flower pot by drawing a stem. You will learn how God can make your life a "bed of roses."

The Lord's Supper

Read 1 Corinthians 11:23–29 and 31–32. Solve the math problems in each box. Circle the words in the box if the math solution is 15. Write the circled words in order at the bottom of the page to learn why Jesus asked us to observe the Lord's Supper.

8+4+4= JESUS	4+3+8= DO	10-4+2= BREAD	15-1+2= BODY
10-2+7= THIS	1+10+3= DRINK	14-5+4= NIGHT	5+5+5= IN
6+10-1= REMEMBRANCE	6+8+2= PROCLAIM	4+3+7= EAT	9-2+6= BLOOD
15-5+5= OF	16-2+3= CUP	2+3+4= THANKS	9+9-3= ME

__ __   __ __ __ __   __ __

__ __ __ __ __ __ __ __ __ __ __   __ __   __ __.

Mixed Fruit

The fruit below is mixed up. Write the letters from the apples on the first set of blanks below to find one fruit of the Spirit. Then do the same for the oranges, lemons, bananas, pineapples, strawberries, grapes, raspberries, and pears. The first fruit shown is an apple, the second is an orange, the third is a lemon, and so on, to help you know which fruit is which. Read Galatians 5:22–23 (ICB).

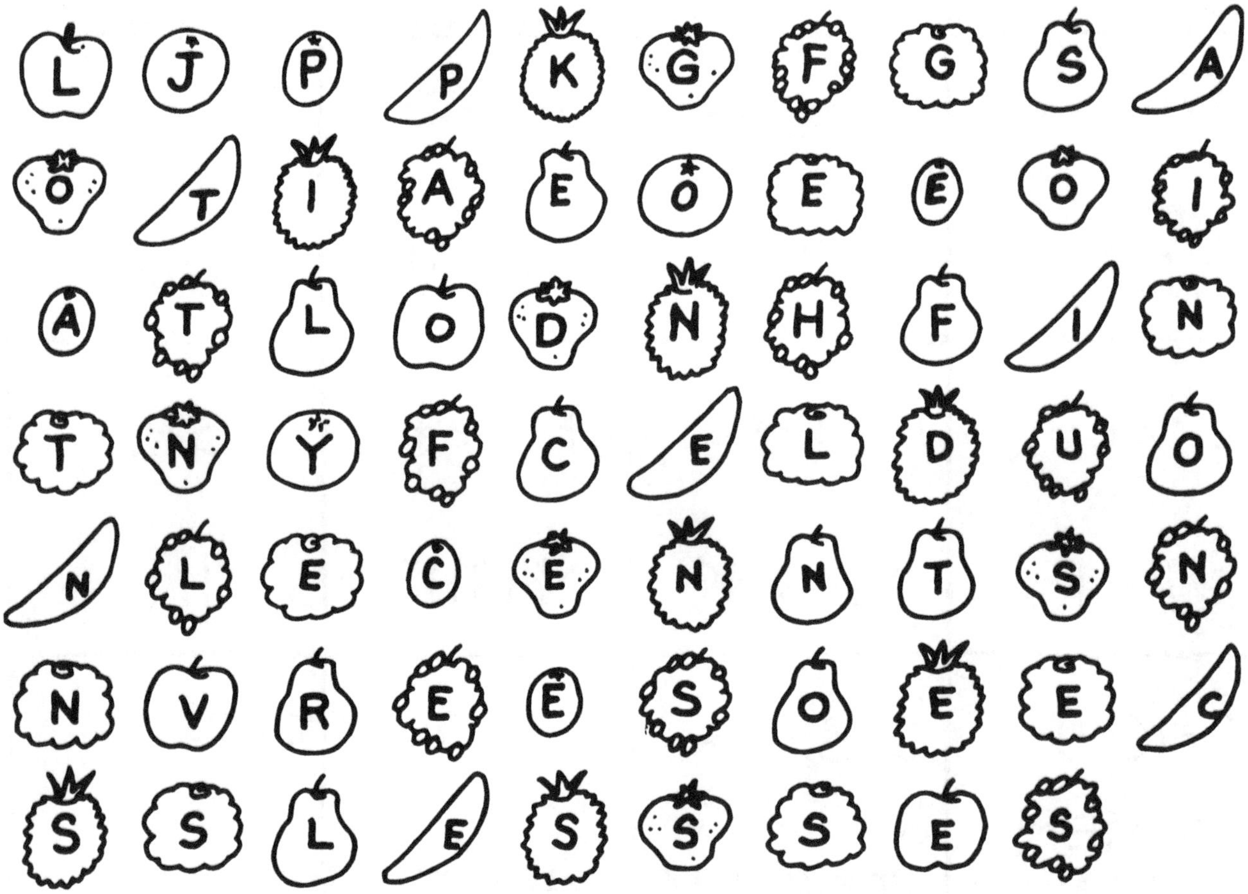

___ ___ ___ ___,   ___ ___ ___,   ___ ___ ___ ___ ___,

___ ___ ___ ___ ___ ___ ___ ___,   ___ ___ ___ ___ -

___ ___ ___ ___,   ___ ___ ___ ___ ___ ___ ___ ___,

___ ___ ___ ___ ___ ___ ___ ___ ___ ___ ___ ___,

___ ___ ___ ___ ___ ___ ___ ___ ___ ___,

___ ___ ___ ___ -   ___ ___ ___ ___ ___ ___ ___.

Helpful Crutches

Romans 3:23 tells us we are spiritually injured because we have sinned. How can we hope to be saved if we cannot walk perfectly, keeping all God's commandments? Use the helpful crutches to solve the message of hope from Ephesians 2:8–9.

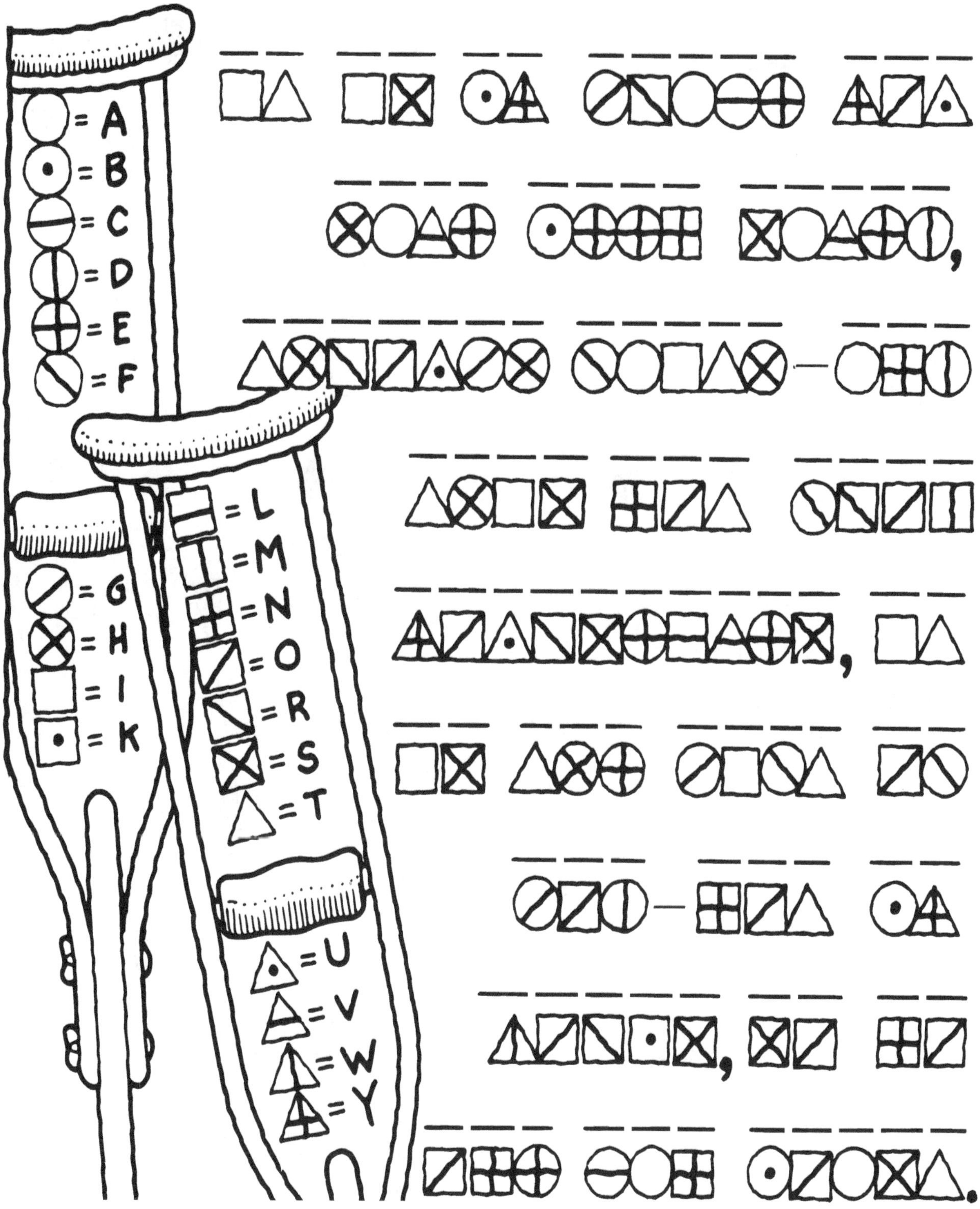

You Can Take It

Read Ephesians 6:10–18 and fill in the blanks below. Using the first or last letter of the word in the blank, follow the lines and write one letter in the box. When you're finished, you'll find a word used four times in Ephesians 6 to describe what believers can do against the Devil.

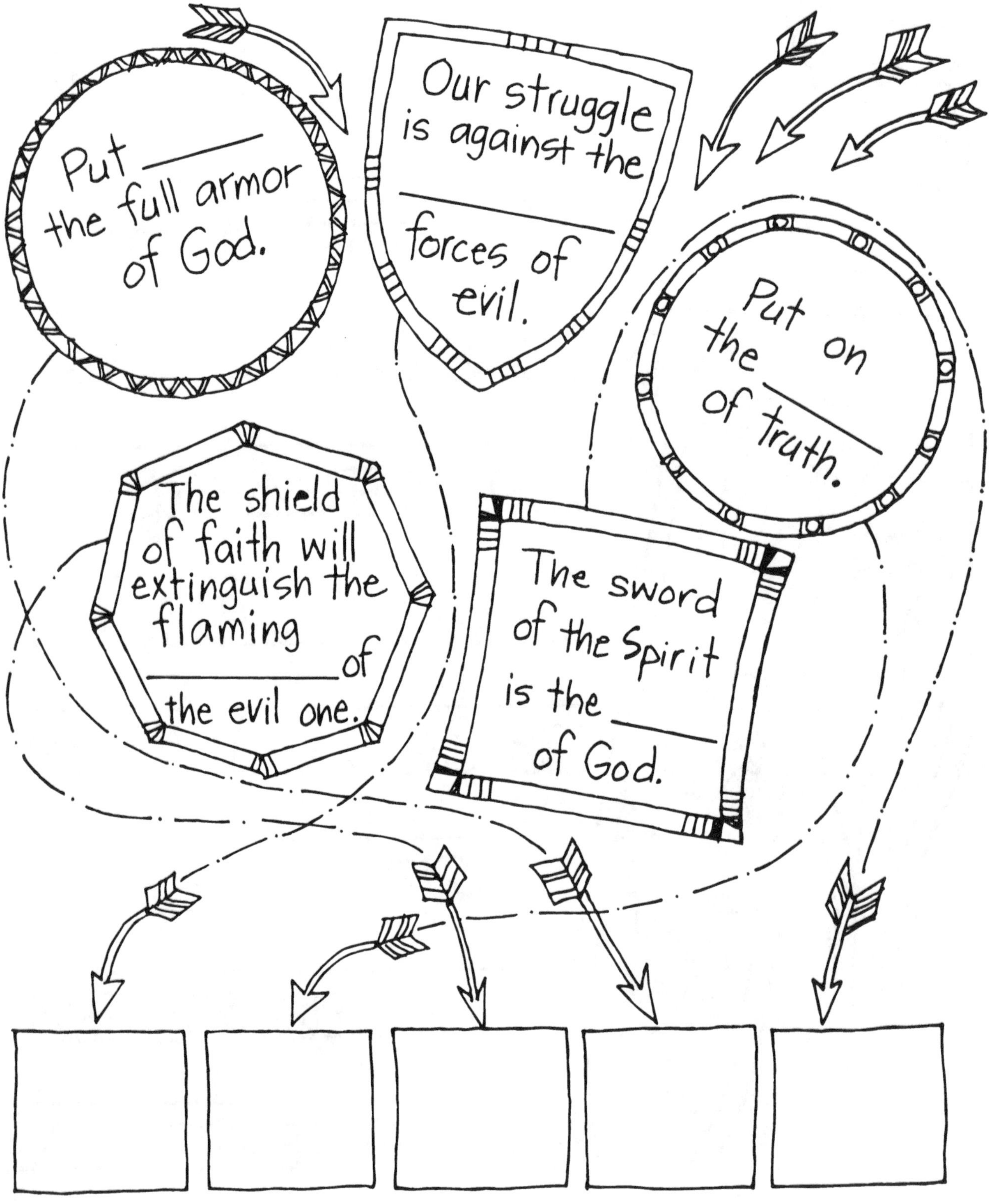

What Should You Think?

Read Philippians 4:4–9 and Colossians 1:9–14. Find your way through the brain maze by "picking up" words that should fill your thoughts.

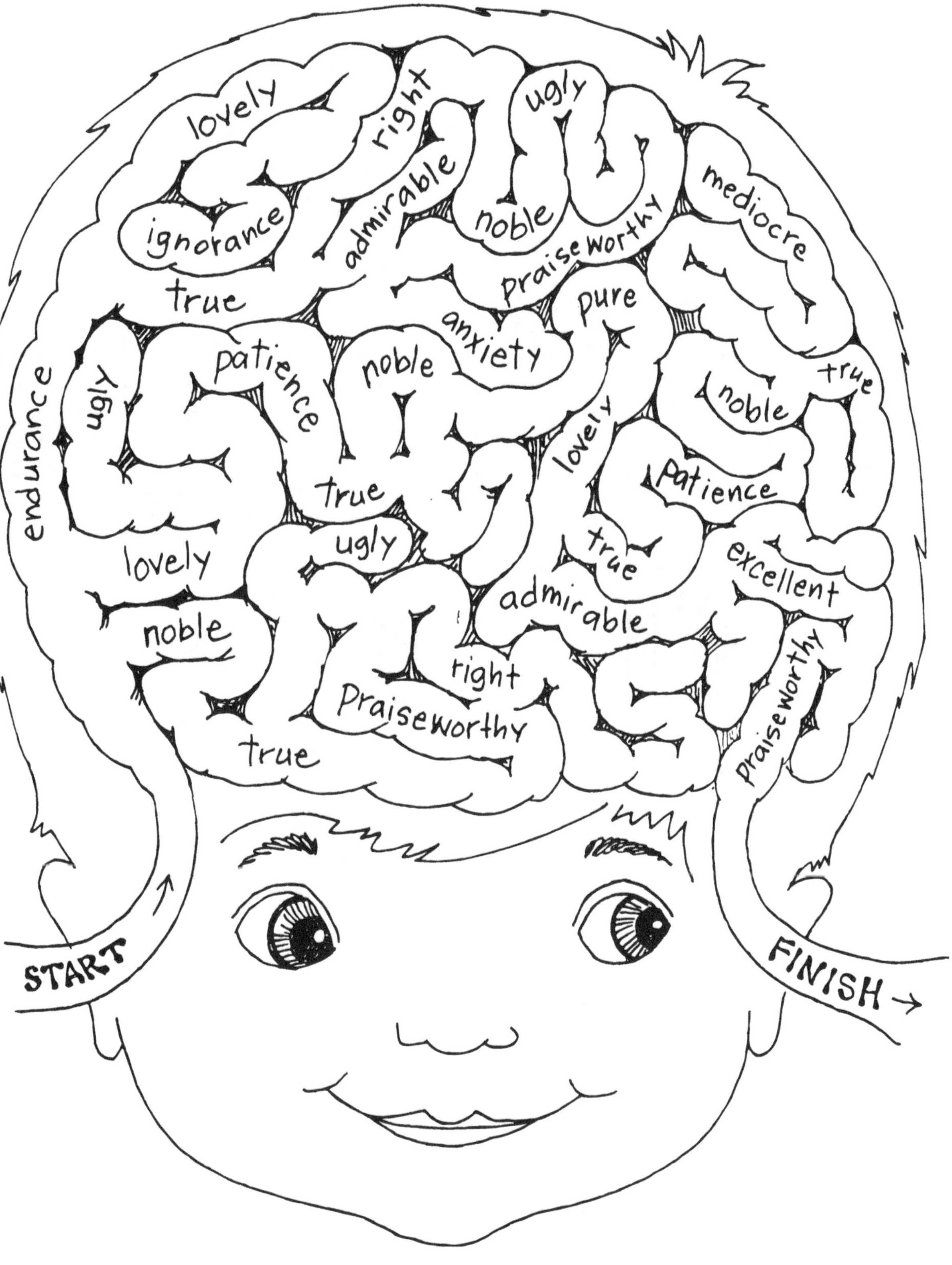

Not to Fear

Read 1 Thessalonians 4:13–18 and Revelation 22:6–7. Start with box A. Put the first letter of the object in that box on the line provided. Then do the same with boxes B, C, D, etc.

Whether we fall asleep in the Lord, or are caught up with Him in the clouds, there's nothing to fear.

____

____

Fight the Good Fight

Read 1 Timothy 1:18–19 and 4:7–12. Paul gave Timothy some good advice. For each line of letters, first write in order all the uppercase letters. Then write in order on the second line all the lowercase letters.

Paul told Timothy to hold on to

goFodcAonITscienHce

____

____

Paul told Timothy to set an example in

SIPEifEeCH

____

____

fLOaiVtEh

____

____

ApNuriDty

____

____

What Is Faith?

Decode the quiz by changing the letters as indicated in the code box. See Hebrews 11:1–6 for help.

From	C	N	W	P	S	D	L	I	A	O	T	F	U	E	R	H	B
To	A	B	C	D	E	F	G	H	I	N	O	P	R	S	T	U	W

OTB DCARI AE

NSAOL EHUS TD

BICR BS ITFS

DTU COP

WSURCAO TD

BICR BS PT

OTR ESS

Active Faith

Read James 2:14–26. Find the message by writing the words in the matching shapes.

Show Love

Read 1 John 4:7–12 and 19–21. To fill in the boxes, begin at one of the lettered boxes. Follow the line that leads from it to another empty box and put that letter in the empty box.

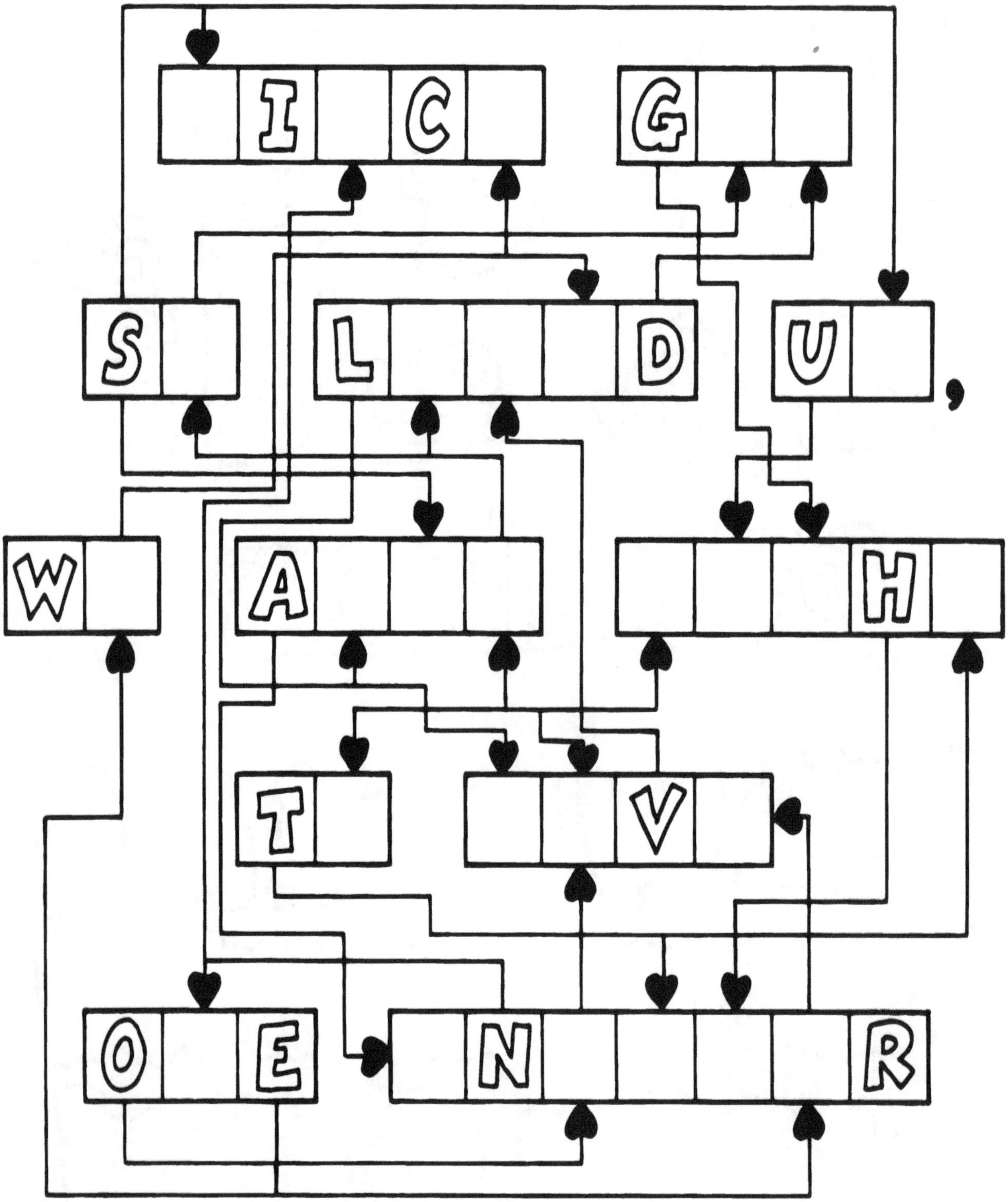

Answers

Let There Be … 9

Day 1. picture 4, light/dark; Day 2. picture 5, water/sky; Day 3. picture 2, trees/plants; Day 4. picture 3, sun/moon/stars; Day 5. picture 1, sea creatures/birds; Day 6. picture 6, animals

The Beginning.................................. 10

God created all things with His almighty power.

Something Special.......................... 11

God created man in His own image.

Strange Tree 12

The first sin came into the world when Adam and Eve disobeyed God and ate of the Tree of Knowledge of Good and Evil.

Where Are You?.............................. 13

Why did Adam and Eve try to hide from God?

Offerings... 14

Abel's offering came from his heart.

Rainbows.. 15

Never again will all life be cut off by the waters of a flood.

The Promise.................................... 16

I will make you into a great nation and I will bless you.

Separation 17

If you go to the left, I'll go to the right; if you go to the right, I'll go to the left.

Who's Who? 18

1. Abraham; 2. three men; 3. Sarah;
4. servant; 5. the Lord; 6. child, promise

A Lot to Learn 19

1. Sodom; 2. Lot; 3. destroy; 4. wife; 5. sulfur; 6. pillar; 7. rising; Sin brings punishment.

Stop! 20

"Do not lay a hand on the boy," he said. "Do not do anything to him. Now I know that you fear God, because you have not withheld from me your son, your only son."

Family Ties 21

Here is Rebekah; take her and go, and let her become the wife of your master's son, as the Lord has directed.

Brothers 22

Esau sold his birthright to Jacob.

Heavenly Ladder 23

This is none other than the house of God; this is the gate of heaven.

Children of Israel 24

Reuben, Benjamin, Naphtali, Issachar, Joseph, Dan, Simeon, Judah, Levi, Gad, Asher, Zebulun.

Oh Brother! 25

Israel, dream, flocks, Reuben, robe, cistern, Midianite, Egypt; Dreamer

Who's in Charge? 26

Pharaoh said to Joseph, "Since God has made all this known to you, … I hereby put you in charge of the whole land of Egypt."

Hunger Strike 27

A. 4, fish; B. 2, banana; C. 3, tomato; C. 1, pickle; B. 4, onion; D. 2, steak; famine.

Family Reunion 28

Three Os diagonally (top left to bottom right)

Egyptian Inscription........................ 29

Reuben, Simeon, Levi, Judah, Issachar, Zebulun, Benjamin, Dan, Naphtali, Gad, Asher

Baby in a Basket............................. 30

When the child grew older, she took him to Pharaoh's daughter and he became her son. She named him Moses, saying, "I drew him out of the water."

Scrambled Plagues.......................... 31

Boils, darkness, flies, waters to blood, gnats, livestock die, hail, locusts; Let the Israelites go.

Eat and Run 32

Passover

Our Passover Lamb 33

1. True; 2. False; 3. True; 4. True; 5. True; 6. False; 7. True; 8. True; 9. True; 10. True; 11. True; Jesus Christ

Walls of Water 34

That day the Lord saved Israel from the hands of the Egyptians.

Food for Thought............................. 35

At twilight you will eat meat, and in the morning you will be filled with bread. Then you will know that I am the Lord your God. Exodus 16:12

The Ten Commandments................. 36

1. gods; 2. idols; 3. name; 4. Sabbath; 5. Honor; 6. murder; 7. adultery; 8. steal; 9. false; 10. covet

Beware of Imitations....................... 37

You shall have no other gods before me.

Respect.. 38

You shall not misuse the name of the Lord your God. Exodus 20:7

Ring the Bells 39

Remember the Sabbath day by keeping it holy.

The Promise.. 40

Honor your father and your mother, so that you may live long in the land the Lord your God is giving you.

Honesty.. 41

You shall not give false testimony against your neighbor.

Leave It Alone..................................... 42

You shall not covet your neighbor's house. You shall not covet… anything that belongs to your neighbor.

The Tabernacle 43

Have them make a sanctuary for me and I will dwell among them.

Written in Stone.................................. 44

The tablets were the work of God; the writing was the writing of God engraved on the tablets.

In Numbers 45

Canaan, tribe, forty, milk, honey, stronger, Joshua, pleased, lead

Thirst Aid 46

Then Moses raised his arm and struck the rock twice with his staff. Water gushed out, and the community and their livestock drank.

But Why, Lord? 47

Follow God's law for a happy life.

Do It Right.. 48

Love the Lord your God with all your heart and with all your soul and with all your strength. Deuteronomy 6:5

Welcome Home................................. 49

No; Yes; Yes; No; No, they crossed on dry ground.

Shout! 50

Joshua, Jericho, trumpets, seven, shouted, collapsed

Achan's Sin...................................... 51

You cannot hide your sins from God.

Remember the Promise.................. 52

1. Your forefathers … lived beyond the river; 2. I led Abraham throughout Canaan; 3. To Abraham I gave Isaac; 4. To Isaac I gave Jacob and Esau; 5. Jacob and his sons went down to Egypt; 6. I sent Moses and Aaron and brought you out of Egypt; 7. You lived in the desert for a long time; 8. I gave you a land on which you did not toil. Now serve God with all faithfulness.

Lead the Way.................................. 53

1. True; 2. True; 3. False; 4. True; 5. True; 6. True; 7. True; 8. False; 9. False; The Israelites defeated Sisera's army with the Lord's help.

Surprise!... 54

They shouted, "A sword for the Lord and for Gideon!"

Samson's Weakness........................ 55

1. slaves; 2. love; 3. Delilah; 4. secret; 5. strength; 6. razor; 7. shaved; 8. hair; 9. asleep; 10. lost; 11. prison; 12. perform; 13. prayed; 14. pillars; 15. temple

What a Friend!................................ 56

She was loyal to Naomi.

Here I Am! 57

Speak, for your servant is listening.

Sounds Like 58

1. ring/king; 2. live/give; 3. can/man; 4. jeweler/ruler; 5. soil/oil; 6. steeple/people

Look Inside 59

The Lord chose David son of Jesse to be king over Israel.

Stones 'n Stuff 60

1. shepherd's bag; 2. Philistine; 3. boy; 4. sword, spear, javelin; 5. Lord Almighty; 6. know; 7. forehead; 8. killed; The whole world will know that there is a God in Israel.

Friends Forever............................... 61

1. kill; 2. warned; 3. loved; 4. friendship; 5. son

Have Mercy on Me! 62

(1) May the Lord judge between (2) you and me. And may (3) the Lord avenge the wrongs (4) you have done to me, (5) but my hand will not (6) touch you.

The Wise King................................ 63

1. Solomon; 2. heart; 3. pleased; 4. riches, honor, long life

Good Advice.................................... 64

Give them a favorable answer; Tell them you will make their yoke even heavier.

Help from on High........................... 65

Bread, water, meat

Rescue Recipe................................ 66

Handful of flour in a jar. Little oil in a jug.

And the Winner Is 67

The fire of the Lord fell and burned up the sacrifice.

Whirlwind Words 68

Elijah, whirlwind, Lord, Jericho, prophets, Jordan, Elisha, cloak, fire, heaven

What a Blessing!............................. 69

1. meal; 2. chair; 3. son; 4. noon; 5. house; 6. eyes; 7. sneezed; 8. call; 9. feet

Who Said That? 70

1. Naaman; 2. young girl; 3. King of Aram; 4. Elisha; 5. King of Israel; "If only my master …"(young girl); "Am I God?" (King of Israel); "Go, wash yourself …" (Elisha); "Are not Abana …" (Naaman); "By all means, go." (King of Aram)

Bad Shape 71

They sinned and worshipped other gods.

What Was Their Downfall? 72

1. sinned; 2. practices; 3. high; 4. stones; 5. wicked; 6. idols; 7. stiff-necked; 8. rejected; 9. worthless; 10. anger

Our God Is Greater.......................... 73

Build, temple, Name, great, Moriah, praise, forever, "He is good; his love endures forever."

Work Boxes..................................... 74

Brought their money gladly.

The Secret of Success 75

As long as he sought the Lord, God gave him success.

Construction Site 76

It had been done with the help of our God.

A Brave Queen................................ 77

I will go to the king, even though it is against the law. And if I perish, I perish. Esther 4:16.

Why Me?... 78

You can do all things.

Lost Sheep...................................... 79

1. pastures; 2. shadow; 3. green; 4. soul; 5. oil; 6. waters; 7. goodness; the Lord.

Wise Up! **80**

1. True; 2. True; 3. True; 4. False; 5. True; 6. True; 7. True; 8. False; 9. True; 10. True; 11. True; 12. True

When the Lord Calls **81**

Here I am. Send me.

His Name Is … **82**

1. Wonderful Counselor, 2. Mighty God, 3. Everlasting Father, 4. Prince of Peace, 5. Son of the Most High, 6. Son of God

Missing Alphabet **83**

God has no equal!

The Prophet **84**

Isaiah

Taking Shape **85**

1. artist; 2. frame; 3. hook; 4. pen; 5. you'd; 6. lily; 7. honey; 8. head; 9. tent; 10. china; Like clay in the hand of the potter, so are you in my hand.

Cistern Escape **86**

1. army; 2. cistern; 3. courtyard; 4. prophet; 5. dies; ropes

Captured! **87**

The captives from Jerusalem and Judah were carried into exile to Babylon.

Follow Directions **88**

Zedekiah became king and did evil. He turned away from God. The Babylonian army surrounded the city. People starved. Soon the army broke in and burned everything.

The Lord's Promise......................... 89

I will put my Spirit in you and move you to follow my decrees and be careful to keep my laws. Ezekiel chapter 36 verse 27.

What's on the Menu?...................... 90

Daniel, Shadrach, Meshach, and Abednego ate vegetables and water. The men from the king's court ate royal food and wine.

God Protects His Faithful................ 91

Shadrach, Meshach, and Abednego were not burned in the furnace because they were true to God.

The King Learns a Lesson 92

1. True; 2. True; 3. False; 4. True; 5. True; 6. False; 7. True; 8. False; 9. True; 10. False; Only God is all powerful.

Handwriting on the Wall 93

The king lost his life, and the message came true because he did not honor God.

Lion Tamer..................................... 94

God's angel shut the lions' mouths.

A Straight Wall................................ 95

1. Amos; 2. Uzziah; 3. Israel; 4. Tekoa; 5. years; 6. hand; 7. sanctuaries; 8. Jeroboam; 9. Amaziah; 10. conspiracy; 11. Judah

Crazy Clues.................................... 96

1. E; 2. T; 3. O; 4. H; 5. A; 6. Y; They came and began to work on the house of the Lord Almighty.

Give and Receive........................... 97

Bring tithes and offerings to God and you will be blessed.

The Genealogy of Jesus.................. 98

Abraham/Isaac; Isaac/Jacob; Jacob/Judah; Salmon/Boaz; Boaz/Obed; Obed/Jesse; Jesse/King David; King David/Solomon; There were 42 generations from Abraham to Christ.

A Gift for Me? **99**

Jesus, because he will save his people from their sins.

Come and Worship! **100**

1. bowed; 2. east; 3. star; 4. Christ;
5. gold; 6. Jesus; 7. Herod; 8. Judea;
9. Mary; Bethlehem

Star Search..................................... **101**

Worshipped him!

Jesus Is Baptized............................ **102**

The Spirit of God descended like a dove on Him.

The Spirit **103**

This is my Son, whom I love; with him I am well pleased.

Yield Not to Temptation................... **104**

Worship the Lord your God.

Calling Followers **105**

Peter, James, John, Andrew, Judas, Bartholomew, Matthew, Thomas, James, Simon, Thaddaeus, Philip; Apostles.

Who Is Blessed? **106**

Mountain

What Am I?..................................... **107**

You are the salt of the earth. You are the light of the world. A city on a hill cannot be hidden. But if the salt loses its saltiness, how can it be made salty again?

A Wise Builder **108**

A wise builder is one who hears these words… and puts them into practice.

12 Men.. **109**

1. Andrew; 2. Simon; 3. Thomas;
4. Judas Iscariot; 5. Simon Peter;
6. Philip; 7. Bartholomew; 8. James;
9. Thaddaeus; James son of Zebedee, John, and Matthew.

Find the Treasure............................ 110

1. treasure; 2. field; 3. man; 4. joy; 5. merchant; 6. pearls; 7. value

Cross It Out.................................... 111

You shall not commit adultery. Herod wanted to kill John.

Jesus Walked on Water.................. 112

Then those who were in the boat worshipped him, saying, "Truly you are the Son of God."

Peter's Confession Hourglass......... 113

1. disciples; 2. Philippi; 3. blessed; 4. region; 5. Jonah; 6. some; 7. who; 8. do; 9. is; 10. you; 11. John; 12. Jesus; 13. Christ; 14. Baptist; 15. Jeremiah; 16. living God

Forgive.. 114

I tell you, not seven times, but seventy-seven times.

Two Sons....................................... 115

Two, first, son, work, vineyard, will not, son, should, father, son, work, vineyard, yes, will, two, first. Change and believe. Enter the kingdom.

When Will Jesus Come?................. 116

Keep watch, because you do not know the day or the hour.

One Talent..................................... 117

Hid it in the ground.

What's the Question?...................... 118

Sheep or goat?

See the Stone? 119

The women went to the tomb and found the stone rolled back. An angel told them, "Jesus is risen."

A Final Message 120

Jesus said, "Go and make disciples of all nations, baptizing them in the name of the Father and of the Son and of the Holy Spirit, and teaching them to obey everything I have commanded you."

Forgiven! 121

Son, your sins are forgiven. That you may know that the Son of Man has authority on earth to forgive sins.

Healing of the Demon-Possessed Man 122

1. True; 2. False; 3. False; 4. True; 5. True; 6. False; 7. True; 8. True

A Rich Man's Mistake 123

He went away sad because he had great wealth.

A Slave 124

Whoever wants to be first must be slave of all.

Important Phone Call 125

Love the Lord your God with all your heart. Love your neighbor as yourself.

The Widow's Offering 126

Everything

Missing Word ABCs 127

Alexander, bottom, curtain, darkness, Elijah, forsaken, Golgotha, heard, in, Jews, king, lots, myrrh, ninth, offered, passerby, robbers, sponge, third, until

Alleluia! 128

1. Arimathea; 2. Pilate; 3. body; 4. wrapped; 5. in; 6. stone; 7. entrance; 8. spices; 9. Jesus; 10. man; 11. robe; 12. right; 13. alarmed; The Lord is risen. Be glad.

Chrono-Code 129

Your prayer has been heard.

The News 130
Child, birth, son, Jesus, Lord's servant, said

It's a Boy! 131
His name is John.

A Savior 132
Today in the town of David a Savior has been born to you; he is the Messiah.

Scrambled Rulers 133
Quirinius, Caesar, David, Augustus, Governor, Christ, Lord; Today a Savior has been born!

Jumble John 134
Tax collectors, soldiers, people, crowd, God, Annas, Caiaphas, Zechariah. Good News.

Fishers of Men 135
1. edge; 2. washing; 3. Simon; 4. catch; 5. night; 6. partners; 7. fell; 8. Zebedee; 9. Jesus; disciples

The Alabaster Jar 136
Forgiven

Good Soil 137
Seed, good, soil, noble, good, heart, word, persevering, produce, crop

Jesus Calms a Stormy Sea 138
He commands even the winds and the water, and they obey him.

Just Believe 139
"My child, get up!" Her spirit returned.

The Glory of the Lord 140

1. eight; 2. John; 3. pray; 4. face; 5. clothes; 6. Two; 7. very; 8. cloud; 9. cloud; 10. listen to; 11. no one

A Good Neighbor.............................. 141

1. b; 2. c; 3. a; 4. c

What Did Martha Open? 142

1. The Lord's; 2. upset; 3. listened; 4. hearing; 5. teach; 6. Mary; her home.

Decode the Prayer.......................... 143

Ask and it will be given to you; seek and you will find; knock and the door will be opened to you.

Rich Man 144

Fool, night, life, demanded, who, get, prepared, yourself, stores, himself, rich, toward, God

Repent! 145

Sink, nut, ear, rake, pen, toes, rain, ghost, one, house; sinner, repents, righteous.

Lost and Found 146

1. cane; 2. lace; 3. bear; 4. ant; 5. end; 6. apron; 7. dew; 8. ants; 9. gull; 10. add; Celebrated and was glad.

The Rich Man and Lazarus 147

Abraham, Lazarus, five, purple, listen, luxury, sores, convinced, torment; Have pity on me.

Amazingly Healed 148

1. Jerusalem; 2. ten men; 3. Jesus, Master; 4. cleansed; 5. praising; 6. Samaritan; 7. ten; 8. well

The Pharisee and the Tax Collector 149

God, have mercy on me, a sinner. God, I thank you that I am not like this tax collector.

A Short Story 150

Sycamore, Zacchaeus, cheated, tax collector, come down, four times, stay, Jericho, salvation. You shall not steal.

Praise God! 151

Blessed is the king who comes in the name of the Lord! Peace in heaven and glory in the highest!

Amazing Love 152

For God so loved the world that he gave his one and only Son that whoever believes in him shall not perish but have eternal life.

Worship 153

God is spirit and his worshipers must worship in spirit and in truth.

One Lunch That Fed More Than 5,000 154

How far will they go among so many? They had enough to eat. Twelve baskets of barley loaves were left over.

Lazarus, Come Out! 155

Many of the Jews put their faith in Him.

Jesus Is Risen 156

Puzzle 1: 3; Puzzle 2: 5; Puzzle 3: 2; He is not here; he has risen.

Easter Morning 157

1. False; 2. True; 3. True; 4. False; 5. True; 6. False; 7. True; 8. False; 9. True; 10. False; Jesus arose!

Miraculous Catch of Fish 158

Across: 1. I'm; 3. with; 4. raised; 6. answered; 7. disciple; Down: 2. him; 3. water; 5. dragged; 6. afterward

Seek the Truth 159

1. True; 2. False; 3. True; 4. False; 5. False; 6. True; Receive the power of the Spirit.

Cross It Out 160

1. wind, fire, sound, tongues; 2. Peter; 3. Pentecost; 4. Jerusalem; 5. repent, be baptized, save yourselves; 6. 3,000; 7. Israel; 8. eleven, apostles; 9. heard, accepted, were baptized; 10. Jews; God made Jesus both Lord and Messiah

Finding Words 161

Breaking, teaching, selling, being, everything, enjoying, praising; believers.

What Did the People Think? 162

1. Peter, John; 2. pray; 3. beautiful; 4. something; 5. gold; 6. Nazareth; 7. jumped, walk; They were filled with wonder and amazement at what had happened to him.

On Trial 163

Peter and John were arrested for talking about Jesus. Peter said the people had crucified Jesus. The rulers were astonished at the courage Peter and John showed but warned them not to speak of Jesus.

What's in a Name? 164

1. believers; 2. shared; 3. great; 4. testify; 5. resurrection; 6. needy; 7. lands, houses; 8. money; Son of encouragement

Stephen's Last Stand 165

Blue: God's grace, power, wonders, miraculous, wisdom, Holy Spirit, Heaven, Jesus; Red: opposition, argue, furious, gnashed, yelling, rushed, dragged, stone

The Ethiopian's Question 166

Look, here is water. Why shouldn't I be baptized?

Saul's Conversion 167

Persecutor, believer, light, blinded, Ananias, sight, called, witness, baptized, Christian

Joy in Joppa 168

1. Joppa; 2. Tabitha; 3. Dorcas; 4. Lydda; 5. Peter; 6. disciples; 7. men; 8. widows; 9. believers; 10. people; Many people believed in the Lord.

Right or Wrong? **169**

Peter learned not to call any man impure or unclean.

Christians Scatter **170**

Stephen, Barnabas, Antioch, Christians, disciples

Good News! **171**

1. Saul; 2. fasted; 3. speak; 4. Jesus; 5. death; Good News

Paul and Barnabas.......................... **172**

The Lord used the early Christians to perform miracles. We are bringing you good news, telling you to turn from these worthless things to the living God.

Prison **173**

The jailer and his family were saved.

The Unknown God........................... **174**

1. from the dead; 2. world; 3. heaven, earth; 4. nation, man; 5. have our being

Spreading the Word......................... **175**

Frauds, beat them. The word of the Lord spread widely and grew in power.

Paul's Mission **176**

Miletus, elders, humility, Holy Spirit, Jews, Greeks, prison, God, nothing, shepherds, watch, tears; Tell the Good News.

Shipwreck....................................... **177**

Keep up your courage, not one of you will be lost.

Love, Love, Love............................. **178**

Share with God's people who are in need. Love must be sincere. Be joyful in hope. Be careful to do what is right. Live in harmony. Practice hospitality.

The Lord's Supper 179

Do this in remembrance of me.

Mixed Fruit...................................... 180

Love, joy, peace, patience, kindness, goodness, faithfulness, gentleness, self-control

Helpful Crutches 181

It is by grace you have been saved, through faith—and this not from yourselves, it is the gift of God, not by works, so no one can boast.

You Can Take It 182

Put on the belt of truth. Our struggle is against the spiritual forces of evil. Put on the full armor of God. The shield of faith will extinguish the flaming arrows of the evil one. The sword of the Spirit is the Word of God. Stand.

What Should You Think?................. 183

Lovely, patience, true, noble, pure, lovely, admirable, excellent, praiseworthy

Not to Fear 184

We will be with the Lord forever.

Fight the Good Fight 185

Faith, good conscience, speech, life, love, faith, and purity

What Is Faith? 186

Now faith is being sure of what we hope for and certain of what we do not see.

Active Faith...................................... 187

Faith by itself, if it is not accompanied by action, is dead.

Show Love 188

Since God so loved us, we also ought to love one another.